T0329109

THE POLITICAL SPECTRUM

THE POLITICAL SPECTRUM

THE RATIONAL FOUNDATIONS OF

LIBERTY AND PROSPERITY

ANTHONY C. PATTON

Algora Publishing
New York

Library of Congress Cataloging-in-Publication Data —

Patton, Anthony C., 1969-
    The political spectrum / Anthony C. Patton.
        pages cm
    Includes bibliographical references.
        ISBN 978-1-62894-168-5 (soft cover : alk. paper) — ISBN 978-1-62894-169-2 (hard
cover : alk. paper) ISBN 978-1-62894-170-8 (eBook)   1. Political culture—United States.
2. Right and left (Political science)—United States. 3. Deficit financing--United States. 4.
Family policy—United States. I. Title.
    JK1726.P365 2015
    320.50973—dc23
                        2015027675

The views expressed in this book are those of the author and do not necessarily reflect
those of his employer.

Printed in the United States

Table of Contents

INTRODUCTION

The inspiration for writing this book was the incessant fighting we see today between Democrats and Republicans in the USA. I am always surprised by how apparently normal people who live similar lives—they put their pants on one leg at a time, go to work, eat food, listen to music, pay the bills, etc.—can have such radically different political beliefs. People who otherwise would probably be good neighbors might choke each other during an argument about abortion or guns. Nations go to war, with tens of millions of people killed in the name of communism and fascism during the twentieth century. People brandish terms like left wing and right wing, communist and fascist, or liberal and conservative, Democrat or Republican, often without sufficient clarity to explain the differences. Thus, I set out to better understand how we arrived at this point of political divide by studying political philosophy with the goal of identifying any fundamental, universal principles that would allow us to better assess and correct our current trajectory.

We know what it means to pass a budget or change marginal income tax rates, but does anyone really agree on how to define left or right in politics, aside from vague intuitions? We believe the left-to-right divide implies a continuum of beliefs, with people on the opposite ends of the political spectrum having often contradictory beliefs (regarding the size of government, abortions, guns, and so on), but people talk about being moderate right or moderate left without clarifying what they mean. How do we know where a set of beliefs can be situated along the political spectrum? What are the key markers along the political spectrum to tell us where we are and to define our own beliefs? Where is the correct place to be on the political spectrum? Is there a correct place? Can all societies be at the same place, or does the ideal place along the spectrum depend on the stage of social progress? If there is such a thing as "the end of history," where will the correct place be on the political spectrum? I soon discovered that it was impossible to answer any of these questions without identifying some fundamental, universal principles that stand the test of time to provide a foundation for our beliefs. Just as every building requires a strong foundation to remain standing, we need a strong foundation in political philosophy to answer these important questions.

We all seem to have an intuitive grasp of what these words mean, such as liberals liking big government and "progressive" values and conservatives liking small government and "traditional" values (though not always), but most people would not agree on all the specifics. Can a conservative ever support a woman's choice to have an abortion? Can a liberal ever support the rights of a fetus? Thus, one of my goals for writing this book was to provide more clarity to the left–right political spectrum by identifying some fundamental, universal principles of political philosophy, which in turn would allow us to promote liberty and sustainable prosperity in a modern state.

Vague Intuitions

One conclusion I reached about political philosophy from looking back on my own life experiences, watching political battles play out in elections, and living in several foreign countries around the world was that many of our core political beliefs—about taxes, abortion, welfare, military, etc.— especially as a young adult but even well into adulthood, *are grounded in emotions and are not the result of a rational thought process.* They are the result of a vague, intuitive process that often trembles in the face of scrutiny. For reasons I do not understand and will not attempt to explain in this book, our experiences and thoughts from a young age lead us down one particular path or another that tends to be associated with *a portfolio of political beliefs*; and once we start down one path, as would be the case with choosing a profession or living in a particular society, it is difficult to change course as the neurons in our brain begin to crystallize and we start looking at the world through one set of lenses to the exclusion of other lenses. We can attribute our political beliefs to our parents, our environment, our food (such as whether we consume enough protein), the media, politics, you name it, but even these variables do not have the power of predicting cause and effect with scientific precision because people in nearly identical environments often end up with conflicting political beliefs as well as different results in terms of political stability and economic growth.

Does geography or climate predispose us one way or another? Does the way the neuron pathways in our brain develop at a young age, even in the womb, predispose us one way or another? Does it matter if we consume breast milk or formula? Are some races or genders more predisposed to certain political belief systems? Some authors have even claimed that the brains of people on the left and the right sides of the political spectrum are different, but this becomes a chicken or the egg situation: does the brain shape the beliefs, or do the beliefs shape the brain? Is consciousness a reflection of underlying material forces, or does consciousness shape the material world we live in? Like bruises after someone hits us, these vague political intuitions stick with us and shape the way we see the world and think about it. Even long after the bruises fade (some never do), the traces remain rooted deep within us and are difficult to eradicate without causing damage to our sense of identity and how we live in the world.

The goal of studying political philosophy is to carefully uproot these vague intuitions and get a bird's eye view of the entire political spectrum by observing the world through the lenses of fundamental, universal principles, which should allow us to make informed decisions about which lenses to use for particular situations and where to situate ourselves along the political spectrum. For example, if we want to achieve artistry in photography, we have to use the correct lenses in a correct manner. The goal is not to shake up the system for its own sake or to leave a trail of destruction, as many radical movements have done. Some of our political beliefs will ultimately be grounded in (clear) intuition or non-discursive thought, because pure reason by itself cannot produce fundamental principles, but at least they will be able to withstand the scrutiny of reason because the proper use of reason will shape the intuitions. Needless to say, doing this is no small achievement.

I do not recall or understand the specific sequences of events that led me down the path of developing what most people would call moderate conservative or "traditional" intuitions about life and politics. While growing up, we did not attend church (I had a peculiar attraction to Eastern mysticism from a young age), we never owned guns, my parents got divorced when I was young, we were the recipients of welfare benefits for a time, and we grew up in Minnesota, a predominantly Democratic state (keeping in mind that Democrats in Minnesota are socially conservative and probably would not get along with many Democrats from California or New York). Therefore, an outside observer who believes in the primacy of material or economic forces might assume that I would lean more to the left, but I did not—quite the contrary. After seeing the movie *Top Gun*, I found myself magnetically attracted to the idea of joining the military and wearing a uniform, for reasons I did not understand, aside from the fact that men at an unconscious level seem to like uniforms and the old adage that women love a man in uniform. What could be cooler than flying a jet? I was first generation military, with no family tradition to move me in that direction, but some mysterious force resonated within me. During college, I drifted more to the right, joined Air Force ROTC and the College Republicans, and accepted the narrative that Democrats are lazy, envious people who want hand-outs, all without ever questioning the foundations of my beliefs. To me, it was obvious, but I was not thinking clearly or rationally, even though at the time I was convinced I was. I was being guided by a web of vague intuitions, or bruises, with a mysterious origin. When Reagan said we needed the Star Wars missile defense system, I believed it, even when the skeptics said it could not be done. History seems to have proven the skeptics correct. When the College Republican brochure spoke out against abortion, regardless of the circumstances, I accepted it without thinking through all the variables and consequences. These ideas resonated with something deep within me, like music, something I could not put my finger on. I believed I was thinking rationally and that the Democrats were not thinking rationally, which made me feel good about myself. That said, by the time I left college to join the Air Force, I started to develop the sneaking suspicion that some of my political beliefs were not my own and that people on the whole tended to believe many things without a rational foundation.

Initially, the study of philosophy was the most important tool I used in recognizing that my vague intuitions were mere shadows in Plato's cave, which allowed me to start the arduous journey of exiting the cave one inch at a time toward the light of day because it forced me to seek fundamental, universal principles for my beliefs rather than relying on my emotional reactions. After majoring in mathematics and philosophy, I continued reading philosophy for over 20 years, to include the complete works in the history of philosophy of Frederick Copleston and Anthony Kenny and the major works of individual philosophers, such as Plato, Aristotle, Kant, Schopenhauer, and others. It was not until I started reading about modern political philosophy (Roger Scruton, Alan Ryan, Karl Popper, John Rawls, Robert Nozick, and others) that I started looking at things in new ways and developing a more systematic approach to the subject that allowed me to set the stage for writing this book. In addition to philosophy, I also found it was important to study evidenced-based subjects to gain insights. Whereas philosophy helped me refine my ideas, it was the work of thinkers like Francis Fukuyama, who used an evidence-based approach to support his findings, that helped me situate my ideas into a more clearly defined context. I still maintain what many would describe as moderate right political beliefs or "traditional" values, such as the prohibition of deficit spending and the sanctity of monogamous procreation (these two topics are the focus of this book), but with a healthy concern for the state of the Republican Party. I remain skeptical of some beliefs on the left side of the political spectrum, but I have grown to understand my beliefs in new ways (in ways that many of my friends on the right side of the political spectrum probably would not support), and my new understanding of how the left thinks has allowed me to be less skeptical of their beliefs and motivations.

Two Fundamental Institutions

According to Fukuyama, institutions are "persistent rules that shape, limit, and channel human behavior,"[1] which is an important point of departure for political philosophy because most political theorists, on the left and the right, agree that strong institutions are the key to good governance, even if they disagree on the specifics. Fukuyama's analysis focuses on three big institutions: 1. the state, 2. the rule of law, and 3. a mechanism for accountability. First, the institution of the state is defined as a central authority that can exercise a monopoly of legitimate force over its territory to keep peace and enforce the law. A patrimonial state, the earliest form of a state, is based on the idea that the polity is the personal property of the ruler and is an extension of his household. Although this type of state has been common throughout history, even today, and can even be stable, it falls short of the ideal. A modern state is based on the idea that a citizen's relationship to the ruler does not depend on personal ties but simply on one's status as a citizen, with recruitment to administrative positions based on impersonal criteria such as merit, education, or technical knowledge. Second, the institution of the rule *of* law is defined as a set of rules of behavior reflecting a broad consensus within the society that is binding on even the most powerful political actors in the society, as opposed to rule *by* law in which the sovereign authority enforces laws but is not bound by them. Third, the institution of a mechanism of accountability is defined by the idea that the government is responsive to the interests of the whole society, which usually, but not always, includes periodic free and fair multiparty elections that allow citizens to choose and discipline their rulers. I suspect that these three institutions will resonate with most people living in modern states, at least those who do not stand to profit from oppressing their people. I cannot imagine any U.S. presidential candidate today speaking out against any of these institutions during a debate.

I cannot do Fukuyama's theory of institutions justice in this book, aside from referring the reader to his splendid books, but he provides a compelling argument for concluding that these three big institutions should be the ideal path or trajectory for any society—a blueprint or playbook, if you will. The

---

1 Fukuyama, Francis, *Political Order* and *Political Decay: From the Industrial Revolution to the Globalization of Democracy*, 6.

only problem I found with this analysis is that, in its most general form, it appeals to both sides of the political spectrum, to both the left and the right, to both liberals and conservatives, to both Democrats and Republicans, although the two sides would probably disagree on some of the specifics. Fukuyama is critical of the American state in ways that would probably appeal to many Democrats, liberals, or people on the left, but his analysis also includes points that would appeal to many Republicans, conservatives, or people on the right. Therefore, when we ask the all-important question— Where should we be on the political spectrum?—the answer is not clear. Even if we all support the three big institutions, we can still disagree viscerally on most of the major issues. I believe Fukuyama has framed the debate in the correct way (in fact, I will assume that the reader supports the three big institutions as a point of departure), but we can keep digging in the fertile soil to find other more fundamental institutions that might help us situate ourselves along the political spectrum. If we think about most plans, such as going out for dinner, there are often one or two variables in the process that ultimately make the decision for us, such as having a coupon that expires the same day or distance restrictions. Regardless of what we might think about the other options, some variables limit our options to one, in which case the discussion ends. We might all agree on the idea of going to dinner, just as we might all agree on the big three institutions, but this agreement by itself is not enough to help us make a decision about where to situate ourselves along the political spectrum. Likewise, there might be other institutions that by their nature help us make a final decision. For example, perhaps there are some more fundamental institutions that are with us from the beginning, prior to the big three institutions outlined by Fukuyama, ones that stay with us in one form another from the most primitive to the most enlightened stages of our political development, ones that cannot be transcended or untethered from reality, without negative consequences. As I developed the two principles in this book—resource management and procreation—I realized that they can be thought of as "persistent rules that shape, limit, and channel human behavior," which means that they can be thought of as institutions. As such, I decided that the focus of this book would be an analysis of these two fundamental institutions.

Society as a System

One of the most important ideas I focused on when writing this book was the idea that society is a system, in the sense that it has inputs and outputs and performs specific functions. I started developing this idea while getting my MBA, where I learned to understand important concepts like "cash flow" and "value." These concepts allowed me to dismiss all theories that ignored these bedrock concepts because they were grounded in math, not in ideology, even though they are often raised in ideological debates. The core premise for thinking of society as a system is the cash flow and value model that all businesses must live by to survive in a system that is based on the free exchange of goods and services. Cash is king, as the saying goes. Rather than focus on whether humans are inherently good or bad, whether our rights come from God or the state, or whether government should be big or small, I reached the conclusion that, given that society is a system, there must be some simple mathematical facts about systems such that when we combine them with other simple truths, a bigger truth would reveal itself like a Polaroid picture that slowly comes into focus or the way a detective collects clues to solve a case. For example, if someone wants to open a microbrewery, he will quickly learn that there is a basic template for success, which he will have to articulate in a business plan.

The microbrew business has a model that does not allow for significant deviation, a model that has been learned over time by trial and error and depends on the technology at our disposal. The rules of the game are brewed into the beer, so to speak. If you do not buy the right equipment, follow the right recipe, or hire the right people to manage the process, you will probably fail or at least not do well. Winging it is never an option, and no bank would approve a loan for such a foray, and yet we elect government officials all the time who wing it and lack the right qualifications for higher office. No, a bad business model will most likely fail, unless the government intervenes to keep it afloat, in which case we enter the world of patronage, clientelism, crony capitalism, and corruption, which are the antithesis of free markets, which are based on the free exchange of goods and services. If you want to succeed in the microbrew business, you have to buy barley or other grains and ferment them in a specific way, which in turn shapes how the whole process plays out. Your intentions or motivations for making the beer do not matter and may actually disrupt the process. The fact that you plan to donate all your profits to charity does not matter as much as the fact that you develop a recipe for a better beer, in accordance with the art and science of brewing. Thus, any plan to open a microbrewery that does not include identifying a source of grains and the right process will most likely result in failure, regardless of good intentions. For many people, making the transition from their own ego to objective reality when discussing political philosophy (or for life in general) is a painful process. It was for me.

Based on this insight, I concluded that there must be some basic laws of society that all rational people must agree with and that do not depend on the political intuition bruises we received while growing up. Just as any business owner can recognize the secret to success, such as a sandwich shop using fresh bread, we should be able to identify some institutions with mathematical variables (that is, not open to debate or interpretation) that underlie any prosperous society and that ultimately shape its trajectory, for better or worse. For example, no one disagrees about the basic recipe for beer. The Germans codified it with the German Beer Purity Law (*Reinheitsgebot*) of 1516. In order for society to survive, it must have inputs and outputs that keep the system running and in balance. This is math, not science, even though managing a society can be thought of as a science. To not agree with this would be self-contradictory, so we should get the math right before we delve into the more complex parts of political philosophy. For example, one conclusion I reached was that people and society must consume resources (food, water, education, police, etc.) to stay alive. If we do not consume enough resources (some we produce by our labor, others are offered by nature), we will die, both as individuals and as a society.

No one can deny this, regardless of political beliefs, but many people reject this simple principle (whether they know it or not) when talking about balancing the books for society, which is tantamount to rejecting math. Where this simple axiom leads us, if we consider it via a process of rational abstraction in a broader context of social life, might surprise some people. I will refer to this as the institution of resource management. To use a second example, if a society is going to survive, men and women must procreate (1 + 1 = 3). Again, this is common sense and cannot be refuted. If people do not produce the next generation of children and nurture them to maturity, we will cease to exist after the current generation dies. Some institutions, such as the Catholic Church, do not allow its own members (the priests) to procreate, which means that it depends on society for its new members from one generation to the next, but this would be impossible if people outside of the Church stopped procreating. Again, as I will show, this simple mathematical fact has important consequences for political philosophy, assuming that we take a rational approach to the idea of procreation that balances the needs of individuals with the needs of children and society. I will refer to this as the institution of procreation.

My political philosophy focuses on these two institutions—resource management and procreation—and the conclusions that follow from a rational analysis of them. The reason for this is that they are fundamental, universal institutions. As long as humans exist, these two issues will have to be addressed. They provide the foundation for all other institutions and cannot not exist in a society, whereas people can survive without the big three institutions of the state, the rule of law, and a mechanism of accountability, as many people have done throughout history and even today. All societies must address these two fundamental, universal institutions and grow from them organically (we can never untether them from reality), or they will fail, just as a microbrew will fail if it does not follow the recipe for beer. (To be clear, every society must also address other institutions, such as the state, the rule of law, and a means of accountability, but these institutions will not be sustainable or even possible if we do not first succeed with resource management and procreation.) At first glance, nothing of particular interest seems to follow from these two institutions—resource management and procreation—in terms of helping us better understand the political divide today in America. However, as I continued my analysis while thinking about society as a system, to include reflecting on the four pillars of my political philosophy—human nature, institutions, wealth, and justice—I realized they were all I needed to create a rational system of political philosophy, which we can use to address some of the most contentious issues today. That is, rather than seeking fundamental, universal principles to justify our own beliefs, we can use fundamental, universal principles to shape our beliefs and resolve the political divide in America.

For example, even though most people agree that education is an important institution, both as an institution in itself and as a way to promote and inculcate other institutions, and an important way to invest in our children for the future, many people ignore what the word "investment" really means from a resource management perspective. In economic terms, in order for the use of resources to be called an investment, it must produce positive cash flow over the life of the investment. For example, if we spend $100,000 on a child during his K–12 education, then if we want to call this an "investment," the child must produce more than $100,000 of additional value plus interest, above and beyond what he would have earned without the K–12 education, to make up for the initial investment. Otherwise, the school would not be an investment, by definition. Some people have a bad habit of referring to most government spending as "investments," which sometimes is the case but often is not, as evidenced by our rising national debt. Granted, 100 percent of the students in our educational system will not have successful results (positive cash flow), and we might even know in advance which children probably might not succeed before the game even begins, but the bell curve distribution of the entire educational institution for the entire population should produce positive cash flow results that can be measured, the same way we would measure the profits of Apple or the S&P 500. Otherwise, we enter a negative cash flow situation that will bleed our economy and result in political decay. Problems arise when people speak about educational spending with no reference to return on investment (math) and no reference to whether spending the money on other projects would have produced better results (opportunity cost). Perhaps all children would benefit from a college education, but many of them would benefit even more from technical training or a stable family environment. Even though the USA spends more per child on education than most other developed countries, the results are not what they should be—not enough "bang for the buck"—especially for poor children, but there are many people who are still calling for even more spending on education rather than for reforms. I would submit that we could actually decrease educational spending, if done correctly, and have better results. However, the vested interests will resist any cuts in spending. The same goes for college spending. Even though the unemployment rate is high for recent college graduates and college loan debt has ballooned to over $1 trillion, a lot of which will never be repaid, there are still many people calling for more spending for college, which is not a wise use of our limited resources.

The Rational Animal

Underlying all political philosophy looms our faculty of reason and the idea of human nature. Throughout history, philosophers have attempted to ground their ideas in a coherent understanding of human nature, with the right tending to be more skeptical of human nature and the left tending to be more optimistic about human nature—from Hobbes' "war of all against all" on the right to Rousseau's "noble savage" on the left. This line of thinking often misses the point because the vast majority of the people who are being analyzed are not living in accordance with reason, at least not in its fullest potential. This would be like trying to assess the nature of a rose if you planted a rose in sand without sufficient nutrients, water, or sunlight. One of the challenges of allowing reason to be our guide is that many important political issues are grounded in emotion, so convincing masses of people to reassess their own beliefs in accordance with the rigors of reason is nearly impossible. In many ways, the history of political philosophy is the attempt to make reason our guiding principle, to heal our bruises, and to move from the shadows in Plato's cave to the light of day, but our two-year election cycles demonstrate that we have a long way to go.

The history of philosophy is filled with disagreements regarding reason and emotion, as if the two were in conflict. On the one hand, a philosopher like Kant suggested that ethics is a science of pure reason and that the rules we live by should be made in the context of reason, exemplified by the categorical imperative of his deontological ethics. On the other hand, a philosopher like Hume suggested the opposite, that ethics is all about emotion and passion, and that reason is there for the ride to steer the ship. I tend to agree with Hume that pure reason is incapable of generating a discussion about values and meaning, but reason is certainly a necessary and powerful tool for discussing them in a systematic manner. No such contrast should exist, even though it often does. The truth is that we are rational animals, animals with a capacity for rational thought, which means that the emotions and passions we experience in many ways are similar but are also in many ways vastly different than what animals experience. Animals have no capacity for aesthetic pleasure or love that transcends their own immediate existence. Therefore, when analyzing human nature and political institutions, while it might be interesting to compare us to our primate brethren, in terms of understanding why irrational people and irrational societies do the things they do, we really have nothing to learn from our primate brethren in terms of improving our society. We should ask ourselves two questions: How would rational people behave, and how do we arrive at the point of being rational? It should not surprise us that many people on the left and the right do not agree.

A Word of Caution

One important point to keep in mind while reading this book is what it is and what it is not. This is a work of philosophy, that is, an attempt to build a systematic abstract model to show how all the political philosophy pieces of the puzzle fit together at the most abstract level in a way that fits with the raw data and intuitions that give rise to the abstract model. Just as a detective might collect all the facts and clues to reconstruct how a crime was committed, I will focus on showing what must be true in order for society to continue to survive, which inevitably includes asking people to make some sacrifices along the way. The idea that society exists for our own sake to pursue our own happiness or our own personal journey will be dismissed as egoism, even though pursuing our happiness or our personal journey should be considered an important part of life. After this book is done, there will still be room for debate about specific issues, such as education and welfare spending, but we will have made great strides to the extent that we can rule out what will not work. Sometimes the secret to life is knowing what not to do. Just as not smoking and not drinking alcohol or sodas are two things you can do to improve your health, knowing what to avoid can help us shape a healthy society. I will not make any abstract assumptions about human nature or justice and then try to build a Utopian society around these vague ideas, but I will talk about what it means to be a rational animal and what follows from that idea.

On the other hand, this book is not a political polemic that is designed to raise all the hot button topics dividing Democrats and Republicans. The acceptance or rejection of my two fundamental principles will certainly have consequences for the ongoing debate between Democrats and Republicans—

as I will comment throughout the book—but my hope is that the two fundamental principles will provide a solid foundation for shaping the debate. This book is also not within the realm of the social sciences. As in the case of education, whereas I will raise the idea of education as an investment, which by definition implies positive cash flow, I will not recommend what level of GDP should be dedicated to achieve the best results or how the curriculum should be changed. These are empirical questions that will require the tools of the social sciences, with the understanding that the findings in this book might place parameters on how we move forward. Regarding healthcare, although I will address the basic of idea of healthcare as an institution and the role of the government, I will not make any specific recommendations regarding how to pay for or reform healthcare. I leave that to the people in the individual cities, counties, states, or at the federal level to decide how they want to live. Life is too short and too many lessons have been learned about what not to do to reinvent the mistakes of the past. In fact, the voters will have to decide all the major issues in this book, even if that means a slightly less efficient model of government that is dedicated to liberty, but this book will place limits or parameters on the decisions made by the voters and should not be subjected to the whim of special interest groups or the tyranny of the majority.

In many ways, this book will raise more questions than it will answer, but it addresses some important questions with some simple answers (simple like the design of an iPhone) that will undoubtedly be difficult to implement in the short term but will pay long-term dividends and get us back on the path of creating a prosperous and sustainable modern state that avoids radical political swings and absorbs the inevitable shocks when they happen. If I can convince people on the left and right sides of the political spectrum to reconsider some of their most basic assumptions and beliefs and to look beyond their bruises, I will consider this book a success.

Part I. Two Fundamental Institutions

Chapter One. Resource Management: The Prohibition of Deficit Spending

Unlike many subjects, political philosophy, and philosophy in general, does not give us clear guidance about where to begin, which is the crucial point of departure for developing a political philosophy.

In astronomy we begin with the planets and the universe, in history with the trajectory of societies over time, and so on, but it is not as clear where we should begin with political philosophy. Do we begin with human nature? Do we begin with material or economic forces? Do we begin with God or inalienable rights? Do we begin with the divine right of kings? Do we begin with the trajectory of societies over time? Where we begin the journey can set us on the right path or doom us to disaster from first sail, and there are no obvious warning lights to tell us whether we are on the right path. The wrong road will not take us to Rome, in this case, regardless of how we travel.

For example, Descartes, the father of modern philosophy, began his philosophy with his subjective, first-person experience, culminating with his famous, "I think, therefore I am" and Cartesian mind-body dualism. This seemed reasonable and intuitive to many people, especially after centuries of Scholasticism, even to some people today, but it led philosophy through a series of mind-bending theories of knowledge (epistemology) and metaphysics (philosophy of being) over hundreds of years that were not resolved until Kant, Schopenhauer, Wittgenstein, and others showed the flaws in the fundamental premise. That is, if we begin with the first-person perspective and attempt to build a philosophy on that foundation (Descartes himself highlighted that he was seeking a solid foundation for philosophy), we can never escape solipsism to get to the objective world of the third person perspective that must be real for any of this to make sense. The reason for this is that the first-person perspective is not fundamental; we cannot address it philosophically until we first address what makes it possible. That is, we necessarily beg the question when we use it as a point of departure because the first-person experience of reality is not fundamental, even if it appears so. By choosing a particular starting point, or fundamental premise, we are baking into the cake, so to speak, most of what follows. Therefore, we should be careful and focus our efforts on where to begin our journey.

Most theories in political philosophy begin with a particular point of departure. For example, the "social contract" theory espoused by philosophers like Locke, Rousseau, and Kant, who were influential in shaping the American and French revolutions, was based on two ideas. First, what are we like in a "state of nature," that is, in the absence of government? No surprise, there is no consensus on the answer to this question, and the earliest speculation was not accurate, as shown by Fukuyama. Second, how did we, after recognizing the limitations of such a social arrangement, take steps to establish a government by a process of consensus (a social contract)?

For example, when the Founding Fathers wrote the Constitution, this could be viewed as a social contract model of government that was used to design our social institutions from scratch, such as the three branches of government with checks and balances, but the Founding Fathers inherited ideas that were derived within a social context over many generations. Many philosophers have been critical of the often-idealized state of nature portrayed by this theory. For example, Hegel argued that the "Spirit" shaped or steered our social progress unconsciously over time, which in turn allowed us to develop socially to the point where rational reflection on our social institutions was possible. That is, the rational individuals who make the social contract are already the product of a society that had the right level of complexity to produce rational individuals capable of thinking about how to form a government. People in a genuine state of nature would be incapable of writing the Constitution. The other critical point is that few people formally consent to the government they live under. No one since the Founding Fathers has had the chance to vote on the Constitution. In fact, many people demand that we revere our founding documents like scripture, even though Jefferson himself suggested that constitutions should be rewritten regularly.

A second point of departure, utilitarianism, was developed by Bentham and Mill in the nineteenth century in England. These two focused on measuring the happiness of each individual in society, without concern for God's will, customs, traditions, society, natural law, or other abstract concepts. The basic idea of utilitarianism was to arrange society in such a way, via the passage of laws and the establishment of social institutions, so as to maximize the overall happiness of society, even going so far as saying happiness can be measured and was the most important variable for assessing the well being of society.

Thus, when deciding whether to pass a law or modify a social institution, we need only calculate how such a change would affect the overall happiness of society. This of course assumes that happiness is the greatest good and that it can be measured, which are no small assumptions. In its crudest form under Bentham, this idea of happiness was reduced to mere pleasure, which taken to its logical conclusion might mean that a life of constant sedation with a morphine drip would be preferable to a life that involves genuine suffering. Under Mill's more nuanced model, the quality of the pleasures was taken into account, to include our concern for the long-term wellbeing of our offspring, which involves sacrifice, but the same basic principle applied and the system seemed willing to accept suffering for a minority if the overall happiness of society increased. This model is also flawed for several reasons, to include the simple fact that happiness is difficult to quantify or measure within a society and that there is no reason to believe that happiness (especially emotional happiness) should be the end all to life, but utilitarianism had the benefit of moving political philosophy in a more empirical direction.

Obviously, when developing a political philosophy, we have to take many variables into consideration, such as human nature; the world we live in, such as geography and climate; and subjective considerations, such as happiness, but this does not mean these variables can be used as a point of departure. Let us suppose we were able to reach consensus about human nature and happiness, from the radical left to the radical right, would that be sufficient for us to hammer out a political philosophy we can all live with? Perhaps, but this is precisely the point: the two ends of the political spectrum do not and really cannot agree on human nature or happiness because the two ends of the political spectrum have more fundamental beliefs or intuitions that shape their conflicting views on human nature and happiness. The disagreement is baked into the cake. The radical left may draft a manifesto on human nature and happiness, and the radical right will disparage it by design, and vice versa. Fair enough, so perhaps our goal should be to draft a model for human nature and happiness that reflects a more central position, where most people live. This would seem like progress, but the "fringe" elements of the center would probably still disagree, and no one would agree on who is in the middle. (Pundits on both sides of the political spectrum often view themselves as "moderate.") In short, the point is that all people along the political spectrum can reduce their beliefs to a portfolio of basic beliefs and intuitions about human nature and happiness that is consistent within its own logic but is not consistent along the entire spectrum or with any fundamental, universal philosophical principles that can withstand scrutiny, which in turn makes compromise a challenge. For example, the right side of the political spectrum tends to be skeptical about human nature and therefore focuses on managing the negative aspects of human nature, with Hobbes' "war of all against all" being a good example. On the other hand, the left side of the political spectrum tends to do the opposite—assuming that humans are innately good (the "noble savage") but are corrupted by the institutions they live under—with Rousseau as a good example. Which side is right? The argument could be made that, absent proper nurturing, people will tend toward misbehavior as a result of their nature, but not always. Or, that because of our nature, proper nurturing will move people away from misbehavior, but not always. Some people are good and other people are bad, for a variety of reasons that we often cannot explain, but whether this is based on any metaphysical or transcendental forces, such as dialectical materialism or Original Sin, is beyond the scope of this book. Rather, this book will focus on the irrefutable fact that we are rational creatures and the consequences that follow from this.

The previous paragraph had an important pointer to get us moving in the right direction. Even if we assume we will never all agree on human nature or happiness, we do live with one simple fact that shapes all political debate: people exist along a political spectrum, with the extremes of the left and the right rejected by most people living in modern states. Just as we can use fundamental ethical principles to help us make rational ethical decisions, I will attempt to show that we can use fundamental, universal philosophical principles to better understand the left–right divide and make wise decisions about society. That is, rather than begin with unfounded beliefs and seek fundamental principles to justify them, I will analyze the basic facts and key concepts underlying political philosophy, put them into a broader context, and then see if we can identify any fundamental principles that transcend place and time. The point of departure for our analysis will be the institutions of resource management and procreation and the conclusions that follow from a rational analysis of them. Only after we have done this will we be in a good position to have a rational discussion regarding the political divide in America.

Net Resource Survival

Most people would agree that survival is a core function of any society and a basic right for all people. No one should be able to take away our right to survive without just cause, such as in response to a threat. This issue is not black and white—for example, people can be arrested for stealing food to survive—but any theory that rejects survival contradicts itself. We have no choice but to embrace survival as a basic principle. Life is its own justification. The reason for this is that if we do not survive, we will cease to exist as a society, in which case this exercise in developing a theory of political philosophy comes to an end, which would be a tragedy. I will assume that all people reading this book, therefore, no matter where they reside on the political spectrum, live in a society that plans to continue surviving, does not plan to commit collective suicide when a comet passes by earth, and therefore grants the right of survival to all people. Survival is a bedrock principle at all points along the political spectrum, even though the two extremes of the political spectrum might not agree on the specifics. I am not invoking the "right to life" as an abstract principle or providing God as a backstop against government tyranny. I am merely invoking survival, continuing our species, as a simple principle, to the extent that the absence of it means the end of society.

Taken at face value, however, it is not clear how survival fits onto the political spectrum. All people believe in a basic right to survival, especially their own. It is true that the right side of the political spectrum has been known to embrace a more robust concept of survival, even at the expense of causing damage to the environment, and that the left side of the political spectrum has been known to accept more limits to our claims to survival, such as by promoting policies in the name of protecting the environment that would reduce agricultural yields, which could result in pockets of starvation, but that is not the type of survival I am talking about. In this chapter and the next, I will address the variables that are essential to survival: resource management and procreation. To move forward on resource management, I will introduce the more complex concept of *net resource survival*. The previous use of the word survival was abstract. How much water? How much food? How much shelter? How much education? How much defense? I will now shift gears to look closer at individual survival in the context of resource management.

As biological creatures, we consume resources to survive. At a most basic level, this includes food and water, but it also includes shelter, education, police protection, and all the other resources we need to sustain society, to include altruism. One important point to keep in mind is that *our own resource consumption begins before we are born.* The mother and father who gave us life, as well as others and society, start using resources to support us while we are still in the womb, to include the additional food the mother eats, prenatal vitamins, regular check-ups at the doctor, hospital expenses, the purchase of baby clothes, and so on. The key point is that others provide these resources—out of love and altruism, out of a broader concern for others, or by being compelled to pay taxes. Thus, when assessing our resource net worth ledger, we enter the world in debt. With time, this debt only increases as we work our way through childhood and the educational system. In modern states, most people do not become net producers of resources until after the educational phase as a young adult, which could be high school, technical training, college, or graduate school. Of interest, we can calculate this cost. We can count the money that was spent to raise us. A parent can calculate the direct cost of food and clothes. Society can calculate the cost of educating a child, which is paid for with tax dollars, but calculating how the costs of traffic lights and police protection relate to each child is more difficult, unless we divide the costs equally for each citizen. Thus, not only must parents use their own money to raise their own children, they must pay taxes to the government to provide other services for their children.

In theory, we could keep a running tab of all the expenses for each child and then ask them to pay it back after entering the workforce and becoming a net producer of resources. However, in addition to being nearly impossible to calculate accurately and given the difficulty of enforcing such a plan (what interest rate would we charge?), the basic idea grinds on our basic moral principles because we tend to view the resources provided to children as altruism, an important concept I will address in more detail as I develop my argument. Simply stated, altruism is selflessness in the form of taking *tangible steps* to provide for the wellbeing of others. It has nothing to do with feelings or good intentions. When I joke with my kids that they will have to pay us back for raising them, they laugh because they understand the idea is absurd.

As I will show later, altruism is one of the most powerful and important elements of political philosophy, as long as we make the conscious decision to harness it in a rational manner, rather than reject it or redefine it in a way that is not consistent with our nature. Both sides of the political spectrum agree with this but disagree with how altruism should be "distributed" within society. To put it simply, during our childhood and youth, when we are incapable of being net producers of resources, other people must provide for us, and in ways that go beyond material resources. In theory, orphans are provided with food and education, but altruism takes it to the next level via love and sacrifice, which is why stable, "traditional" families have a proven track record of accumulating more wealth over generations. This is not a book about psychology, but as a parent I can attest to the importance of physical contact and love for raising a child. The children who have two parents and other people who are willing to make sacrifices for them will, all things being equal, benefit more than children who do not receive this same level of altruistic support.

At this point, without getting too political, the resources, to include altruism, to raise a child come mostly from one of two places: the family (which includes the extended family or kinship network) or society (everyone else). It is a well-known law of human nature that nothing is stronger than the bond between parent and child. As I will address in the next chapter, it gives rise to the kin selection and reciprocal altruism model that is so important to political philosophy. It is also a fact that not all parents provide for their children the way they should, due to neglect, ignorance, or a lack of resources. In these cases, and even when parents are doing a splendid job, there is often room for society to play a positive role in providing resources to ensure that each child reaches his or her potential, within reason. So far so good, but we start to enter the political debate when we say that *some forms of altruism are better than others*. To use the language of economics, we can ask which form of altruism is the cheapest and most reliable. As a general rule, all things being equal, biological parents can be relied upon to provide altruistic love and even sacrifice their own interests for the sake of the child. As Plato observed:

> First they are sick for intercourse with each other, then for nurturing their young—for their sake the weakest animals stand ready to do battle against the strongest and even to die for them, and they may be racked with famine in order to feed their young. They would do anything for their sake.[1]

All things being equal, in a bell curve kind of way, not on a case by case basis kind of way, which is what matters most for philosophy and social policy, biological parents can be relied upon to provide the altruism their children need—for free, that is, without raising taxes or creating any government programs, as has been the case throughout most of human history. Therefore, any political system would be wise to tap into what is

---

1 Plato, *Symposium*, 207b.

perhaps the most powerful force of human nature: the natural bond between biological parent and child. On the flip side, it is not clear that the same thing can be said for society. Many people would argue that it would be a good thing if all people were altruistic with society at large, but there are no historical examples of this happening and it could even result in resources being misallocated due to a lack focus. Do we really want people giving away all of their resources at the expense of their own children? That said, we should consider an important variable: not all parents perform their duties as expected—because they lack the resources (we cannot live on love alone), because of ignorance, or because, dare we say, they are bad parents who are motivated by egoism at the expense of their own children or expect others to shoulder the burden for them. Returning to our analysis, the important part is that until we reach adulthood and become net producers of resources, we are net consumers of resources and someone else has to provide those resources. The resources do not appear out of thin air. Thus, when looking at society and the political philosophy we will embrace, we have to account for how these resources will be produced and allocated. The children cannot provide the resources, unless they work or have a way to earn an income, which should be avoided, and we will rule out keeping a running tab for children to pay after they reach adulthood. With the net resource consumer phase of youth out of the way, we can shift to the phase of being a net producer of resources.

At some point, usually after we finish the educational phase of our development, we enter the workforce to become net producers of resources. For the moment, we will assume that the debt of childhood is paid. At first glance, it might seem sufficient to earn enough resources to provide for our own survival, but this misses the point. In addition to providing for our own survival, we have to consider taxes, providing resources for our children (paying it forward), and planning for retirement with savings when we again often become net consumers of resources. Just as important, we have to understand work as anything that has to be done, whether we get paid for it or not, such as changing the oil in our car or paying someone to change the oil in our car. When considering the options of a parent taking care of children during the day or working a job to earn a salary to pay someone else to take care of the children during the day, we should consider both options as work. Someone has to take care of young children during the day—it is important work that has to be done—so whether or not a person actually gets paid for the work he or she does is not as important as the fact that the work gets done. In fact, by doing work that does not involve receiving a paycheck, we avoid paying taxes, whereas we have to pay taxes on the salary we use to pay for daycare. As the saying goes, a penny saved is a penny earned, which means that the pay for being a stay at home parent is whatever would have been paid to a daycare provider (and all the other work that gets done in a home). I add this important caveat because I have encountered many people, unfortunately, who do not consider being a stay at home parent a legitimate or productive form of work. Nothing could be further from the truth. For reasons that are not clear, there is an incorrect perception that work is not legitimate unless we directly get paid for it.

During our working years, which last from roughly 25–65 (about 50% of the average life), our own lives and society at large depend on the resources we produce and the work we perform. For every working age adult who is not a net producer of resources, someone else has to pick up the slack for raising children (schools), running government programs (such as national defense and welfare), and contributing to retirement planning. Circumstances will dictate that some people, sometimes for reasons beyond their control, will struggle with becoming net resource producers, but it is precisely for this reason that our educational system should focus on moving people along this path of personal development and resource production, as opposed to teaching people that government exists to take care of them or assume the major risks of life. One of the goals of our educational system should be to help people become net resource producers; if we do not, we will not produce the resources we need to survive and thrive as a society.

Given that the phases of our lives before (youth) and after (retirement) our working age years more often than not involve being net resource consumers, the argument could be made, with math, that we have a social and moral obligation to produce enough surplus resources during our working years (above and beyond our own consumption) to offset our net resource consumption during the other two phases of our life—youth and retirement. That is, we have a mathematical way to calculate whether or not we have fulfilled our most basic social obligation. To repeat, we do not owe the debt of our childhood, but we will be expected to provide resources to our own children during their net resource consumption years, and to society at large via taxes, which is a way of paying it forward.

In other words, if we were to create a bar chart (see below) to track our net resource consumption during different phases of our lives, to include before we were born, with negative bars for youth and retirement and positive bars for our adult working years, the sum of the bars should add up to at least 0 to avoid being net consumers of resources during our lives. The idea of leaving the world a better place—being a net resource producer— should be enshrined in our educational system and social values.

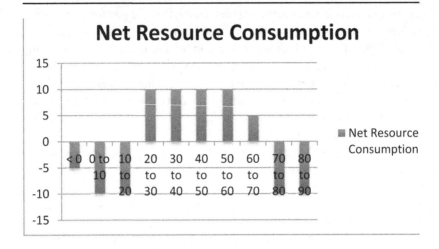

With this chart, in which the 10 bars add up to 0 (-5 + -10 + -10 + 10 + 10 + 10 + 10 + 5 + -10 + -10 = 0), I would like to highlight one of the primary differences that separates the right from the left in politics, generally speaking. Although both sides of the political spectrum have to accept the math of the above chart, both sides do not agree on how our social obligations are derived or defined by the math.

Whereas people on the right tend to link the net resource production years (the positive bars) to the net resource consumption years (the negative bars) via family or tribal ties, with working age people taking care of the youth and elders, people on the left tend to link the two via the government, with social programs funded with tax revenue taking care of the youth (such as public schools) and elders (such as Social Security).

Whereas the right will often call people on the left lazy for wanting to pass the buck and avoid their social responsibilities, the left will often call the right greedy for not wanting to establish social programs for the youth and the elderly. As I will address in the next chapter, although society certainly benefits from a safety net, I believe the argument from the right is more sustainable than the argument from the left, for two reasons. First, the bonds between family members as a matter of fact are stronger than the bonds between strangers, even people from the same society, which means that family members can be relied upon *in a more consistent and predictable manner* to make the necessary sacrifices for their own family members. This is how humanity survived for millennia before the rise of the modern state. Second, given the amount of tax revenue that has to be collected to fund these social programs (local, state, and federal government spending in the USA recently accounted for 41% of GDP), they can become a net drain on the economy, often via deficit spending, and ultimately do not produce the desired outcomes that many people envision, which results in calls for even more tax revenue. There is no doubt that providing a safety net is an important function of government, especially in a modern state, but these programs are no match for the strength of family networks (both emotionally and financially), which give the family members important advantages over others.

Before moving on to retirement, I should say a few words about a topic that plays an important role in our lives: *debt*. For most people, taking out a loan to buy a home or a car is an economic rite of passage, but as the recent financial crises have shown (2000 and 2008), debt can be a double-edged sword. Most people who understand finance know that a healthy level of debt can be a good thing, even necessary for success, what Rich Dad calls "good debt." For example, without debt, most people could never buy a home or start a business or would have to save a long time to buy a decent car. Our ability to absorb debt, of course, depends on our assets and our income, that is, on our ability to pay the debt back with a certain degree of predictability. When banks or individuals lend money, the first thing they want to know is whether they will get their money back, with interest. To measure this, banks look at income, assets, other debts, and so on (creditworthiness), to make an informed assessment about the quality of the loan. As such, we have rules of thumb, such as a 20% down payment for a home or a monthly mortgage payment that does not exceed a fixed percentage of someone's income, which helps prevent failed loans.

If debt is used wisely (rationally), it can help you grow your wealth more rapidly and make you a net producer of resources and an asset to society. Any real estate investment book will mention the benefits of debt or leverage. However, if debt is used recklessly (irrationally, that is, in violation of math), it can lead to bankruptcy and make you a net resource consumer and a liability to society. The key variable in determining whether you are using debt wisely or recklessly is *solvency*: as you accumulate debt, can you service the debt payments, along with all your other expenses, keeping in mind that you should have a savings buffer to fill the gap during short-term disruptions to your income. This still sounds somewhat abstract, so I should mention a different concept that has a more quantitative connotation: *deficit spending*. With deficit spending, we have a clear, unambiguous concept that politics cannot modify or twist. If your total expenses, to include servicing your debts, exceed your income, you have deficit spending, whether you are on the left or right side of the political spectrum. If your total expenses, to include servicing your debt, are equal to or less than your income, you do not have deficit spending. You have positive net resource consumption.

This is one of those few but important facts that all people must accept, and the honest acceptance of it will have profound consequences for political philosophy.

Granted, there will always be times when we have to dip into our savings to make ends meet during short-term income disruptions (even Keynes did not support sustained deficit spending), but the deficit spending we see today for families and governments takes it to dangerous levels. Not only are many families not saving, they are using deficit spending to sustain a lifestyle their incomes cannot support. This makes them net resource consumers, which is not a sustainable way to promote economic growth. The same goes for most governments. Thus, if they have income problems, they cannot pay their debts and have no savings to survive in the meantime. Needless to say, any family or government that does this in a sustained way, year after year, is on the path to bankruptcy. We should regulate the issuance of credit and debt to avoid debt traps precisely because our modern financial system is conceptual and rational. Not only that, we as members of a society should rightly judge such a person or government as irresponsible, as not "living within their means." As the deficit spending increases and servicing debt payments eats up more of our income, it becomes more difficult to remain a net resource producer. This means other people will have to pick up the slack, which is not fair to the rest of us. Thus, when we say people are net resource producers, we are saying that, at the end of the day, when all the accounts are settled, they still have something to show for their work, whether in the form of savings or other assets.

Regarding retirement, given that work takes a toll on our bodies and that most people would like to take a break before death, planning for retirement should be an important part of our net resource model. If all goes well, we will have saved enough resources or acquired enough assets so that we can shift back to being a net resource consumer during retirement. If all goes really well, we will continue to be a net resource producer during retirement, such as by running a business or renting out real estate, while still slowing down to enjoy life.

A review of the federal budget shows how important retirement entitlements are, with Social Security and Medicare/Medicaid making up about 50% of the total federal budget. That is a stunning number from an historical perspective. Although Social Security seems like a nice entitlement, it is really nothing more than a paternalistic program by the federal government to force people to save for retirement or the prospect of disability. (Some people insist on referring to this program as "insurance"; but given that decisions regarding the program are often based on political winds, not on mathematics or actuarial charts, evidenced by the looming insolvency of the programs, we cannot call it insurance in the technical sense of the word.) Absent this program, left to their own devices, many people would not save enough money and would end up destitute, in which case, in the absence of government programs, their children or other family members would likely have to assume responsibility for taking care of them. (This is a trend I predict will gain momentum as we see a return to multi-generational homes.) Given that so many people pay into the program for so many years, it is no surprise that Social Security is a political hot potato that few are willing to touch, even though the model has broken down and we are moving toward insolvency. The input and output model for the system is not sound because we have fewer and fewer workers taking care of more and more retirees, and the proper adjustments to the system are not being made because the program is driven by politics, not by math or actuarial charts. At some point, we will have to do a combination of the following three options: raise contributions, raise the retirement age, or lower the benefits. We can either make the choice now or have the decision made for us later.

To avoid a political debate, we should step back and take an objective look at the mathematics of retirement finance. At this point, we are still talking about the life of an individual person, not society, even though society is nothing more than a collection of individuals. If we assume a scenario in which Social Security or no other such programs exist, what could a person do to plan for retirement, keeping in mind our net resource producer model? As a general rule, we have two models: defined benefit programs or defined contribution programs. With defined benefit programs, in exchange for investing a set percentage of our income, we receive a predictable stipend after we reach retirement age. For example, if we invest 10% of our income in a retirement program for 40 years, we will receive a stipend of 40% of our income when we reach the age of 62. The specific numbers do not matter; what does matter is that we know how much money we will receive each month when we reach retirement until the day we die, even though we might not know the purchasing power of the money in the future. A pension of $50,000 thirty years from now might sound good but might barely buy groceries when the time comes. This is known as an annuity. On the other hand, with a defined contribution plan, we invest a fixed amount or a percentage of our income into a fund and watch it grow. When we reach retirement, we make withdrawals from the account until no money is left. This is the 401(k) model. We can withdraw a flat rate annuity, as in the case of a defined benefits program, but the key difference is the money might run out. Or, there might be money left over when we die, in which case we can pass it on to our family.

Simple enough, but the consequences are significant. In the case of a defined contribution plan, we know exactly how much money we have at all times in our account, but we lose some predictability because we do not know how long we will live or how the value of our account will change with inflation. How much should we take out each month? What happens if the money runs out? In the case of a defined benefit program, however, we know exactly how much money we will receive during retirement, often with a built-in adjustment for inflation. What is not to like about this model? After all, it is difficult or impossible to anticipate the return on investment to predict an exact monthly stipend. To do this, you will have to "sell" your 401(k) retirement account to a bank or insurance company, which will make a calculation based on many complex variables in the actuary tables (math). The key is that, in exchange for the bank assuming the risk (you might live to be 110 years old, or the economy might crash), the bank or insurance company will require a fee, which means less money for you, just as a person might sell a recurring lottery payment for a lump sum now. Many people, especially in their later years, are willing to give up some potential gains for security or predictability. The important point is that this risk calculation is based on math. Some politicians will make promises they cannot deliver on, but we should tune them out.

Given these two models, people can make a rational decision about how to plan for retirement, perhaps using a blend of both. With defined contribution plans, we assume all of the risk and make all the decisions. With defined benefit plans, a third-party such as a bank or insurance company assumes some of the risk in exchange for providing predictability. If the bank miscalculates, it suffers the loss, not you or the taxpayers. If you die early, they win. If you live longer than expected, you win. However, what happens when the government enters the world of defined benefit programs, such as Social Security, and uses the ballot box and polls, not math or actuarial charts, to make decisions? (The government will certainly hire mathematicians to run the program, but the political process itself will inevitably run the program.) What happens if the government miscalculates and does not collect enough money to pay all the future liabilities? Or worse, what if the government does not care about the math and instead promises more generous Social Security benefits for political purposes, such as gaining votes to win elections? Which politician will do the rational thing and reduce benefits or raise the retirement age if math dictates we should? Which constituents would vote for someone who proposed reducing Social Security benefits?

Just as we can use the idea of prohibiting deficit spending as a rudder to steer us safely though our net resource producer working years, we can use the concepts of defined contribution and defined benefit programs to steer us through the net resource consumer years of retirement. Granted, as we move from the individual to society, we can talk about whether poor people will receive additional benefits, above and beyond their contribution to the retirement program, but this raises an important point to consider. If Social Security were to convert from being a defined benefit program to a defined contribution program, such that the benefits people received would equal the amount of money they contributed into the program during their working years, plus interest, as in the case of a 401(k), could we ever have a solvency issue? The answer is no, for the same reason that the money we are allowed to withdraw from our 401(k) is limited to the amount of money we paid into the account. We will never have to bail out the 401(k) program (knock on wood). Granted, the critic might argue that poor people could never contribute enough money to their own accounts to have enough money to survive after retirement. That is, the critic might argue that the Social Security program, in addition to being a retirement and disability insurance program, is also a *wealth redistribution program*. This might be true, but we could address this by supplementing poor people with money outside of the Social Security fund. Thus, this would be a fair and mathematically objective way to resolve the Social Security debate—you get what you invest, nothing more, nothing less, and we forever avoid the possibility of default. Not to mention, and just as important, we remove the possibility of political corruption from the game because politicians will be unable to promote irrational benefits (not based on math) in exchange for votes. For this reason, to avoid the potential collapse of pension systems in the public and private sectors and to ensure their solvency forever, without the potential for political manipulation, *I would propose that we eliminate all defined benefit programs in the public* sector and replace them all with defined contribution programs.

Before moving on, I should say a few more words about being born into debt. Just as we would never expect adults to pay back the money that was used to support them during their net resource consumption years of youth, because the debt is paid at birth, which is an idea I assume most people on the left and the right would agree with, the same idea applies to society. Some people have argued that we are indebted to society at birth and that people who succeed in life owe a larger percentage of their income to society because "they didn't build that." On an intuitive level, the idea makes some sense—others built the roads that I use to run my trucking company—but the same rule applies. The previous generations that built those roads did so on their own by paying taxes in accordance with the laws. The fact that they built those roads does not obligate us to pay them back any more than we have to pay back the military for protecting our country during World War II, aside from honoring them. Our debt to society today is nothing more than the current tax bill we pay today in accordance with the law. Today, we too are paying taxes to build new roads and repair old ones, but we have no right to expect people 20–30 years from now to pay us back. As long as we are paying our taxes in accordance with the current tax laws, we are paying our debt to society and do not incur any special debts because we take advantage of what has been produced by society in the past, whether roads, schools, or other technology, just as children do not incur any additional debts just because their parents spent a lot of money prior to their birth. Obviously, most intelligent people recognize that they could not have achieved success on their own or without the society they live in, and some rich people certainly avoid paying some taxes or reduce their tax burden because of corruption, but this does not mean they should be forced to pay additional money, above and beyond what is required by the law. It might be true that "they didn't build that," in the sense of the roads that someone uses for a trucking company, but neither did we, and nothing stopped us from pursuing the same profitable business opportunity. As long as we pay taxes in accordance with the law, we have paid our debt to society.

State Arbitrage

While I was studying for my MBA, I studied the Black-Scholes Option Pricing Model. The basic idea was that if we wanted to buy an option on a stock (the option to buy a stock at a future price at a fixed price), which is a financial derivative, how do we calculate the fair market value of the option? For example, if Apple is currently trading at $100 and I think the value of the stock will rise to $150 in three months, I could buy an option to buy the stock in three months for $125. If I am right and the stock rises to $150, I can execute my option to buy it at $125 and pocket a $25 profit (if I sell the stock immediately for $150), less the cost of the option. If the stock does not rise to $125, or even drops, I do not execute my option and I lose the cost of the option. The complexity of this calculation is driven by several factors, such as the riskiness (volatility) of the stock, the time until the option expires, and the risk-free rate of return, which is beyond the scope of this book. In the end, a formula was devised that received the Nobel Prize for Economics in 1997 (which is why it took almost an entire semester to understand the formula).

One of the insights that led to the formula was the idea of using combinations of other financial assets to simulate an option as a way to calculate the fair price. For example, if I can use the combination of buying a stock and selling short a bond with a risk-free rate of return, I can *simulate* the returns of an option without buying an option, the details of which are beyond the scope of this book. If I can do that at a price that differs from the current market price of the option trading on an exchange, I can arbitrage (simultaneously buying and selling an asset with different prices to earn a risk-free profit) the opportunity. For example, if I am watching the markets closely and see a moment when gold is selling for $1,300 in New York and for $1,310 in Tokyo, I can simultaneously place a buy order in New York and a sell order in Tokyo to pocket a $10 profit risk-free. My profit was based on the simultaneous buying and selling of the gold (arbitrage), not on speculating whether the price would rise or fall. The same goes for an option. If I see the three-month $125 Apple option selling for $15 and I can simulate the same option for only $10, then I can arbitrage the difference to make a risk-free profit of $5.

Shifting back to our analysis, one of the most important questions we should ask when talking about the creation of a modern state is how such a state would compare to a state we could simulate on our own. For example, in the USA, local, state, and federal spending recently accounted for 41% of GDP. If 41% of my income goes out in taxes to pay for all that government, but I could create my own government-like organization by paying only 30% of my income, I would have to weigh the pros and cons of both options—just as I would have to weigh the options of buying an option on the exchange or simulating my own option. (If this sounds crazy or far-fetched, consider the option of moving to a foreign country with lower taxes.) For example, even though I could save 11% of my income by creating my own government-like organization, would the quality of service be as good? As they say, you get what you pay for.

Let us suppose that after years of hard work we found ourselves living in a self-sufficient farm with good soil, crops, domesticated animals, and plenty of fresh water. We are able to achieve net resource producer status. We can survive day-to-day, build some assets over time, such as the house we live in, and pass the farm onto our children. We might keep guns for protection and trade our surplus goods and services for other goods and services. At some point, as our farm grows, we might use some of our resources to hire a full-time security guard to serve the role of security so that we can focus on farming. As we accumulate more wealth, we might hire a tutor to educate our children. As we accumulate more wealth, we might hire a doctor to treat us, and so on, using our own wealth and resources to hire people to perform the services that a government would normally be expected to perform. In this way, we will have simulated the creation of a government, to the extent that services are being provided, the key difference being that we can fire any of these service providers at any time. They work for us. They cannot force us to pay them for their services, which is a nice option to have. The important point is that we now have a baseline for assessing the value and effectiveness of government.

It should not take long to see that such an arrangement, although possible (and a reality for many wealthy people living in developing countries with weak states), is not the most efficient way to do business. After all, my neighbor could hire a dozen security guards and have them attack my farm to kill us and take over the farm. To prevent this, I could hire 24 guards, and so on, but at some point all the people who are living in a particular geographic area and with a common sense of identity would benefit from pooling their resources to create one institution that has a monopoly on legitimate force, call it the police or the military. This should be with the understanding that once this is done, it will be difficult or impossible to fire them (they have the guns), so we would be wise to demand a means to defend ourselves or even remove them from power if they abuse their authority. The same goes for school and doctors. Rather than hire one tutor to teach all of my kids, I could pool my resources with other families to hire teachers who specialize in various subjects and ages. Rather than hire one general doctor, I could pool my resources with other families to hire doctors who specialize in different areas, and so on. In the case of teachers and doctors, we could still fire them more easily, because they do not have a monopoly on legitimate violence, but we would all benefit from establishing stable institutions.

As we expand our analysis, two points stand out. First, just as humans need resources and nurturing to develop and mature as organic creatures, governments need only one thing: money (tax revenue). Money is the lifeblood of government. If we give money to the government, it has everything it needs to perform its functions, to include hiring and training qualified employees. (As I will address later, many governments have the authority to print money under a fiat currency system, which changes the rules of the game.) Second, as we create different social institutions—military, police, education, medical, etc.—we can measure their effectiveness vis-à-vis our simulated state. That is, we can measure the value of government by the value it creates above and beyond our simulated government. For example, if I can reduce my security expenses and receive better services from the national police, it is in my rational self-interest to pay taxes rather than establish my own police force. The same goes for education and medical services: if pooling my resources with other people to make institutions creates efficiencies and improves the predictability and the quality of service, it is in my rational self-interest interest to pay my taxes. The important point is that we have a baseline to assess the real value of government, and it stresses the idea that government exists to serve the needs of the people who pay the taxes.

In short, there is an objective way to assess the value and effectiveness of government. For example, if we are spending more money on education and the results do not improve, we have a problem. My guess is that most people would fire a private tutor if the results were not positive and tangible—soon after the services begin, not after several years or decades—or even demand their money back. Could you imagine making such a demand to the government? In many cases, spending even more money alone probably will not solve the problem, so we have to look for other underlying variables, such as what is being taught, how it is being taught, and who is doing the teaching. If we spend less money on police and crime starts to rise, we have a problem, and so on. We might have to spend more on the police to reduce crime to a level we can live with, keeping in mind the principle of diminishing returns: reducing crime rates to zero could be achieved only at an exorbitant cost and with a significant reduction in liberty. The same logic applies to terrorism, which has received a disproportional response relative to the actual damage it does to our country in the average year. Just as we can assess the value of the person who changes the oil in our car by considering the value of his service relative to other service providers, we can assess the value of our government by the services it provides relative to what we could do on our own or with commercial vendors. That said, all governments work with some tolerable levels of inefficiency to achieve desirable results that market forces alone are unable achieve. For example, we might spend millions of dollars in the justice system to put someone behind bars, even if the future crimes we might prevent will not save us millions of dollars. Or, some children might need special services at school, which might or might not pay off in the end, but we want to prevent them from falling too far behind, especially if they are late bloomers. That is, in addition to serving as an efficient service provider, governments provide others services that are harder to quantify, especially in the short term. However, this does not mean we cannot place rational limits on government inefficiency to prevent abuse, such as prohibiting deficit spending.

Deficit Spending

At this point, we can begin addressing the first fundamental institution of political philosophy, which means that some readers will probably start to more strongly agree or disagree with what I am about to say. If I presented my analysis correctly, most people should nod, however reluctantly, to acknowledge this simple mathematical truth, which has profound consequences. If we keep in mind that governments do not exist independently in a state of nature—we have to create them—we have to start from the position of no government as a baseline and slowly add government institutions to the mix until we achieve the right balance. As a general statement, we will begin by saying that people on the right side of the political spectrum prefer smaller governments and people on the left side of the political spectrum prefer larger governments, at least in terms of the role government plays in our daily lives, but there are always exceptions to the rule. For example, some people on the right support the idea of funding a large military, which has contributed to deficit spending, and some people on the left support the idea of the state dissolving at an advanced stage of communism.

The primary debate between left and right hinges on the legitimate functions of government, which in the end boils down to how much money will be collected in tax revenue to fund the various programs. If we are working under the assumption that we are living in a modern state, such as the USA, then the democratic process is really nothing more than a process for achieving consensus about the role of government. As sentiments shift to the left, we will tend to see a call for larger government; as sentiments shift to the right, we will tend to see a call for smaller government, with the whole process shaped by our culture. We want government to reflect the will of the people, *but we also want the will of the people to reflect the reality they are living under and the realities about how people and institutions behave.* This is a healthy tension that exists in every election and can be used to advance our society, or at least prevent us from regressing. What we cannot allow is a group of self-appointed experts who believe they know what is best for us rise to power and disrupt the will of the people, unless the people freely recognize that these people have a positive vision for the country and vote for them. For example, if a left leaning government pushes a radical left-wing agenda, there could be a backlash in the next election, with a shift to the right, which makes implementation of the radical left-wing program difficult or impossible. The same works the other way with a radical right-wing agenda.

Between this battle of left and right is the government itself. And the government, like any system, needs resources to survive. If we do not provide enough resources to the government, it weakens and fails to perform its primary function—serving the needs of the people. On the other hand, if we provide too many resources to the government, or if the government finds ways to extract resources from the people against their will, such as by force or by printing money, it could become tyrannical and fail to perform its primary function—serving the needs of the people. Thus, we have to walk a fine line when talking about the size of the government and keep in mind that the government at any moment should reflect the current status of the struggle between the voters on the left and the right, which is often a function of the level of social development. If the extreme right has its way and government is bled to a minimum, we could face the tyranny of special interest groups and businesses that pay off judges to avoid justice or manipulate the banking system to steal money. If the extreme left has its way and the government grows too large and takes on a life of its own, beyond the control of the voters, then tyranny is probably not far away because a radical left-wing agenda requires centralized power to be implemented.

I am not suggesting how large government should be, what specific institutions should be created, or which specific laws should be passed, but I would like to propose one fundamental philosophical principle that would shape how we resolve the political divide in American: *a prohibition on deficit spending*. On the one hand, this prohibition would serve as a rational check on political ambition, hubris, and corruption. If deficit spending is prohibited, many political promises would ring hallow and many special interest groups would scatter to the winds. In other words, this prohibition would keep the government in line. On the other hand, this prohibition provides us the discipline we need to focus on creating wealth rather than seeking ways to receive entitlements or other financial benefits from the government. Just as we should want our children to face the rigors of homework rather than plagiarizing from the Internet, the rules of the game should demand that we all stick to the path of hard work and discipline rather than take the easy way out by demanding entitlements or special favors. In other words, this prohibition would keep the citizens in line.

Prohibiting deficit spending is the best way to keep our society on a positive track and to avoid radical swings one way or the other. Just as we make school a requirement to help children stay on the right path, we can help the government and the citizens stay on the right path by requiring balanced budgets. With this fundamental, universal principle enshrined in our beliefs, we will be one step closer to resolving the political divide in America. If the government cannot resort to deficit spending to achieve its objectives, it will be forced to take steps to help society create more wealth to collect in taxes, which is more difficult than borrowing or printing money. To repeat, *a prohibition of deficit spending is not a prohibition on debt*. Governments at the federal, state, and local levels should be free to take on debt as a rational way to fund projects, as long as there is enough current revenue to service the debt. For example, if a city collects and spends $1 million per month in tax revenue and wants to build a school that will have monthly loan payments of $50,000, the city should issue a bond as long as it reduces its other monthly expenses by $50,000 per month. Or, if such a reduction would be difficult, the people could vote to raise an additional $50,000 per month in tax revenue. What should not be allowed to happen is $50,000 per month in deficit spending because once the genii is out of the bottle, we will never get it back in, which is what we are seeing today. Deficit spending is an addictive drug that chips away at the discipline that is required to create wealth and build a prosperous society based on liberty.

The key issue here is that government should be accountable to the people and the people should not look to the government as a way to drain the wealth of society. If the political landscape today is such that the government can raise only $1 million per month in tax revenue, based on current tax law (assuming special interest groups did not manipulate the tax laws), then the government has a solemn responsibility to spend only $1 million per month because the laws passed by the people's representatives determine how much they collectively agree to pay in taxes. Just as the person who changes the oil in your car cannot raise prices on a whim, because you can go to other service providers, we need a mechanism to restrain government so that it does not pursue its own interests. At the same time, we should make sure government has the capacity and the autonomy to perform the functions we need them to perform on our behalf. Government officials who know their portfolio can make recommendations for budgets or advise us what will happen if budgetary goals are not met, but they should have no authority to dictate how much the taxpayers spend, any more than a private businessman should be able to dictate which products we buy or how much we pay for them. When we allow the government to introduce deficit spending, the system slowly breaks down and allows the government to assert itself over the will of the people. For example, suppose I am running for mayor of a city that collects $1 million per month in tax revenue and decide I want to defeat my opponent at any cost. In such a scenario I might offer to sweeten the pensions of the teachers and police in exchange for their votes, even if the city does not have enough money today to add to the pension system to fund such a future liability. This, in turn, initiates a race to the bottom as politicians scramble to make promises in exchange for votes because voters are told to "vote their interest." We can kick the can down the road and have our children pay the bills when the teachers and police officers retire, but this would not be fair to the people who did not vote for this spending (our children). Just as we do not inherit a debt at birth (either our own debt or the debt of our ancestors), we should not be allowed to give our grandchildren a debt that they will have to pay for with their own income.

Why stop there? Suppose I as a candidate make promises to build a new weapon system in a military base in my home state or promises to increase Social Security benefits, even though we lack the current tax revenue to fund such promises. In short, by giving government the power of deficit spending, we open the door for politicians or government looking out for their own interests at the expense of the people who sent them there to work on their behalf, which leads to a breakdown in fiscal discipline. It also opens the door for special interest groups to manipulate the political system to gain benefits, such as funding for specific programs, knowing full well that the government will simply issue new debt to fund the deficit spending. We also see the Federal Reserve print money out of thin air to buy back billions of dollars of debt via Quantitative Easing to keep interest rates artificially low, which allows highly paid pundits with esteemed credentials to use prestigious publications to make the specious argument that we do not have a debt problem because interest rates are low. "Lead us not into temptation." Once corrupt people know there are hundreds of billions of dollars sloshing around the system without any check by the voters, they will flock there to take advantage of the situation. If that money dries up and the potential for corruption is squeezed out of the system by prohibiting deficit spending, the corrupt people will look for other ways to make illicit money, but at least they will not have the opportunity to do harm to the government.

If we know one thing about human nature (that is, humans who do not have a refined faculty of reason, which, unfortunately, is a larger number than most of us are willing to admit) it is that most people will say yes to free stuff, so the candidate who promises the most free stuff will often win the election, unless people have the courage to avoid the destructive "vote your interest" mantra and vote for the person who will "do the right thing" for the good of the country, not what is good for our own particular situation, even if that means spending cuts and discipline. Therefore, if we could prohibit deficit spending such that all those promises of free stuff would ring hollow, the candidates who campaign on that message would not succeed and would be forced to sell their snake oil elsewhere.

Another equally important reason to prevent deficit spending is its impact on society as a whole. Setting aside government corruption for now, what happens when more and more resources are funneled into the government for less (or even negative) return on investment? The same thing that happens in our own lives if we do not spend our money wisely. If we keep spending more money on education and the results do not improve, what is the rational thing to do? If we offer more government loans for college and the unemployment rate for recent college graduates rises to 50%, what is the rational thing to do? If we spend billions on new fighter aircraft even though we no longer engage in air-to-air combat, what is the rational thing to do? As more resources are wasted in the government, resources that could have been put to better use in other ways (opportunity cost), we begin to damage our ability to remain net resource producers, which in turn limits our ability to invest in the next generation, which leads to a vicious cycle. A prohibition on deficit spending would help us avoid this vicious circle.

I am not proposing that eliminating deficit spending will produce Utopia—in my opinion, references to Utopia in political philosophy are the hallmark of undisciplined thinking—but it would create a new level of trust in government and would change the rules of the game by imposing discipline and squeezing out corruption and the influence of special interest groups. It would also encourage government agencies to save money rather than spend all excess funds at the end of the fiscal year to ensure the same or a larger budget the next year. If there is room for the government to grow and it is doing a good job of serving the needs of the people, then by all means let it grow. But once we reach the point of making the shift to deficit spending, this should be our line in the sand, no matter what we believe are the potential benefits. If we cannot achieve it this generation, we will achieve it next generation. If the people want more tax revenue to fund more programs, they will have to take their ideas to the ballot box and be willing to fund those programs with their own money. If the people want less tax revenue to cut government programs, they will have to take their ideas to the ballot box. After the dust settles and the tax revenue is collected, the job of Congress will be to spend it wisely.

Eating the Seed Corn

Before concluding, I should address deficit spending from a different angle to give the reader a better understanding of why it should be prohibited. If we imagine a situation in which we are stranded on a remote island with only one banana tree, we will have to structure our eating habits around how many bananas the tree produces. If we assume the tree produces 10 bananas per week, then we can eat 10 bananas per week, perhaps less but certainly not more (unless we save some from the previous week and eat them before they spoil). However, what if one week we are particularly hungry and want to eat 14 bananas? In this case, we have two options: first, we can grow a second banana tree to increase banana production (that is, create wealth, which should always be the first answer when discussing economic issues); or second, continue eating 10 bananas per week, perhaps less but certainly not more. But what if we do not like that answer? What if we really want 14 bananas per week—"now!" with a foot stomp—and do not want to be burdened with planting another banana tree? The short answer is nothing. You are out of luck. On a remote island, that is, *in a state of nature, deficit spending is impossible*, which is why the prohibition of deficit spending is rational and grounded in reality.

The point I am trying to make with this simple example is that you cannot create wealth out of thin air (you can plant a new banana tree, but this takes time and effort), but you can create fiat money out of thin air, as I will address in the chapter on wealth. Paper currency on an island will not help the banana tree produce more bananas, but paper currency in a modern economy will allow us to buy more bananas than we can afford at the moment. For example, if I have no money, I can go to the grocery store and buy 14 bananas with my credit card. At the end, I could default on my credit card to avoid payment, but I still got 14 bananas, unlike the poor sucker on the island who was limited to 10 bananas per week. To state it clearly, *modern fiat currency can be a rational achievement*, if used properly, an abstraction grounded in reality that allows us to facilitate economic transactions, in ways that allow us to escape the burdens and limitations of a barter economy, which is a positive game changer for most economies. However, precisely because paper currency is a rational abstraction, it can be abused, what I will address later as a black magic concept. I am reminded of *The Clouds* by Aristophanes, in which a failure to be rational resulted in deficit spending on horses and in the end a rationalized ploy to avoid paying the debts.

To raise one final point, deficit spending is not possible in a state of nature, but eating the seed corn conveys the same idea. If we are hungry during the winter, we might be tempted to eat the seed corn to avoid starvation, rather than go ice fishing or hunting. But if we do that we will be unable to plant our fields in the spring, which will result in certain starvation later. With proper planning, we should save enough food during the summer and fall to survive the winter. If we do not, the temptation to eat the seed corn might get the best of us—a short-term gain with disastrous long-term consequences. Deficit spending is the modern equivalent of eating the seed cord in the sense that growing interest payments on our debts takes away money we could have spent on other programs (opportunity cost). Granted, we can dip into our savings during a dry spell, but once we start tapping into future income, with no plan or means to grow our income, we start down a road to financial ruin. In politics, the path of least resistance will most always triumph over the path of discipline, unless we have the strength and courage to reject it.

CHAPTER TWO. PROCREATION: THE SANCTITY OF MONOGAMOUS
PROCREATION

In the first chapter, I addressed one of two fundamental facts of life that
provide a foundation for my political philosophy, the first of two fundamental
facts that no one on the left or right can disagree with. The first fact was that we
must consume resources to survive, which raised the idea of the institution of
resource management and the prohibition of deficit spending as a way to place
a rational limit on how we run our government. The two sides of the political
spectrum might disagree on how much we should consume or how consumption
should be managed, but not the fact of consumption itself. For example, if humans
need about 2,500 calories per day to live a satisfactory life, this is a fact, not a
theory, keeping in mind that we can discuss which foods are best for deriving
those calories and whether environmental considerations for producing our food
supply should trump scientific nutritional considerations when making dietary
recommendations.

The fact of resource consumption was used to develop a model of net resource
consumption over our lives to break down life into three phases, the net resource
consumption phases of youth (from birth up to 18–25 years old) and old age
(roughly more than 65 years old), and the net resource production phase of our
working age bridging the other two (roughly 25–65 years old). I added the caveat
that work means anything that has to be done, whether or not we get paid (a
penny saved is a penny earned), such as a stay at home parent taking care of
the children during the day or working a job to earn a salary (and pay taxes) to
pay someone else to take care of the children. We should not make the common

mistake of equating work with receiving a salary because most of us perform many jobs that we do not get paid for. The age ranges are flexible, obviously, depending on the person and the society where he or she lives, but the important point is that for our own lives to be in resource balance, the total production during the years of net resource production (to include setting aside money for family, retirement, and taxes) should be equal to or greater than the total consumption during the years of net resource consumption of youth and retirement. Any proposal to reduce national production should be offset by a reduction in national consumption.

This is simple mathematical symmetry. For example, if you take out $50,000 in student loans during college (resource consumption), you must pay the loan back with interest after you start working, above and beyond your other obligations. The same goes for life in general. If we consume $250,000 of resources during our youth and $500,000 of resources during retirement, then we should produce at least $750,000 of resources (above and beyond what we consume for personal use) during our working years to balance this out. The resources are used in four primary ways—personal consumption, taxes, retirement planning, and raising our family. Granted, we do not inherit the debt of our youth or our society—we pay it forward—but the basic concept of balancing net resource consumption with net resource production during our life applies to everyone, regardless of their political beliefs. The mere fact that we live in a modern state does not relieve us of this burden. This is a goal to strive for, with the understanding that some people will have surplus resource production and others will have deficit resource production, but that the accounts for society as a whole should at least balance if not have a surplus. If everyone did this—if we structured our society in such a way as to set this as a primary goal this for each person— many of our social and political problems would go away. Instead, many people focus on things like their personal journey and emotional happiness, which are all worth pursuing, but do not always pay the bills.

With this model of net resource consumption established, I introduced the concept of debt and the creation of government. Similar to a human, a government is an entity that must consume resources to survive. It is a system. As history has shown, if people do not provide enough resources to the government, it grows weak, fails to provide necessary services, and falls prey to powerful special interest groups or outside enemies. On the other hand, if people provide too many resources to the government—or worse, if the government finds a way to commandeer resources from the people against their will or to print money against their will—and thus takes on a life of its own, we run the risk of tyranny. Somewhere between a weak state and tyranny is a sweet spot of liberty where government serves the needs of the people in a mostly efficient way that most people would be unable to achieve on their own in a state of nature. For example, we could ask each family to be responsible for its own security by hiring security guards (which is how many wealthy people live in developing countries), but this would be an inefficient way to provide protection and could result in fighting among the various groups that are struggling for power. Rather, if we all agree to create a single institution, such as the police, this will be the most efficient and effective way to provide for our security. The left and right can fight about how large government should be and what functions it should perform—these issues are decided in the ballot box—but there should be no doubt about the need for government and the benefits of a modern state.

Finally, I took the idea of government and debt to identify the key principle that should keep government in the sweet spot and avoid drifting too far to the left or too far to the right. Just as a person can use debt to help him become a net producer of resources ("good debt"), to help jumpstart the transition from subsistence farming to civilization, a government can as well. The concept of debt, as I will address in the chapter on wealth, is a rational achievement that can benefit us greatly if used in a rational manner, or cause destruction if used in an irrational manner. Just as individuals would have a difficult time buying a home without debt, governments would have a difficult time paying for most projects without debt, such as roads and schools, which would undoubtedly result in social stagnation. To repeat, I am not proposing that governments stop issuing debt. They should issue debt. However, just as individuals can run up too much debt, to the point where they become insolvent (we have mathematical models for this, not abstract theories), the same goes for government. The key variable for determining whether a person or a government has too much debt—whether we are using debt in a rational or an irrational manner—is the inability to pay it back with current income. If not, this results in deficit spending—when expenses exceed income. Granted, there will always be times when we have to dip into our savings for the short term if we are having income problems (thus, we should all consider it our responsibility to have savings), but deficit spending as a matter of course is unsustainable and results in bankruptcy, not to mention a lack of discipline that tends to follow from such spending habits. Also, reliance on deficit spending distorts the political process and promotes patterns of behavior that are not consistent with promoting our personal development or the sustainable growth of the economy.

To avoid this, I said the rational conclusion of the first fundamental institution of political philosophy, the institution of resource management, should be the prohibition of deficit spending. The government budget for any given year should not exceed the tax revenue collected during the year.

(The corollary to this is that defined benefit retirement programs in the public sector should be prohibited and be replaced by defined contribution retirement programs. Governments, by the nature of the political decisions they make regarding these retirement programs, are incapable of running these programs in accordance with mathematics and actuarial tables.) This is the best way to keep the game fair, honest, and sustainable. If a political party or a government does not like the results of the most recent election, they should not be able to use deficit spending to achieve their political objectives, which often means helping some people at the expense of others. People pay taxes in accordance with the law, and the government should be limited to spending that amount of money, or using the ballot box to ask for more. In many ways, deficit spending violates the trust between voters and the government. Granted, in theory, a government could use sustained deficit spending to achieve some objectives, just as we could improve our own quality of life by running up a credit card bill. However, by opening up the floodgates of deficit spending, we open the door to special interest groups and corruption, so the potential benefits do not outweigh the risks, and it is not clear who we could entrust with such authority. Not to mention, we still have to pay the tab at the end of the day. For example, a senator who wants to win votes might promise to buy an advanced weapon system from a defense contractor from his state, and then use deficit spending to pay for it as a way to deepen the debt burden on our children and grandchildren. This race to the bottom of making promises in exchange for votes perverts the system and invites corruption. Or, a mayor who wants to win votes might promise more generous retirement benefits to the police and teachers (long-term promises that affect the next generation) but does not have enough current tax revenue to add additional money to the retirement system to cover the long-term liabilities. Unfortunately, people often "vote their interest," but a prohibition on deficit spending would prevent this tendency from running rampant.

In summary, deficit spending (when spending exceeds revenue), which includes the printing of fiat money to avoid the burden of tax collection, is a gateway drug for special interest groups, corruption, and a loss of discipline on the left and the right. This downside outweighs any possible benefits of deficit spending and threatens the government sweet spot of balancing the demands from the left and right sides of the political spectrum via the ballot box. If both sides of the political spectrum would agree to give up their claim to spend money that cannot be paid back, the rules of the game would change dramatically. Corrupt people would have to find other ways to be corrupt and politicians could not make promises they could not keep. It is precisely this lack of discipline that creates so much of the gridlock we see today, which in many ways defines politics—the pursuit of policies for political gain without the tax revenue to pay for them. The beauty of this simple conclusion (simple like the design of an iPhone) is that it makes no assumptions about whether the left or right is correct about how big government should be or what functions it should perform. The only assumption it makes is that the amount of government spending should reflect the will of the people because government should serve the people, not the other way.

With the institution of resource management out of the way, we can shift to the institution of procreation. If we are working on the assumption that we want our society to survive, then in addition to each person needing to produce and consume resources, the people living in a society must produce the next generation for society to survive. History has shown us different ways of procreating—monogamy, polygamy, groups, even laboratory test tubes—but it is an irrefutable fact of life, whether you are on the left or right side of the political spectrum, that we must produce and nurture the next generation to maturity in order for society to survive. In fact, I would argue that how we manage procreation (that is, how we institutionalize it) is one of the most important decisions we will make as a society—creating and preparing the next generation to take over after we reach retirement. As was the case with resource consumption (if we do not consume resources, we will die), we cannot reject procreation without contradicting ourselves. If we do not produce the next generation and nurture them to maturity, there will be no one here to discuss political philosophy, which would be a tragedy. And just as the fact of resource consumption provided a foundation for rational analysis that resulted in the prohibition of deficit spending, as I will show in this chapter, the fact of procreation provides a foundation for rational analysis that will result in society promoting the sanctity of monogamous procreation.

Kinship Networks

Returning to Fukuyama, he addresses a variety of topics, such as the state, the rule of law, a mechanism for accountability, development, political parties, corruption, decay, human nature, and other important topics, which I encourage everyone to read, but for now I would like to focus on how particular procreation models give rise to the modern state. Procreation includes sperm from one man and an egg from one woman uniting to produce a fetus in the womb of the mother. Ideally, this should be a cooperative effort based on love and mutual respect, but procreation throughout history has often involved coercion or a lack of mutual respect, often resulting from coercion, arranged marriages, or demands from the state to grow the population in support of strategic objectives, such as war. From the most fundamental act of procreation between two people to the most complex societies, our continued survival on this planet depends on people forming societies to live a shared experience. No man is an island, and we cannot survive by facing the forces of nature alone, especially during childhood, so some form of human cooperation is essential, as Aristotle noted:

> The proof that the state is the creation of nature and prior to the individual is that the individual, when isolated, is not self-sufficing; and therefore he is like a part in relation to the whole. But he who is unable to live in society, or who has no need because he is sufficient for himself, must be either a beast or a god.[1]

We can develop ways to cooperate for our own mutual benefit, as well as for the greater good, but Fukuyama addresses two forms of natural human cooperation or sociability (natural in that they are not learned but are genetically coded and emerge spontaneously as individuals interact) that play a critical role in how human societies have evolved over time. The first form of natural cooperation or sociability is *kin selection*—the survival of our genes. It is a law of nature that, all things being equal, the love we have for people is proportional to the genetic similarity we have with them, which is why children given up for adoption will often spend years or decades tracking down their biological parents, even if the adoptive parents did a superb job of raising them. Dozens of apathetic people will watch a person get murdered on the street but a mother will risk her life by lifting a burning car to save her baby. Parents who have experienced the rush of emotions that accompany looking their newborn baby in the eyes know what I am talking about. Implicit in this bond is knowledge of the genetic similarity. (For this reason, it is crucial that the institution of procreation in each society includes taking steps to ensure the father knows who his biological children are and is held responsible for providing for them.) If a mother were to give up a child for adoption and then by chance stumble upon her child twenty years later in a shopping mall (without knowing who the child was), it is unlikely they would both suddenly be overcome with a rush of emotions. They might pause and find their similar appearances intriguing, but the rush of emotions would not flow until after they could confirm the truth. If we want parents to tap into the natural outflow of love and altruism, on a society-wide bell curve kind of way, not on an individual case-by-case basis kind of way, which is of primary importance for political philosophy and policymakers, they should know which children are theirs and should be educated, guided, and pressured by society to take care of them.

---

1 Aristotle, *Politics*, 1523a 25.

This first form of natural cooperation or sociability leads to the second: *reciprocal altruism*. One of the primary obstacles to social progress is overcoming the prisoner's dilemma—motivating people to cooperate and play by the rules rather than cheat or live like freeloaders. For example, if our village saves up money and needs to buy some irrigation equipment, we might entrust one person from our village with our savings to travel to town to buy the equipment while the rest of us stay back to protect the village and continue working. To ensure this person completes the task, we can take one of two approaches. First, relying on kinship bonds, we could send a trusted family member (which could be an immediate family member, a trusted person from the same tribe, or a person with whom we have established a pattern of trust building measures over time) to complete the task, taking comfort in knowing that the person would never put personal gain above performing the task for the greater good and run away with the money. Second, relying on a criminal code mindset, we could hold the person's family hostage, perhaps with a threat of death, until he returns with the irrigation equipment. Either way, the goal is ensuring that the person does not take the money and run. Setting aside the criminal code mindset for now—Who would want to live in such a village?—the point is that people as a matter of fact are more likely to cooperate with and make sacrifices for people who share their genes or with whom they have established a pattern of trust building measures at the expense of others, which historically has meant people from the same tribe or family network. Having lived and worked in Pakistan, I can attest that the power and influence of tribal networks is alive and well today.

Some people might balk and say that even though people give family members and close associates special treatment as a matter of fact, we *should* have full cooperation and altruistic love for all people equally, even if we do not naturally. However, this view ignores the most basic facts of life, such as that life is short and that we have limited resources. Love is a precious resource that cannot be diluted too much. Just as a full dose of morphine is required to kill the pain, not a few drops, love must flow in a natural way and in a full capacity to have the desired effect. With the rare exception of a saint, we cannot love all people with equal intensity, just as our paycheck cannot feed all people equally. The same goes for cooperation. Trust takes time to build, so it would not be rational for us to expect people to treat all people the same, especially when limited resources are at stake. The point is, given that these two sources of natural cooperation and sociability—kin selection and reciprocal altruism—are natural and universal, it should not surprise anyone that they have played a key role in shaping how societies have survived and developed over the millennia.

Returning to idea that we inherit a debt with our birth (our parents and society took care of us until we could take care of ourselves), given that most people throughout history have lived in abysmal conditions (relative to people living in developed countries in the twenty-first century) and without the benefits of a modern state, it is no surprise that people who showered their offspring with altruism at the expense of other children were more likely to survive for many generations or that tribal affiliation became the predominant form of social cohesion. This was the only option because there was not a modern state with police protection and social programs to provide the same benefits in a way that is not linked to tribal affiliation. People needed a way to ensure they were taken care of during old age. In fact, using analogies from the theory of evolution or game theory, it is safe to say that any society that did not structure itself in such a way as to tap into these two natural sources of cooperation and sociability probably ceased to exist, which is precisely why most societies around the world and throughout history have these conservative, tribal origins. It should not surprise anyone that history is not replete with prospering communist empires, precisely because the basic premise of communism is at odds with the ideas of kin selection and reciprocal altruism. We know what worked because we still see it today, which is not to say that the old models should never change. The modern state cannot cast off all elements of the conservative, tribal model without running the risk of weakening the foundation.

With these two sources of natural cooperation and sociability established, we can now look at how societies actually evolved over time, as opposed to how the social contract thinkers or communists imagined they did. This will allow us to begin developing a theory about how society should manage the institution of procreation. The key finding was that *people were socially organized from the beginning*; they did not start out as isolated individuals who formed societies over time. As Aristotle observed, man is a political animal. According to Fukuyama, the first stage of social development was the *band*, which consisted of small groups of individuals who were mostly genetically related and lived by hunting and gathering, with the land supporting 0.1 to 1 people per square kilometer. People living in bands have no private property, no economic exchange, no individualism, and are overall guided by a sense of egalitarianism. In many ways, this sounds like the Utopia some people today aspire to, although it was a brutal way of life that few people in the modern world would want to endure. The second stage of social development, which started about 10,000 years ago, was the *tribe*, which could sustain 40–60 people per square kilometer. Agriculture was the most important technology that allowed people to make the transition from bands to tribes and increase population density. Although tribes allowed for some division of labor, they consisted of self-sufficient segments rather than being a collective whole. Some segments would fail and others would succeed, but the tribe remained and the segments were expected to survive on their own. Another important development during the tribal stage was religion, which was organized around a belief in the power of dead ancestors and unborn descendants to affect the health and happiness of one's current life and facilitated large-scale action by the tribe by pushing back the dating of common ancestry. (It would subsequently take thousands of years of intellectual development from these crude origins for people to conceive of a universal, loving God who was the creator of the universe and not beholden to any particular tribe.) As Fukuyama notes, the first two stages are dominated by kinship and egalitarianism and lacked a central source of authority or third-party enforcement of laws.

The next important transition was from a tribal to a state-level society. Unlike tribes, states possess a monopoly on legitimate coercion and exercise this power over a defined geographic territory, which might include people outside the tribe of the leader or even groups of people who might be hostile to the leader. And because states are centralized and hierarchical, they tend to produce more social inequality than we see with bands and tribes. Fukuyama highlights that there are two types of states. First, the patrimonial state, as defined by the sociologist Max Weber, in which the polity is considered the personal property of the ruler and the administration of the state is an extension of the ruler's household. Similar to a tribe, the natural forms of cooperation and sociability, kin selection and reciprocal altruism, still play a key role in how the patrimonial state is run. Second, a modern state, on the other hand, is more impersonal because a citizen's relationship to the ruler depends on one's status as a citizen, not on personal ties. The administration of the modern state is less concerned with the ruler's family and more concerned with impersonal criteria such as merit, education, or technical knowledge. Although the natural forms of cooperation and sociability, kin selection and reciprocal altruism, continue to play an important role in the daily lives of citizens, they play a less important role in ruling the modern state.

The key point is that as we move from the dominance of kinship networks and patrimonial states toward the development of a modern state, there will often be a conflict between modern states and the kinship networks that provide the foundation for modern states, for two reasons. First, large kinship networks will be able to influence the government in ways that benefit the kinship networks at the expense of the whole population. We see this problem today with families that have people rise to political power based on name recognition, such as the Kennedy and Bush families. If we want to live in a fair society in which each vote counts equally in terms of shaping policy, we should take steps to prevent powerful kinship networks from manipulating the government. Second, kinship networks often act as governments within a modern state, performing state arbitrage functions for its own members. For example, kinship networks can use their size to protect and support the kinship network members at the expense of others, such as offering jobs or loans for businesses, help with childcare, assistance for college, and even performing judicial functions for conflict resolution within the kinship network. To the extent that kinship networks perform traditional government functions within a modern state, it opens up the possibility of conflicts with other kinship networks. This can lead to blood feuds and other problems, which require the judicial system of a modern state to resolve the conflict in a way that an objective outsider would judge as fair. In many developing countries around the world with weak states, kinship networks (tribalism) often play a key role in performing the functions of a modern state.

At first glance, the simple solution would seem to be to eliminate kinship networks and give all authority to a modern state, but this misses the key point that *we never could have progressed socially to the point we are today without kinship networks.* Kinship networks are the raw fuel that provides the foundation and stability we need in life—our base camp, so to speak. Kinship networks made social progress possible in the absence of a modern state. Just as we cannot stop producing food and other basic functions to survive, we cannot throw out the baby with the bathwater with kinship networks. The reason for this is that almost half of our life depends on the altruism of others, in terms of providing the resources we need to survive during youth and retirement, when we are net resource consumers. Given that the only two natural forms of cooperation and sociability—kin selection and reciprocal altruism—are inextricably linked to kinship networks (kin selection, in particular), not to modern states, we would be wise to continue to tap into these two natural sources of cooperation and sociability as a way to ensure that all people receive the altruistic love they need to survive and thrive. In theory, the modern state could assume the role of the "great altruism distributor," but that would require a significant increase in tax revenue (in the USA, local, state, and federal spending recently accounted for 41% of GDP) and probably would not be effective. We should not move in the direction of having children bond with the state rather than biological parents. If children were forced to bond with the state, it would in all likelihood disrupt their natural organic growth and maturity (arrested development) and instill a dependency mindset. Kinship network altruism is mostly free in the sense that it often does not involve the exchange of cash or the collection of taxes. Parents and extended family members often gladly assume these altruistic responsibilities, so a society would be wise to embrace what are probably the most powerful forces in human nature, while at the same time taking steps to ensure that the kinship networks do not grow to the point where they are able to unfairly manipulate the political system.

"Traditional" Procreation

From time immemorial, men and women have united to produce the next generation, sometimes eagerly, sometimes against their will, but always with the goal of continuing the species. The specifics of how procreation has evolved and changed over time are beyond the scope of this book, but it is worthwhile to address how procreation has been viewed from two opposing sides of the political spectrum—tribalism and communism—as a way to find a rational solution in the middle that balances human motivations with social responsibility. One of the most interesting passages about the union of men and women is Aristophanes' speech about love in Plato's *Symposium*. After describing how men and women were once united in one body, which has evolutionary implications, and how Zeus split us in two, he goes on to say:

> Love is born into every human being; it calls back the halves of our original nature together; it tries to make one out of two and heal the wound of human nature.[1]

This is a beautiful and poetic way of thinking about love—most husbands refer to their wives as their "better half," with no expectation that the wives will reciprocate—but it also provides insights about procreation by telling us what it is not. That is, *we do not produce asexually*. We have two genders— male and female—that contribute sperm and eggs, respectively, to produce babies in the womb of a woman. This is one of those rare irrefutable facts of life that no one on the left or right can challenge. If we reproduced asexually, men and women would not unite to procreate because we would not have genders. We would all be the same. The idea of pair bonding would never enter our minds. There would be no battle of the sexes. We might sit around drinking wine and talking about when our time will come to produce a baby, in ways that would most likely be beyond our control. We might even bemoan the fact that it will interfere with our personal journey. There would be no stay at home mothers and no negligent fathers abandoning their families to procreate with other women. There would be no such thing as cheating because people would not have sex and would not seek sexual

1 Plato, *Symposium*, 191d.

gratification or commitments. We would probably interact with each other and find ways to cooperate, but we would not have sexual feelings for each other. In fact, *romantic love would not exist*. Both sides of the political spectrum can talk until they are blue in the face about gender roles and procreation, but no one can disagree about how babies are made and the fact that this is the only way to perpetuate the species.

For this section, I intentionally put the word "traditional" in quotes to highlight the fact that what many people today refer to as traditional is not really traditional at all, as many people are quick to point out. The idealized "traditional" nuclear family of the 1950s, which was based on the rational principle of romantic love, not on tribal affiliation, female oppression, or lust, is still thriving today and is a rational creation that has not been common in history. The institution of monogamous procreation correlates with low levels of poverty and gives a woman the right to freely choose her mate. Given that kinship networks (tribalism) governed most elements of our lives before the rise of the modern state, it should surprise no one that the institution of procreation has changed with the creation of the modern state. For example, as many romantic comedies make clear, kinship networks often make demands on us in terms of our procreation partner, when we start having children, where we should live, where we should work, how many generations should live in our house, and so on. In fact, many tribes, even today, expect marriages to happen within the tribe, to include first cousins or polygamy. The relatives often scoff at childish and irresponsible notions of romantic love. Greek families want Greek babies, and so on.

The basic idea is to keep the kinship network strong, and this means having babies and taking care of them, even if it means compromising on our personal dreams or not mating with an outsider or the person we truly love. Any kinship network worth its salt knows that the kinship network with the best plan for procreation is the most likely to survive and accumulate wealth over multiple generations, which will provide the tribe members with the altruistic safety net they need to live into old age. In many romantic comedies, the star-crossed lovers complain that their families have no right to pressure them to get married and procreate, and almost without exception they fail to realize until the end that their kinship networks played the key role in making them the people they are today. For example, their parents probably made similar sacrifices, as did their parents, and so on, so they should be grateful. The kinship network provided them the support and nurturing they needed to reach the point of rational reflection and a desire to live a meaningful life, which takes us back to the idea of paying it forward. For most of history, people fought to assume a leadership role within the kinship network or family business, so the modern state narrative of escaping the "bonds" of a kinship network by marring an outsider or avoiding the family business is relatively modern and in many ways peculiar. On the one hand, it reflects a rational desire to escape the often quirky traditions of our kinship network, but it also reflects an irrational desire to ignore what made us possible and how most people find true meaning in the personal journey of life: family.

Most people in a modern state would cringe at the idea of arranged procreation between a man and a woman, whether to strengthen the kinship network or because the elders believe the match will result in feelings of genuine love and affection after the children are born. However, just as most people in a modern state have no problem with expecting people to work and pay taxes (the resource management institution side of the equation), most people do not have the same expectation regarding procreation. Taxes are not optional, but the modern state ethos seems to have relegated procreation to the optional file, an "other" category that no one, not even the government, should be able to discuss or regulate, even though the proper management of it (the institution of procreation) is critical to our survival. If we are going to work to pay taxes to support our family and the modern state, it would be ideal to have a job we love, but we generally frown on people who avoid their financial responsibilities by quitting a job because they are not happy, especially if it means leaving the family without an income. In fact, many people work long hours for "the man" at the expense of their family, but they do not apply the same logic to procreation. Producing the next generation is just as important as paying taxes—even more so in terms of helping society survive, because we can live without a modern state—but many people believe they are free to avoid procreation or to leave their procreation partner as soon as they are not happy, which suggests that for many people, their personal happiness trumps the social responsibility of raising children. Ideally, we will procreate with a person we love, but once children enter the equation, we assume new responsibilities that in many ways trump the importance of our own happiness, with the caveat that it is hard to find true fulfillment in life until we put the happiness of others ahead of our own.

In short, kinship networks take a more pragmatic approach to procreation, a model that has stood the test of time. Some kinship networks will promote monogamous procreation, others will promote polygamy (which can be rational, depending in the circumstances, but has a tendency to produce a large population of young men without access to women, which is a recipe for social disaster), but at the end of the day they are all focused on the survival and prosperity of the kinship network. All members should place this obligation above personal self-interest, just as we expect people to pay taxes at the expense of their personal self-interest.

Hence, we reach a dilemma. Given that the modern state is often at odds with kinship networks, it is no surprise that the modern state promotes a form of procreation that is often at odds with the form of procreation for kinship networks. For example, modern states tend to eliminate kinship as a condition of procreation by allowing anyone to procreate with anyone over the legal age, with no pressure to procreate at any particular age. Even though we know with scientific certainty that the odds of complications (such as autism or down syndrome) rise rapidly with age, we are taking no rational steps to publically revise the narrative for people waiting to have children until later in life, often into their forties. Some modern states provide tax incentives that favor couples with children, as a way to encourage people to have children or to ease the financial burden of parenting, but the modern state does not provide the same pressures that a kinship network would. As a result, the institution of procreation under modern state authority is more likely to end up in divorce than the institution of procreation under kinship network authority, which is not to say that people in kinship network marriages are happier. The reason for this is that the modern state is not a kinship network and does not care which particular kinship networks survive (although some modern states have focused on particular kinship networks). The modern state wants productive workers who provide tax revenue to the state. The modern state also wants children to swear their loyalty to the modern state, not to kinship networks. However, if the institution of procreation is weaker within a modern state than it is within a kinship network, the inevitable result will be that children born into strong kinship networks within a modern state will have many advantages over children who rely on the social services provided by the modern state, which could promote inequality.

The modern state concept of procreation focuses on satisfying two important objectives: producing the next generation and personal fulfillment via romantic love. This is the single most important two-for-one we have in society, the elusive bridge between social responsibility and personal fulfillment. Modern people do not want procreation to be a duty and they do not want to procreate with someone they do not love, and most certainly not with someone who has the authority to force them to procreate, as is the case with some women in societies dominated by tribal networks. That said, with this increased emphasis on personal fulfillment, an increase in the divorce rate has been an inevitable consequence, just as we would see a rise in high school dropouts if school attendance were decreed optional. As a result, the idea of romantic love, at the expense of social responsibility, now plays a more prominent role in the institution of modern state procreation, even though procreation can exist without romantic love. (Some people marry their best friend or a political or economic ally.) We can procreate without romantic love, so romantic love is not essential to the institution (the same way that having a formal education is not essential for having success in life), but that does not mean romantic love is not important (the same way that having a formal education is important). In fact, many people, the author included, consider romantic love between one man and one woman for the purpose of procreation to be the pinnacle of a happy, rational life.

One of the problems with modern love is that it tends to ignore the fact that there are different kinds of love. The kind of love we feel initially, call it passionate or erotic love, is not the love that grows to define the relationship after procreation enters the equation (although it is often what motivates many people to procreate in the first place). The kind of love that a man feels for the mother and his children is not the same kind of love that a woman feels for the father and her children. Men and women have different hormonal systems and experience love in different ways, in ways that most of us will never understand, as evidenced by the steady stream of romantic comedies that appeal to the two genders in different ways. In fact, it is precisely the complementary nature of love between men and women with children that creates a feeling of wholeness in the relationship. A singer of a band I saw in Memphis once wisely said the blues is nothing more than the expression of love between men and women with children. The wisdom of kinship networks is that they recognize that procreation is hard work and requires sacrifice, like anything in life that is worth pursuing. The institution of procreation is not a morphine drip to keep us in a state of bliss until the promise of a new high presents itself.

The primary weakness of modern state procreation is that it defines it primarily in terms of feelings, emotions, and personal fulfillment, not in terms of social responsibility. If we fall out of love or find that we have "irreconcilable differences," we can go our separate ways with "no fault" and no one to blame, regardless of how it affects the children. (I wonder what the IRS would say if we decided that we were no longer happy with our current tax obligations.) Granted, I do not believe that anyone should be forced to stay in a relationship, especially when abuse is involved, but I believe the modern state institution of procreation would benefit from some lessons from the kinship networks, such as putting more emphasis on social responsibility, as it relates to raising children, and less emphasis on personal fulfillment, because being socially responsible is one of the best ways to achieve personal fulfillment. Otherwise, kinship networks families will grow stronger and modern state families will grow weaker. It is cliché to call education the great equalizer, but the numbers also show that, all things being equal, children raised in "traditional" families have many advantages over children raised in broken families. Given the left's eagerness to promote equality and level the playing field, the unwillingness of the left to actively promote the nuclear family model is nothing short of puzzling.

Test Tube Love

The previous section on "traditional" procreation probably resonated with many people who are to the right on the political spectrum. Promoting "family values" is a consistent theme on the right, even if some of the political leaders promoting these family values fail to live up to their own ideals. However, the more extreme forms of tribal marriage—marriage only within the tribe, arranged marriages, etc.—probably did not resonate with many of these same people. Most people on the right in modern states would prefer to keep the basic idea of "traditional" marriage (with nostalgia for the 1950s) and eliminate the historical tribal baggage. That is, if we use the previous section to identify the extreme right side of the political spectrum to begin looking for a rational solution in the middle, it is now time to shift to the extreme left side of the political spectrum, to help us find a rational solution in the middle that we can use to shape the political debate and resolve the political divide in America.

As odd or surprising as it might sound, some people throughout history have actively argued for the end of the "traditional" procreation model of husband, wife, and child, usually with the goal of having the state assume responsibility for raising children. One of the earliest examples of this comes from Plato in the *Republic*, where he says:

> [t]hat all of these women are to belong in common to all the men, that none are to live privately with any man, and that the children, too, are to be possessed in common, so that no parent will know his own offspring or any child his parent.[1]

If it is safe to say that most people in modern states today would reject the extreme form of tribal procreation (the tribe dictates who procreates with whom), I am confident that most people in modern states today would reject this extreme version of procreation (the state severs the bond between biological parent and child). However, oddly enough, this belief has been a mainstay of the radical left throughout history. Plato, like many of his followers, was concerned that the love of parents for their biological children clouds their objectivity when making decisions about society and opens their hearts to dynastic ambitions for generations to come. To avoid this, some societies or institutions have resorted to eunuchs or eunuch-like members (people who are not allowed to procreate), such as priests

---

1 Plato, *Republic*, 5.457d.

in the Catholic Church, but such ideas can have no place in a society because society is not an institution and depends on an orderly process of procreation to avoid extinction. Obviously, many societies have suffered from royal families squabbling over who should be heir to the throne, at the expense of all rational discourse regarding the nature of legitimate political authority, but the reason I highlight this quote is to show that procreation and the nature of the relationship between biological parent and child is one of the most fundamental issues of political philosophy. In many ways, how a society chooses to manage the institution of procreation and the relationship between biological parent and child *is the most fundamental issue of all*. If we cease to procreate, we cease to exist. Therefore, it should be no surprise that the institution of procreation should be front and center for political philosophy.

If we consider a scenario in which the state benefits from severing the ties between biological parents and children and then take this thought process to its logical conclusion, we see the science fiction that moves procreation to the test tube, as shown in chilling detail in *Brave New World* by Aldous Huxley. As every radical left-wing ideologue knows (tongue in cheek), the secret to establishing an all-powerful global state is the breakdown of traditional procreation and keeping the population in a state of arrested development, to prevent them from achieving their rational potential. With "traditional" procreation of any form eliminated, tyranny is one sunrise away. If you want to have complete control over a population, they must serve the state rather than their own biological children. Even though there are benefits to limiting the power of kinship networks (even conservatives in modern states today do not support the procreation model of tribes), there are limits beyond which we start to cause damage to the social fabric, *precisely at the point where we cease tapping into the benefits of kin selection and reciprocal altruism*, the two natural sources of cooperation and sociability.

Moving forward in history to another germane voice, Karl Marx, the founder of modern communism during the nineteenth century, also made a clarion call for the abolition of the traditional family in *The Communist Manifesto*, a sentiment shared by many of the fringe members of society today who adhere to communist ideology. Marx went to great lengths to clarify that he was attacking the "bourgeois family," which he claimed treated women as mere instruments of procreation and concealed a hypocritical and legalized community of women. Marx was not a free-love kind of guy in his own affairs, unlike some of his communist comrades—in fact, he was largely seen as a happily married man who set up barriers between his daughters and male suitors—but he believed the bond of love between two people should matter more than the material and economic forces shaping the structure of society. Marx believed that all societies and ideas were the result of material and economic forces, such as climate, geography, and the Industrial Revolution (which was actually the product of rational minds), but he apparently failed to appreciate that, if true, this would include his own philosophy, in which case he would be incapable of transcending his own situation to promote social change. Thus, ironically, Marx gives us the rope to hang his own theory. In order for Marx's ideas to be true, there has to be something true and essential about human nature, independent of material and economic forces, that allows us to steer the ship in a positive direction, rather than merely described the events as they happen. However, this cannot be true without contradicting Marx's claim that material and economic forces are fundamental.

Marx, Engels (his benefactor who, ironically, owned a factory—"the means of production"), and other communists of the day all agreed that the system of capitalism (to be accurate, crony capitalism) had distorted human relations, most notably in the form of bourgeois procreation, which, they claimed, led to prostitution and child labor, even though they knew full well that prostitution and child labor predated the rise of (crony) capitalism. He argued that the material and economic environment in which we live shapes how we behave and how we relate to each other, which by necessity—not by conscious choice—compelled us to create the institution of bourgeois procreation. What Marx seemed to ignore was the fact that the institution of procreation for kinship networks was functional and focused on survival, not only on personal fulfillment, so he was correct to point out that the institution could be demanding and driven by material forces, but that was not the end of the discussion. That is, kinship networks knew full well that their institution of procreation often involved coercion or personal sacrifice, but they also knew they had limited options. According to Marx, by being slaves to private property and industrial production, we have debased ourselves and perverted our true potential, which is a claim that has some merit given the common sentiment that we should not be slaves to consumerism. Many people do live in wretched conditions, then and now, which makes it more difficult for them to achieve their full potential. However, this has always been the case for all people in all societies in history, especially during the band and tribal stages. The first glimpses of economic prosperity, however, were invariably linked to the rise of capitalism.

Marx, like Plato, wanted to see children removed from the family environment for educational purposes and with the goal of preventing families from subjecting them to the grim conditions of child labor. On the surface, this sounds like a noble objective—keeping children out of the factories and providing them an education—but this is where the problems begin. Even if Marx's intentions were noble, by removing children from their parents he was breaking an important bond that is critical for helping children grow and develop to achieve their full potential—the biological bond of altruism. As an unbending materialist, Marx would have to accept the conclusion that material resources could also replace the altruism of a biological parent, which was probably why he was not apparently concerned about removing children from their parents. According to Marx, consciousness is the product of material forces, not the other way around, so any adult providing the right resources to a child should be able to nurture the child with the same results as the biological parent. Given that the strongest and cheapest force of altruism in the universe is between biological parent and child—in a bell curve kind of way, not in a case-by-case kind of way—it is not clear why any society should waste so many resources paying so many people to raise children with whom they have no biological bond. *Why the insistence on fighting what nature has given us for free?* This is like burning down fruit trees that sprout effortlessly and replacing them with fruit trees that require our labor. And second, it is not clear why the modern state is any more enlightened or benevolent than the kinship model it proposes to replace. Kinship networks have the benefit of having survived over time, although many of them could be accused of refusing to change with the times. Although it is true that kinship networks are guilty of protecting their own interests, the same could be said for modern states.

It should be clear that both extremes of the institution of procreation addressed in this chapter—tribalism and communism—should be avoided, which means that the rational solution is probably somewhere between. On the one hand, most people who are living in modern states do not want to compel people to procreate against their will, especially with people they do not love. On the other hand, we do not want to give the state the power to sever the bond between biological parent and child, which brings us to the second principle of political philosophy.

Modern Love

With this analysis behind us, we can now assemble the pieces of the puzzle to develop the second principle of political philosophy regarding the institution of procreation. Our goal should be to find a rational and sustainable position between the two extremes, with powerful kinship networks (tribalism) on the right and an all-powerful, centralized state on the left. Both sides have good and bad points, so we should be able to select a rational sweet spot that gives people enough freedom and liberty to live the life they want to live while also taking rational steps to ensure that our society continues to prosper and thrive, rather than die on the vine or transform into a totalitarian nightmare.

First, regarding kinship networks, although people should have to right to participate in one, with all the attendant benefits, the modern state should take steps to prevent kinship networks from becoming too powerful (to prevent them from unfairly manipulating the political system) and to help people who want to leave the bonds of their kinship network if they do not want to belong. For example, if a woman belongs to a kinship network that pressures her to procreate with a person she does not wish to procreate with, the state should intervene, if necessary, to prevent that from happening. No one should be forced to procreate with anyone. Thus, as a tip of the hat to the left, the state has a positive role to play in making sure that kinship networks are not allowed to violate our individual rights, even if that is how the kinship network has always done things. People should be free to choose their own destiny, to include their own procreation partner, but many people would probably benefit from listening to their kinship network rather than their hearts, especially at a young age. Perhaps that nice girl down the street our parents told us about would have been the right choice. Most of us are alive today because past generations of people in our kinship networks made the necessary sacrifices for us, long before welfare programs played a prominent role in our society. People should remember the debt they owe to their kinship network and keep in mind that if they choose to take advantage of the benefits of their kinship network, they are obliged to play by the rules and pay their debt forward to the next generation, even if that means starting a family with the person who was not their first choice. They should not be surprised when the kinship network makes demands of them. Membership is not free, and you cannot have your cake and eat it.

Second, continuing with kinship networks, although the modern state should be active in limiting the negative influences of them, to include protecting our rights, the modern state should not throw out the baby with the bathwater and ignore two of the most powerful forces in human society: kin selection and reciprocal altruism. If we are going to establish a state institution of procreation based on personal freedom at the expense of kinship networks, we should tap into these forces by *ensuring that the bond of love and altruism between parent and child becomes the foundation of our state institution of procreation*, not something to be severed. Thus, the most important social bond transfers from being among tribal members to being between biological parent and child. Biological parents, all things being equal in a bell curve kind of way, not in a case-by-case basis kind of way, which is of primary concern for political philosophy and policymakers, can be relied on to make the necessary sacrifices for their children, often at a great financial and emotional sacrifice to themselves. Granted, some parents will not perform their duties, and for these occasions the state or kinship networks can intervene to protect the interests of the children, but we as a society must make a conscious decision to tap into the forces of kin selection and reciprocal altruism as the primary way to raise the next generation. The alternative is collecting massive levels of tax revenue to establish social programs that will be run by people who are not emotionally invested in the children they are serving (relative to the parents). Not to mention, if the modern state institution of procreation does not tap into kin selection and reciprocal altruism, the children born into the modern state institution will often be at a disadvantage to the children who are born into kinship network institutions of procreation, which could tip the political and economic scales in their favor over time. If the left truly wants fairness, equality, and a level playing field, they should actively promote the "traditional" family.

Third, shifting to the modern state, although the modern state has an active role to play in the institution of procreation, we also must impose limits on the modern state so that it does not drift toward tyranny by the state, just as we should impose limits on kinship networks to stop the drift toward tyranny by the tribe. The most effective way to do this is to stop the modern state from severing the bond between parent and child. *The best way to do this is to sanctify the union of one man and one woman*—monogamous procreation—*as the foundation of our state institution of procreation.* (I will take it as axiomatic that most modern states will not embrace polygamy or other models of procreation.) Most people seek emotional fulfillment in the institution of procreation, which is a good thing, but it is first and foremost a sacred *duty* to produce and raise the next generation, and only secondarily an institution of personal fulfillment. As luck would have it, procreation is one of the most fulfilling things most people do during their short lives. For most people I know, the love that grows from rearing children is the most profound love of all, a love that is difficult grasp without having children and one that makes the required sacrifices all the more satisfying. It is important to keep the flame of passion lit, of course, but most mature people recognize that this cannot be the foundation of raising a family, and our social obsession with sexual gratification, even after the Social Security checks begin to arrive, merits scrutiny.

As a society we must take the position that raising a family is hard work and a social obligation, not a way to tickle our fancy and move on to the next love interest when the first loses its spark. Without this discipline, we are left with the broken homes that are so prevalent today, with many single parents living in poverty and transferring those challenges to their children—whereas the people who subject themselves to the rigorous demands of monogamous procreation will be more stable and will accumulate more wealth over several generations, which will tip the economic balance in their favor.

To conclude, when I say we should sanctify monogamous procreation as the foundation of our state institution of procreation, I am talking about taking active steps to promote the institution. Just as we sanctify education with compulsory school attendance and make it a rite of passage for upward movement in our society, we should promote monogamous procreation the same way and accept no substitutes. The reason for this is that, like education, raising a family is hard work. Just as children, especially boys, will have a tendency to slack off in school without pressure to keep them on the right track, many adults, especially men, using our high divorce rate as proof, will have a tendency to let their families break down without some pressure to keep them on the right track. Active steps to promote monogamous procreation would include public service announcements and social celebration of the institution, above and beyond what we see in romantic comedies. Just as people should not give up on public schools, even though many are failing our children, people should not give up on monogamous procreation, even though divorce rates are high. We should recognize that our failure to sanctify monogamous procreation is a self-fulfilling prophesy. Our failure to sanctify it sucks the life out of it and sets the stage for institutional decay and divorce. The rising divorce rate is our failure, not a failure of the institution.

Final Comments

I will consider this chapter a success if most readers are unaware of the fact that I never once, up to this point, used the word "marriage." All of my references were to procreation and family. This was intentional. Like so many issues in our society today, some of them boil down to semantics. Keeping in mind that we are rational animals, the way we procreate will be similar to how other animals procreate but at the same time dissimilar, just as the way we seek shelter and food is similar but dissimilar. For other animals, procreation is mostly an unconscious act. Male animals do not sit around when the females are not in heat and talk about sex or how many babies they hope to have. Procreation for animals is driven by instinct and chemistry. Animals do not reflect on the meaning of life or assess the potential for overpopulation and then make a conscious decision regarding whether to procreate. When it is mating season, they try to mate, all of them. Animals are not bashful. They are not self-conscious. They do not have the equivalent of a 40-year-old virgin. They do not have celibacy. Some animals will succeed, others will not, which is all part of the circle of life, but the fundamental fact of procreation remains.

Humans, on the other hand, have the opportunity—some might call it a burden—of thinking about procreation, which in many ways is the counterpoint to thinking about death in the circle of life. We can imagine our ideal mate, we can choose the right time, we can choose the right place, we can choose how many children to have, and so on. The experience of having a children for many will be the single most fulfilling thing they do during their short lives on earth, even if (nay, when) it is filled with moments of frustration. During history, the human institution of procreation has changed, partly in response to environmental demands, partly in response to religion and awareness of our innermost desires, and this entire narrative seems to have flowed in the direction of romantic love, from the Troubadours, to Schopenhauer's essay on romantic love, to the love songs we hear on the radio, to the formulaic romantic comedies that draw large audiences year after year. In fact, for many people the terms romantic love and procreation go hand in hand, to the point where most people today could not imagine procreating with someone they did not love in a romantic way. This has certainly refined and elevated procreation to a new level of personal fulfillment, which only a rational animal could experience, but we also run the danger of untethering the concept of romantic love from procreation, which would threaten the institution of procreation and the idea of romantic love itself. As we dance to the music of life and ponder life's profound mysteries, we should understand romantic love as the music of our sacred participation in the joy of life. Otherwise, if we untether romantic love from procreation and make it a journey of personal fulfillment rather than a surrendering to the mystery of life, we risk demeaning the institution of procreation, which opens up other debates about marriage that should be moot before they begin.

This concludes my analysis of the two fundamental institutions—resource management and procreation—which resulted in two important findings: the prohibition of deficit spending and the sanctity of monogamous procreation. These two fundamental, universal principles, taken together, provide a strong foundation for helping us make decisions regarding how to resolve the political divide in America. If a majority of Americans were to agree on these two principles and use them as a foundation for making decisions in the ballot box, many of the more complicated issues would fall into place. In the next part of the book, I will analyze four pillars of political philosophy—human nature, institutions, wealth, and justice—to provide more depth and a stronger foundation to my analysis.

PART II. THE FOUR PILLARS

CHAPTER THREE. HUMAN NATURE

Attempts to develop a cohesive political philosophy often focus on human nature as a point of departure. For example, Hobbes argued that human nature was essentially bad ("the war of all against all"), which prompted him to create the all-powerful Leviathan state to keep everyone in line. On the other hand, Rousseau argued that human nature was essentially good ("the noble savage") but was corrupted by social institutions (as opposed to being civilized by them), which prompted him to want to change how society was organized. As a general rule, the right tends to have a more skeptical or demanding view of human nature, exemplified by the concept of Original Sin, and therefore sees the primary role of the state as protecting us from ourselves and from others. On the other hand, as a general rule, the left tends to have a more optimistic and tolerant view of human nature, exemplified by the idea that criminals can be reformed and that everyone has the potential to go to college and be successful, and therefore sees the primary role of the state as helping us achieve our potential. Obviously, both sides have correct and incorrect insights about human nature, but the tendency to focus on one aspect of human nature at the expense of others tends to produce an incomplete political philosophy, which makes it difficult to use as a point of departure. My political philosophy will make no assumptions about whether people are inherently good or bad, but will rather focus on the important fact that we have the potential to manifest something that is unique in the animal kingdom: *reason.* If we focus on the fact that we are rational animals, the consequences for political philosophy are interesting.

You Have Great Potential

Unlike most animals, humans are not born ready to live. We cannot exit the womb and get down to business. We spend a long time in the womb and have no survival skills immediately after we are born, although we instinctually suckle the breast of our mother. All animals benefit from parental nurturing, but humans are especially vulnerable to the forces of nature for many years. Not only that, even if we have the right nurturing to keep us alive, we lack the sufficient instincts to make a quick transition to self-preservation. Baby turtles do not have to be taught to run to the water (really, they don't), but we humans must learn to do most of what we do via a process of imitation, trial and error, and education, and we still often make mistakes. Not only that, the development of our character does not happen the same way that a plant or an animal grows to maturity. When a lion is born, it immediately starts down the path of becoming a flesh-eating hunter merely by following its own instincts. Lions do not read books or attend boot camp to hone their martial skills, although they do watch and learn. In particular, and this is the key difference, they cannot pause and consider the option of becoming a vegetarian, that is, of not living in accordance with their nature. In the case of a human, he might or might not develop a character that is consistent with his true nature and that he needs to survive. Many do not, even though nature gives us all the equipment we need to survive. We have to take proactive and persistent measures to shape our own biological growth and maturity (to avoid getting off track) in a way that is consistent with our nature as rational animals. That is, we must walk the razor's edge, which opens up the possibility of error and incorrect behavior, as well as an inability to detect whether we are on the wrong path.

Aristotle was the first philosopher to systematically address the difference between the essence of something and its potential for change, which was important because philosophers before him, such as Plato, struggled with the idea of explaining the idea of eternal truth in the flux of experience. Heraclitus said we never stepped in the same river twice and that the world was in a constant state of flux, like fire, with eternal truth being an illusion. On the other hand, Parmenides postulated the existence of the eternal One and eternal truth, with the state of flux being an illusion. What followed from this was Plato's doctrine of the Forms and Aristotle's essentialist reaction to it, a legacy that has shaped Western philosophy to this day. As Whitehead observed, the history of philosophy is largely a footnote to Plato. Aristotle defined man (his essence) as "rational animal," but he also recognized that not all people manifest the full potential of their power of reason, especially people outside of Greece (the barbarians). Reason is like a seed waiting to receive water, soil, minerals, and sunlight—the seed is really there and distinguishes us from all other animals—but we have to work hard to manifest, nurture, and train this potential, just as a gardener has to tend his garden in accordance with the art and science of horticulture. To explain this model more clearly, Aristotle spoke of the four causes—material cause, formal cause, efficient cause, and final cause. To use a classic example, in the case of a statue, the block of marble is the material cause, the sketch or plan for the sculpture is the formal cause, the sculptor himself is the efficient cause, and the finished product is the final cause. Michelangelo was famous for saying that sculpture was the art of taking away, not adding on—that is, releasing the sculpture hidden within the stone. This four-cause model can apply to many scenarios in life, but this chapter will focus on humans and our capacity for reason. To cut through the analysis, Aristotle would say that the final cause of man—that is, the final result if we are properly nurtured during our organic growth and maturity—is a life of rational reflection and action in accordance with virtue.

This way of looking at humans—the idea that we have a natural organic end state (maturity) that we fulfill only if we live in accordance with our nature—is known as *teleology*. (By extension, if we do not live in accordance with our nature, we will not fulfill our proper end or teleology.) To use a biological analogy, if the purpose of a stomach is to digest food and the purpose an eye is to see, then the purpose of being a human is to live in accordance with reason and virtue, as well as to perpetuate our DNA via procreation. This is our highest good, how we measure our progress as humans. In the language of modern political philosophy, this type of teleology is known as *perfectionism*, which, as we will see, is not popular with some schools of thought, especially on the left. To keep the concept as simple as possible, I will use teleology to mean nothing more than the idea that *if we provide people with specific types of inputs progressively over time (nutrition, love, education, etc.), we should expect predictable outputs (a mature, rational adult), and that we would be wise to seek only the types of outputs that are consistent with our nature.* If we believe it makes sense to say something is consistent with our nature as human beings, we are talking about teleology. For example, if we teach kids arithmetic, we set the stage for teaching them algebra, and then geometry, and then calculus, and so on. If we start with calculus (jump ahead too far) or teach the arithmetic incorrectly (get on the wrong track), we most likely will never arrive at the desired destination of lucid, mathematical thinking to solve complex equations. Likewise, if we teach kids to delay gratification and work hard for every dollar, we will set the stage for a productive adulthood that is defined by net resource production. If people did not have teleology of some sort, some basic end state that is the result of correct behavior in accordance with our nature, our lives would be chaos. Perfectly normal children could spontaneously become criminals; drug addicted criminals could spontaneously become saints; and so on. As I will address, both the left and the right believe in teleology; they just do not agree on what our final cause looks like. Going back to our lion example, does anyone doubt that lions were designed to hunt animals? Does anyone deny that lions have teleology?

To add more clarity, we should consider Aristotle's understanding of virtue. Aristotle believed that all people have a capacity for virtue but recognized that virtue did not come easy, even to the most wellborn Greek aristocrats. In fact, many Greeks were deeply troubled by the fact that virtuous men often had children who lacked virtue, despite a good upbringing, as discussed in Plato's *Meno*. We have to work hard to achieve virtue, the same way we have to practice an instrument or a foreign language for the right amount of time and with the right amount of intensity to achieve mastery. For example, if we take the virtue of courage, Aristotle would place the behavior of a person between two extremes, with a coward on one end and a fool on the other. A person who quivers and runs away at the first sign of danger is a coward (deficiency), and therefore lacks courage. On the other hand, a person who rushes recklessly into a dangerous situation is a fool (excess). The courageous person finds the difficult and rational middle ground—doing the right thing, at the right time, for the right reason, despite the fear. In terms of how to train someone to be courageous, Aristotle said the two extremes of the courage spectrum (deficiency and excess) are not the same (one is less easy than the other) and that the middle ground is not necessarily the arithmetic mean between the two extremes. For example, if eating one egg is deficient and eating 11 eggs is excessive, we should not eat 6 eggs—the arithmetic mean—to find the middle ground. The rational middle ground between the two extremes is just that—a rational middle ground, not a mathematical mean. In this case, 2–3 eggs might be the rational middle ground. Thus, if we want to train people to be courageous, *we have to train them slightly on the less easy side of the spectrum—that is, slightly on the side of foolishness.* This is important. For example, most humans, left to their own devices without any training or assistance, would drift toward being cowards rather than fools, in life and in combat, which is why we have to train soldiers to fight. (We will assume the soldiers are being trained to fight a morally just war.) Therefore, to train their virtues to find the rational middle ground of courage, we have to train soldiers to be slightly foolish so they can ease their way back to genuine courage as they develop their skills. If we train soldiers at a level of intensity slightly on the coward side of the spectrum, they will never rise to the level of real courage when combat begins, which is not to suggest that we have precise gauges or methods to measure how courageous a person is. The upshot of this is that *we should think about political philosophy not only as a pursuit of truth, but also a process of helping us achieve our potential as rational individuals and as a rational society.* Just as most people view education as indispensible for shaping our character, the way we structure society itself to promote social virtues should be in such a way as to always keep us moving along the path of personal development to fulfill our teleology.

The same logic that applies to people developing their virtues between the extremes of behavior also applies to society developing its social virtues between the extremes of the political spectrum. Just as most things in life that matter do not come easy, such as accumulating wealth by hard work and frugality, we should structure our society (the social virtues) in a way that avoids the two extremes of the political spectrum by training citizens slightly on the less easy side of the political spectrum. It is easier for a hard working person to slow down than for a comfort-seeking person to speed up, just as it is easier for a frugal person to start spending than it is for a spendthrift to start cutting back. Likewise, if we offer too many generous social programs, we should anticipate that many people will opt for the benefits rather than face the rigors of hard work, whereas people who are taught the virtue of hard work will be less likely and even reluctant to become dependent on the state. This is a question of "caring" in the sense that we should care that people stay on the right path rather than fall off the path and fail to live up to their potential. Not only that, once a pattern is established, it is hard to break, which is why we have to set our car keys in the same place 21 consecutive days to establish the habit of not losing them. Thus, when creating social programs, we should be concerned with the general welfare of people, of course, but we should also be concerned with keeping people on the difficult path of self-improvement. As Aristotle would admonish us, this should result in a life of rational reflection and action in accordance with virtue.

Given that we are rational animals, we cannot look to other animals as models of behavior. It does not matter what monkeys or dolphins do, although human behavior in a fallen state (when we fail to live in accordance with reason) often resembles animal behavior, and we cannot always use reason when relating to irrational people. The social virtues do not come easy. In fact, we naturally resist them and naturally drift toward the less difficult side of the virtue spectrum (religious people might attribute this to Original Sin). This requires training and discipline to achieve. For example, given that we are rational and capable of abstract thought, we can introduce into our economic transactions the concept of fiat money that is linked to the underlying economy, which I will address later. However, given that this abstraction (fiat money) can be duplicated via the printing press, like counterfeit money, it can be untethered from reality, so we have to structure our use of this abstract model to keep us on the path of social virtue while taking advantage of the benefits. As I showed in chapter one, this means the prohibition of deficit spending. Without this, we will stray from social virtue and end up with hyperinflation and people who do not understand the value of a dollar. Likewise, given that we are rational animals that are capable of procreating in a variety of ways (monogamy, polygamy, test tubes, groups, etc.)—all other animal species procreate in accordance with instinct—we should choose a rational model for procreation that relies on a level of abstract thought that is grounded in our own nature. That is, it should be hard work, but it should also be fulfilling, like anything in life that is worth having, such as achieving mastery of a musical instrument. We might resist monogamous procreation and it might not always feel natural, in the same way that resisting violence or laziness is not always easy, but it is the best way to channel our natural energies as individuals and as members of society. The fact that we tend to see poverty with broken families and wealth with "traditional" families is proof that monogamous procreation is a social virtue—it is the result of hard work, does not come easy, and makes society better for everyone. It ensures that we produce the next generation and that nearly all children have a mother and a father who will provide for them altruistically.

The Power of Reason

One of the best ways to understand what reason is and how it impacts our lives is to understand how life would be without reason. In *The World as Will and Representation*, Schopenhauer provides insightful analysis that is useful in this context. According to Schopenhauer, the life of most animals is dominated by what he calls *understanding*, which is the world that is presented to us by our sense organs—eyes, ears, nose, mouth, and touch—and depends on a complex nervous system. When we open our eyes, observe the world, and act in accordance with what we see, without any abstract thought, we are using understanding. The key variable in the world of understanding is *causality*, pace Hume. By observation alone, we can gain intuitive insights about the nature of cause and effect, even without the power of reason. I have watched my dog many times as he watches the world around him and responds in a correct manner to many simple situations. He clearly understands the cause and effect of some situations and rarely makes mistakes when he does. Granted, his grasp of cause and effect is limited to simple actions, such as a bouncing ball, but his grasp is apparent. For example, once he has assessed that he has to elevate himself six inches to snatch a piece of salami from my hand when my wife is not looking, he does it perfectly, over and over, and then asks for more. When he chases a ball, he anticipates the bounce and jumps to grab it, again, usually without error. Clearly, the ability to assess causality is not dependent on reason, although we undoubtedly need reason to understand the more complex levels of causality.

When my dog wakes up, he wants breakfast, which must include low carbohydrate dog food mixed with meat. Given his physiological features (canine teeth, forward looking eyes, etc.) and his digestive system, he is a carnivore. He will never wake up one day and decide he wants a salad or a low protein diet. He has no moral compunction for the lizards or birds he kills in the back yard. In fact, it seems to excite him. He is a dog. When I grab a ball and throw it, he chases it with excitement every time, unless he is tired or occupied by something more interesting, like the massive bone of a pork leg. When I ask if he wants to go "bye-bye" for a walk in the park, he jumps in the car full of excitement, without exception, every time. He is a dog. Of interest, he is sometimes confused about mating, especially when he was young, and he has been known to attempt to mount things that could not produce offspring, such as pillows, but he now goes crazy around female dogs in heat, without having a talk about the birds and the bees. If he were to meet a female dog in heat now, he would try to mate. There is no circumstance in which he would pass, say he was not in the mood, or complain that there are too many unwanted rescue puppies in the world. The point I am trying to make with these examples is that *dogs cannot choose to behave contrary to their nature, that is, their teleology.* Animals behave in accordance with their nature, their teleology, because they live in the world of understanding, which does not allow for non-teleological behavior. They do not possess a capacity for rational reflection. They also do not have a capacity for making life choices that would move them to one side of the canine political spectrum. Have you ever met a conservative or a liberal dog? Huxley's insights on reason are useful.

> Non-rational creatures do not look before or after, but live in the animal eternity of a perpetual present; instinct is their animal grace and constant inspiration; and they are never tempted to live otherwise than in accord with their own animal dharma, or immanent law. Thanks to his reasoning powers and to the instrument of reason, language, man (in his merely human condition) live nostalgically, apprehensively and hopefully in the past and future as well as in the present; has no instincts to tell him what to do; must rely on personal cleverness, rather than on inspiration from the divine Nature of Things; finds himself in a condition of chronic civil war between passion and prudence and, on a higher level of awareness and ethical sensibility, between egotism and dawning spirituality.[1]

1 Huxley, Aldous, *The Perennial Philosophy*, pg. 141.

Reason is what separates humans from other animals and allows us to rise above (or fall below) the world of understanding. To use a metaphor, reason allows us to step out of the river of life (the world of causality), take a deep breath and look around, then see where we want to go and jump back into the river. We can look back (past), admire where we are (present), and see what awaits us (future), whereas other animals would be stuck navigating the river, maneuvering a perpetual present, with no awareness of past, present, future, or death. We are still subject to the cause and effect parameters of the world of understanding—if we watch an egg fall, it breaks when it hits the floor, no matter how hard we wish or pray to the contrary—but reason gives us powerful tools that other animals do not have. Reason thus opens our lives to exalted things like art and philosophy, but reason also brings with it the potential for abuse, as Schopenhauer observed:

> With abstract knowledge, with the faculty of reason, doubt and error have appeared in the theoretical, care and remorse in the practical. If in the representation of perception illusion does at moments distort reality, then in the representation of the abstract error can reign for thousands of years, impose its iron yoke on whole nations, stifle the noblest impulses of mankind; through its slaves and dupes it can enchain even the man it cannot deceive. It is the enemy against which the wisest minds of all times have kept up an unequal struggle, and only what these have won from it has become the property of mankind.[1]

Before continuing with the potential down side of reason—some psychologists, such as Albert Ellis, believed in the primacy of cognition in psychopathology—we should take a look at its essential function, as this will help us understand how reason can be abused. According to Schopenhauer, the essential function of reason is *concept formation*. Exactly what concepts are and how they are formed is beyond the scope of this book, but we are all familiar with the basic idea. If we see pretty colorful objects in nature, we can create the concept "flower" to put them into the same category. The human brain naturally strives to conceptualize the world, and the creation of each concept shapes the way our brain works. We can combine flowers with other similar leafy objects to create the broader concept "plant," and so on until we reach the highest degrees of human abstraction, with a concept like "substance," what Aristotle called a category. The important point is that, given the world we live in and the language we speak, our conceptual web or hierarchy will take a predictable shape given the nature of reason and the world we live in. We might have one or twenty words to describe snow, depending on where we live. Going in the other direction, we can create concepts for subspecies of flowers, such as roses or orchids, or even a

---

1 Schopenhauer, Arthur, *The World as Will and Representation*, Vol. 1, pg. 35.

lower level by creating concepts for subspecies of roses, such as Hulthemia, Hesperrhodos, Platyrhondon, Rosa, and so on. As long as the process of abstraction is grounded in reality (the understanding, although we also have psychological concepts of inner world emotions, such as anger or joy), we should avoid errors and our conceptual network should assume a relatively predictable shape that is capable of drawing consistent and accurate conclusions. On a more practical level, if we can think abstractly in such a way that it allows us to pack 20 canteens of water (five canteens per day for a four-day trip across the desert), we can plan for the future and improve our chances of survival. Or, if we can develop an abstract concept for money that allows us to transcend the limits of physical gold and silver but remain grounded in reality as we exchange goods and services, we can grow our economy in ways that were never possible before. Reason is the ultimate tool, and the ultimate double-edged sword if used incorrectly.

As our conceptual toolbox grows each year, both organically and via education, and our brain synapses form complex webs, it changes the way we think and feel. For example, although art in general expresses emotional or non-discursive truths, not concepts or logical truths, our ability to express ourselves artistically depends on our capacity for concepts and reason, even though art is not or should not be conceptual in nature, which a complex and paradoxical idea that is beyond the scope of this book. Animals cannot create art or experience artistic emotions. For this reason, it does not make sense to philosophize about human nature unless we are talking about people who have a developed faculty of reason. If people who are living in a stone-age level of existence are prone to violence, it does not make sense to use these people as a basis to argue that people are naturally violent, unless by that we mean that people in an unrefined stage of rational development are prone to violence. Along the same lines, if we recognize that a group of people or a society lacks reason, we cannot always relate to them in the same way that we would relate to rational people. If a tribe in the Amazon lives in peace and harmony but their idea of technology is a bone through the nose, it does not make sense to use these people as a basis to argue that people are naturally peaceful and harmonious. The question of human nature requires us to assess people in their most refined form—that is, when the faculty of reason guides their lives—but I am not sure we could make universal conclusions even in that situation, which is why speculating on human nature is not a good point of departure for political philosophy. Granted, not everyone achieves a refined level of rational thought, so we have to base our legal system on a slightly lower common denominator, such as the laws we pass and how we treat criminals, but we should always look to reason when defining our potential.

One of the most important tools in our conceptual toolbox is language. As we think about the world in terms of flowers and fiat dollars, we are able to use our brains in ways that other animals cannot. I highlighted that concepts change the way we think, without yet making any reference to language. Just as most changes in the evolutionary process affect individual behavior, not collective behavior (because not all people live in large societies), it makes sense to talk about the primary function of concepts as changing the way we think and only secondarily as providing a foundation for language, but such an important claim is beyond the scope of this book. Many animals communicate with varying degrees of complexity, without the benefit of reason, so it seems reasonable to claim that concepts do not provide the foundation for language as much as they allow us to transform language into a higher level of complexity. The philosophical implications of language are also beyond the scope of this book, but as Fukuyama observed, language played a key role in shaping how human societies evolved. Even the most evolved primates do not grow beyond a band and always live within a small area, which Fukuyama attributes to a lack of human-like language, which in turn means a lack of reason. Thus, if reason plays the critical role in allowing us to develop a complex language, which in turn is required to develop a modern state, then *civilization as we know it depends on our capacity for reason.*

Black Magic Concepts

If someone wants to make a sword, he has to find the right metals, blend them and heat them to the right temperature, and then shape them and cool them according to the art and science of metallurgy. If we want to have a sword that works effectively and does not break, we have to make it step by step in accordance with the laws of science. Granted, this process might have been learned by trial and error over time, probably with some luck, but the art and science of metallurgy is something we discover, not something we invent. The laws of metallurgy will never change, no matter how much we hope or pray. As our knowledge of metallurgy grows with time, we can develop concepts to provide structure to our understanding of it, so that we can better understand it and teach it to others, to avoid having each generation reinvent the wheel. Just as we benefit from and are limited by the roads and infrastructure that were made before we were born, we all benefit from and are limited by the language we inherited. If concepts are going to be useful, they have to be grounded in reality.

As I addressed in Part I, during the earliest stages of our social development, we were not always fully aware of what we were doing, to the point where by the time we started to reflect on our social institutions, many of them already had been formed and were shaping how we were thinking about them. The same goes for the development of language. By the time we could reflect on language, we were already using language to reflect on language, which in turn shaped how we reflected on language, a cycle that is possible to break only if teleology is fundamental to our nature. No doubt, a process of trial and error combined with luck shaped how we developed as a society—keeping in mind that the societies that made the wrong choices probably disappeared from the face of the earth—but it should be clear that many mistakes were made along the way. Shifting to the present topic, concepts, it should be no surprise that many false or invalid concepts were developed in our earliest stages (even now), mostly because we lacked scientific understanding. For example, we might create concepts that are not grounded in reality or do not function in accordance with cause and effect. This is all a long-winded way of saying that people make mistakes when creating concepts. We cannot plant a stone to grow a fruit tree, but we can observe the world and create false concepts. Unlike other animals, which act in accordance with instinct in the world of understanding, humans have the power to create concepts, to include false ones, which allows us to make errors and stray from our nature or teleology. After a period of reflection, a lion will never switch to a vegetarian diet and then die a slow death death due to lack of essential nutrients. However, humans can reflect on life and make life choices that actually damage their chances for survival, something that would have been impossible if the person was living in the world of understanding, in accordance with his teleology. Thus, when using reason, we should ensure that we are doing so in accordance with the world of understanding, or we run the risk of hastening our own demise.

If we look at the political spectrum from left to right, we can apply the same idea to reason. If we lacked reason, like other animals, we would live in accordance with understanding and our lives would be more predictable, probably similar to other higher primates. That is, we would not have political parties on the left and right extremes of the spectrum. We would probably have alpha males and a hierarchy based on power (as we do now, in some ways), but there would not be a left–right divide. Given that we do have reason and therefore possess a capacity to transcend the world of understanding, the normal conclusion would be that the introduction of reason into human life moves us only in the direction of progress. However, given that we can make false concepts, we can regress to a level of existence that is in many ways lower than other animals because whereas animals must act accordance with understanding and their teleology, and therefore in accordance with reality, humans are capable of acting contrary to understanding, that is, contrary to reality or their teleology, and even contrary to their own survival. For example, if we pray for food rather than hunt for it or gather it ("God helps those who help themselves"), we might die. Or, we could establish a pattern of deficit spending and currency devaluation as a way to fund our government, which would lead to hyperinflation or currency collapse, not to mention breaking down the work ethic and virtues of the population. Thus, the first challenge of civilization is making sure that our most fundamental concepts correspond to reality and the world of understanding, just as we must get the fundamental institutions of society right (resource management and procreation) before we address the more complex institutions (the state, the rule of law, and a mechanism of accountability). Only after we have done this can we begin to talk about growing our concepts to achieve rational reflection.

Along these lines, given that we cannot rely on instinct alone to shape how we live, to include our social institutions, it is important to understand the difference between natural and normative laws, a topic Karl Popper addressed in *The Open Society and Its Enemies*. Popper defined normative laws as the norms, prohibitions, or commandments that influence and control how we live, things that can be enforced, that are within our control, and are subject to change. For example, we can choose to establish a kingdom with polygamy one year and then switch to democracy with monogamy the next year. On the other hand, we cannot decree that men and women change genders, that people start living for 1,000 years, or that gravity stop working. There are underlying physiological and scientific facts that shape how we ultimately structure our society, but the fact that different societies in different times and places have different forms of government and institutions proves that they do not fall under the rubric of scientific law.

Given that natural and normative laws are interrelated, one of the most important questions is whether normative laws can be grounded in or derived from natural laws. Since the creation of the USA by the Founding Fathers, it is popular to talk about "natural rights," such as the right to life, liberty, and the pursuit of happiness. However, given that these so-called natural rights are clearly normative—we could in theory live without them; they do not regulate our lives in the same way that gravity does, even if they are consistent with our teleology—does it ever make sense to say that the norms we choose to live by have the gravitas of natural law? Popper answers this question in the negative, but with a qualification. According to Popper, humans have passed through phases of growth regarding how we understand the difference between natural and normative laws.

Naïve Monism: In this stage, the distinction between natural and normative laws is not yet made, which is common for primitive tribes. The idea here is that a tribe of people, in a blind process of striving, stumbles across particular ways of behaving that promote survival, sometimes confusing the natural for the normative, or vice versa. For example, they might project human motivations into the movements of the sun and believe that the sun decides whether or not to rise each day, just as a person would, and then devise rituals to ensure that the sun rises each day, apparently unaware that the sun will continue to rise even without the ritual (or they derive spiritual benefits from the ritual). On the other hand, they might believe that their taboo against incest, which could have been otherwise, at least in theory, has the force of natural law, to the point where they could not even consider the possibility that they could make a conscious decision to abolish the taboo. Thus, we see that people can develop false concepts to make them believe that what should fall under the laws of nature actually falls under the laws of human motivation, and vice versa. These false concepts can prevent us from developing intellectually to the point of rational reflection. Out of this naïve monism, Popper considers two modified versions:

Naïve Naturalism: According to this version, all regularities we experience in life, whether natural or conventional, are felt to be beyond the possibility of alteration. Popper considers this an abstract possibility that has never been realized.

Naïve Conventionalism: According to this version, all natural and normative regularities that we experience are expressions of, and dependent upon, the decisions of man-like gods or demons. Both natural and normative laws are open to modification by the gods and demons, such as by magical practices. Even natural laws are upheld by sanctions, as if they were normative laws. Heraclitus said: "The sun will not outstep the measure of his path; or else the goddess of Fate, the handmaids of Justice, will know how to find them." Once again, we see that people made errors when abstracting concepts from reality, which can be pleasant in poetry or literary language, but not in science.

The key here is that in the early stages of history, when people were first gaining consciousness of themselves and the world they lived in, they were overwhelmed by the fire hose of perceptions and crude concepts, unable to discern or disentangle which elements were due to them and which elements were due to nature. (According to the esoteric tradition, religion is primarily about the evolution of consciousness and only secondarily about the creation and evolution of the material world, which would explain the recent "creation" of man.) Just as a newborn baby struggles to process his perceptions, people in this stage of historical development struggle to differentiate the inner world from the outer world, the normative laws from the natural laws. According to Popper, the breakdown of magic tribalism is closely connected to the realization that the taboos that regulate behavior are different in different tribes. This gives people the first insight that their normative laws are imposed and enforced by man, and can be broken without unpleasant consequences if sanctions can be avoided by others in the tribe. You can imagine what might happen when a person forgets to pray to the gods, at a specified time and place, and he is not punished—no lightning bolt. He might forget to do it the next day, and the next day, fearing the lightning bolt but slowly reaching the conclusion that the failure to pray does not summon a lightning bolt. Then again, by not praying he might sense how his lack of humility before the divine causes a negative emotional reaction within him. His ego might swell and he might start to believe that he can use other people as means to an end or that material goods are the most important things in life. Popper highlighted the fact that Athens had a trading economy, which exposed them to other tribes around the Mediterranean, for its acceleration away from primal tribalism to the beginning of philosophical reflection when the great Ionian philosopher Thales predicted an eclipse on 28 May 585 BC.

Popper credited the Sophist philosopher Protagoras for first achieving a clear distinction between normative and natural law. Popper calls the goal of this process (of understanding and living by the difference of normative and natural laws) *critical dualism*. However, before reaching this advanced stage of development, Popper identifies three intermediary stages, which he claims arrive from the misapprehension that conventional or artificial, in the context of normative laws, means arbitrary.

Biological Naturalism: This theory claims that in spite of the fact that moral laws and the laws of tribes or nations are arbitrary (not grounded in scientific law), there are some eternal unchanging laws of nature from which we can derive such norms. In other words, norms can be derived from facts. Food is a good example. After all, we know from science that we should not eat too much food or too little food. We know how many calories we should eat each day and of which kind to maintain our weight and good health. We can use scientific method to determine which foods are good for us, such as analyzing the nutritional content (water, proteins, carbohydrates, fats, vitamins, minerals, etc.), and in which quantity. So far this makes sense. However, Popper claims that this way of thinking has been used to defend contradictory positions. For example, different views of human biology have been used to promote both equalitarianism and the rule of the strong. Popper is not denying that our biology is a valid ground for establishing norms, but he is denying that all of our particular norms can be derived from our biology alone, absent, I would assume, rational thought. Popper might be right that normative factors determine whether our diet is based on beef and potatoes rather than chicken and rice, but it is not clear how Popper would respond to the more abstract and rational claim that our diet should be based on particular ratios of protein, fats, and carbohydrates. That is, once we introduce the power of reason, which is capable of reflecting on our biology, we are in a better position to ground some of our norms on biology.

Ethical or Juridical Positivism: This theory shares with biological naturalism the idea that we must try to reduce norms to facts. According to Popper, positivism maintains that there are no other norms but the laws that have actually been set up and which therefore have a positive existence. The individual does not judge the norms of a society. The society provides the code by which the individual must be judged. According to Popper, this system is often conservative, authoritarian, and often invokes the authority of God, although the same could be said about a system that is liberal, authoritarian, and often invokes the omnipotent power of the state. This model seems to apply to any society that values revelation, whether theological or Marxist, rather than philosophy or science.

Psychological or Spiritual Naturalism: This theory is a combination of the previous two. The biological naturalists are right in assuming that there are natural ends or aims (teleology), but they overlook the fact that our natural aims are not necessarily focused on health, pleasure, food, shelter, or propagation. Some people have higher, spiritual aims, which is true, especially after we reach the stage of rational reflection. The ethical positivists are also right in emphasizing that all norms are conventional, but they overlook the fact that they are an expression of the psychological or spiritual nature of man, and of the nature of human society. According to Popper, this theory is often used to justify the natural prerogatives of the noble, elect, wise, or natural leaders, often in support of a Utopian agenda, with Popper using Plato as an example.

Before moving to the final stage of critical dualism, Popper addresses two tendencies that often get in the way. The first is a general tendency to monism, that is, the reduction of norms to facts, which was addressed above. The mere fact that some people have different colored skin, different natural capabilities, or different genitalia does not allow us to extrapolate a complex system of normative laws. (However, as I showed in chapter two, the fact that humans have two genders and procreate via the union of man and woman does allow us *to set rational parameters* on how society should regulate procreation *to achieve the best results*—for individuals and for society as a whole.) As we will address later, norms that contradict natural laws can be eliminated, but particular norms cannot be logically derived from particular natural facts, except through a process of abstraction and trial and error over time. The second is based upon our fear of admitting to ourselves that the responsibility for our ethical decisions is entirely ours and cannot be shifted to anybody else. Many humans take comfort in the idea that the rules and norms that shape our lives are grounded in a solid foundation that transcends our own personal beliefs or desires, such as God or a written document. As Dostoyevsky said, "If there is no god, everything is permitted." This is not true, of course, but it suggests that many people are more likely to follow moral principles if they believe they are backstopped by a divine power than they are if some guy just made them up.

The primary reason I reviewed Popper's ideas regarding normative and natural laws was to provide a better context for understanding the idea that the misuse of reason can result in incorrect conceptual models that often cause confusion at best or damage at worst. If we keep in mind that reason is what allows us to stray from the inflexible world of understanding and causality, for better (rational reflection) or for worse (magical thinking), then it makes sense to say that *the existence of the political spectrum is due to the improper use of reason.* People who go down the path of joining the radical left or the radical right camps of the political spectrum do so based on false conceptual models, ones that stray from the cause and effect of understanding and legitimate abstraction in accordance with reason. And the more errors they make, the further they move from the center. Just as some ancients mistakenly believed that human motivations governed the sun's motion and that the laws of nature governed some human institutions, both the radical left and the radical right can trace their false beliefs to the improper use of reason. As we wipe away the cobwebs of our dilapidated thinking and polish our power of reason to a brilliant shine, to the point where we are capable of rational reflection, we move toward the middle of the political spectrum. However, just as Aristotle said we have to train people on the less easy side of a the virtue spectrum to achieve the golden mean, in order for society to achieve the highly desired rational middle position, we have to train society on the less easy side of the political spectrum, which is *the path of discipline and frugality.*

Alchemy

I have made reference to manifesting our potential, especially as it relates to reason. Unlike most animals, which can wake up each day and stay on the path of biological growth and maturity by instinct alone, humans have to work hard, make decisions, and take action each step of the way, and we can get off track at any time, sometimes never to return. Therefore, rather than focus on human nature per se, this last section will focus the process itself—the process of achieving biological growth and maturity in accordance with our nature as rational animals.

Alchemists during the Middle Ages and the Renaissance practiced an esoteric craft that blended science and magic. The goal was to transform base metals into gold, which was considered by many to be a metaphor for personal transformation and purification of the soul. It was not clear exactly how they did it—their books are filled with references to mercury, sulfur, and salt—but it is probably safe to say it included some oblique references to romantic love and sexual activity. The "fleshy sword" of Paracelsus comes to mind. Most likely, these thinkers were discovering things about themselves— the inner laws of consciousness, which had corresponding outer laws in nature and the planets (the microcosm and the macrocosm)—to include techniques for shaping our biological growth and maturity. They encoded them secretly into books to avoid charges of heresy from the Church. Again, I do not claim to be an expert on the alchemists, but their quest to transform human nature is appropriate for our analysis.

In a previous section I addressed the art and science of metallurgy, the idea being that metal must be transformed by a process in order for a sword to be sharp and resist breaking. To achieve this, we cannot simply heat up some metals, pour them into a mold, and let it cool. If we use the language of the alchemists, human nature is like a sword that must be heated to a specific temperature to be molded and acquire new properties. Some people refer to this as transformation within a crucible, the idea being that we can only transform ourselves and achieve our teleology within the fiery heat of life itself. Ilya Prigogine coined the phrase "dissipative structure" to refer to the patterns that self-organize in far-from-equilibrium systems. Whether or not it is true in physics is not as important as the fact that it can be used metaphorically to understand how people experience the process of organic growth and transformation. The properties of steel or other metals change when they are heated to extremely high temperatures, after which it will have a sharper edge and resist breaking after it cools. To use a human example, new recruits who go to boot camp are transformed into soldiers via a process of hard work, exercise, and discipline. This process transforms people in ways that could not be achieved by watching television on the couch.

A similar thought process also applies to the concept of a hero. During a story, the hero faces progressive challenges that push him to the limit, at which point he is ready to slay the dragon, which is often a metaphor for the internal conflict that set him on the journey in the first place. The same idea applies to a professional athlete or an artist achieving mastery, a topic that Robert Greene addresses masterfully in *Mastery*. A professional runner will train his body to exhaustion, for a certain amount of time and at a certain level of intensity, until he breaks through a plateau, which allows his progress to accelerate asymptotically, or the pianist who trains for thousands of hours, year after year, until the notes eventually roll off his fingers effortlessly as if he were playing a game. The one thing all of these transformational examples have in common is a sustained amount of time and a sustained level of intensity in whatever they do, to the point where they begin to transform the person from within, just as the properties of metals change when heated to high temperatures. In the case of reason, a modest form will reveal itself in all of us with minimal effort, like a tool that does not quite fit but can get the job done with persistence. Basic nutrients and day to day living will give life to reason, but if we hope to nurture the growth of our reason to the point where we are capable of the kind of rational reflection that would make Aristotle proud, we must work hard and continually grind ourselves to new levels of refinement.

CHAPTER FOUR. INSTITUTIONS

There is generally consensus on the left and the right that building strong institutions is a key to good governance. Having lived and worked in several developing countries, I can attest that there is nothing more frustrating than working with broken institutions, especially ones that often do more harm than good, and nothing more refreshing than seeing a small investment in an institution pay big dividends. In every country there are many people who are willing to work for the common good. You just have to find them and focus some effort on keeping out the bad ones. The firing of a few corrupt people and steady investment in people who really want to work can make all the difference. The good news is that both sides of the political spectrum, left and right, tend to agree on the importance of institutions, at least in the abstract, but there is often serious disagreement on the types of institutions we should have, how many we should have, how big they should be, and whether they should be controlled by the private or public sector.

The purpose of this chapter is to step back and think about what institutions are and how they fit into a theory of political philosophy, rather than discuss the nuts and bolts of running specific institutions. That is, I will not look at institutions in the same way that someone from the social sciences would. I will not make any specific recommendations for institutions—most countries have similar ones (police, military, education, health, welfare, procreation, etc.) that are tailored to the local population and environment—but the conclusions we arrive at should help us start our journey on the right track when it comes time to make decisions regarding our institutions. For example, I will not argue that a certain percentage of GDP should be spent on education, or that any particular society should have a certain number of policemen per capita, or doctors per capita, and so on. Just as a general should understand the nature of the battle before making strategic decisions, we should understand what institutions are before creating them, changing them, or eliminating them. In this book's introduction, I noted that Fukuyama defined institutions as, "persistent rules that shape, limit, and channel human behavior"; in this chapter I will address the questions of, "To what end?" That is, how can we know whether an institution is working well? If we are successful in gaining a good understanding of what institutions are, it will clear up some of the conflicts between the left and the right and set the stage for rational decision making.

The basic idea of an institution, such as a private business, an educational system, or a military or police force, is that *the whole is greater than the sum of the parts*—simple (like the design of an iPhone). This can be achieved by economies of scale, expertise, division of labor, corporate culture, or other variables. For example, an automobile manufacturer that successfully exploits the concepts of division of labor and economies of scale can grow its output, profits, and market share. In fact, it is not possible to be profitable in the mass-market automotive industry today until a minimum production threshold is met. That is, the *business model* for the mass market automotive industry has parameters for success that shape the industry—the business model. Or, a judicial system that promotes a culture of integrity and expertise can put more criminals behind bars. If the prosecutors or judges are corrupt or incompetent, the possibility of justice is elusive, and the legal system becomes a mechanism for powerful people to protect their criminal activities and to put their law-abiding enemies behind bars. Thus, when assessing the value of an institution, we should consider first and foremost whether the net result of the institution (the net resource production, to include intangibles like people feeling safe) is that the whole is greater than the sum of the parts, quantitatively, qualitatively, or both, and that powerful forces (criminal, tribal, special interests, etc.) cannot use the institution to manipulate the political system for their own benefit. If the institution works, we should probably keep it. If not, we should reform it or eliminate it. Of note, culture and tradition, even if sometimes inefficient, can play an important role in shaping our institutions. For example, should we collapse our five military services into one service in the name of efficiency or should we allow the five services to compete and maintain their traditions, even if we have to hire more people and pay more money? We should never throw out the baby with the bathwater in the name of progress or efficiency, but our basis for assessing institutions should always be whether the whole is greater than the sum of the parts. If individuals or other groups of people acting on their own could achieve similar or better results at a lower cost (state arbitrage), then we should reconsider whether the institution merits our resources.

Before diving into our analysis, let us begin with an example. Most people on the left and the right agree that the military should be a single institution run by the federal government. The left might prefer a smaller military with a less aggressive role around the world, unless we are averting humanitarian crises or nation building, but the right certainly would never want to establish 50 independent militaries under state control, in the spirit of the 10ᵗʰ amendment, which is often the basis for how the right side of the political spectrum believes the government should be run. Clearly, there are many benefits to having a national military—nationwide recruiting, training and equipment standards, and so on. If each state were to run its own military, the same way municipalities, counties, and states run their own police forces, we would have problems with training and equipment standards and organizing all the disparate elements to unify for a common cause in the event of a war. What if individual states did not support a particular military operation? Would they reserve the right to veto or opt out? For anyone who has seen the U.S. military in action, the whole is definitely greater than the sum of the parts. We have the greatest military in human history. The coordination of operations and logistics on a global scale has never been matched, but this is in large part because we have chosen to make it a federal public institution rather than subject it to the economic laws of supply and demand that define most private sector institutions.

Out of Chaos

Today, we tend to think of institutions as rational organizations that are designed to serve a specific purpose, such as a newly incorporated municipality establishing a police force by using demographic and socio-economic data to determine how many policemen to hire for a given population density, or analyzing the demographic and economic data of a state to make a plan for building a chain of fast food restaurants. Things were not always this way (and often are not today). As Hegel observed, as opposed to the social contract theory of political philosophy, which assumed that societies begin when rational people of their own freewill come together for a common purpose, the historical evolution of human institutions was largely a process of trial and error, often without rational reflection and often grounded on things other than reason or the greater good, such as ego, power, bad science, or black magic concepts. By the time we had developed to the point where we were able to reflect on our institutions, we were already knee-deep in them; and the way the institutions developed shaped the way we thought about them. As a result, self-criticism or empathy for other cultures is difficult for most societies, which is why a play like *The Trojan Women* by Euripides should be viewed as a major accomplishment. The same goes for language: by the time we could reflect on our own language and grammar, we were already using them, which in turn shaped how we reflected on them, and so on. Or, to use a different analogy, imagine a computer filled with a mix of random software programs and fragmented files. At some point, we become aware of this problem and begin the rational process of deleting old programs and files, adding new ones, downloading security patches, and then cleaning the whole thing up with anti-virus and defragmentation programs. In the end, we will have a highly efficient machine (fulfilling our teleology)—order out of chaos—but it would be misleading to say we had a rational plan from the beginning or that we could have arrived at the stage of rational planning without first passing through the more chaotic phases of trial and error. Just as kinship networks survived or died based on a process of trial and error (we could use words like "invisible hand" or "evolution"), some institutions worked and others did not. Going back to Part I, for a society to survive, at a minimum, it must find a way to rationally institutionalize resource management and procreation.

One thing that stands out in the political debate between left and right is the importance of institutions. The left tends to focus on the value of state institutions, such as health, education, and other social services, and the right tends to focus on the value of private institutions, such as businesses that that create the wealth to pay for social services, which should not surprise us given the analysis in Part I. The left has a tendency to want to shift important institutions to the state side of the equation, such as healthcare, to focus on social justice rather than profits. The right has a tendency to want to keep institutions on the private side of the equation, such as healthcare, to prevent them from growing stagnant or pushing our nation toward bankruptcy (even though most developed countries with single-payer healthcare systems spend a lower percentage of GDP on healthcare). The reason for this is that the debate between left and right is primarily about the role of government. The Founding Fathers were fairly clear on this issue, even if some people choose to ignore them or to interpret them in creative ways, even in the Supreme Court, but the debate continues. People who tend to agree on the proper role of government tend to agree on the types of institutions we should have. However, just as we do not always understand the origins of our institutions, most people cannot always provide a clear explanation for why they hold particular political beliefs. Most of us have some core political beliefs or intuitions (bruises) that cannot withstand scrutiny, such as how we understand the "right to life" or the "right to choose," but if we take a step back and let the raw facts and the mathematics of life be our guide, we might be surprised by what we find.

The Business Model

To gain a better understanding of institutions, we should start with ones that are based on economic activity, such as businesses, ones that could in theory exist in a state of nature (without government) in a society that allows for the free exchange of goods and services. In fact, we will begin with the assumption that government is minimal or at least lacks the power to artificially prop up weak businesses that would fail if left to their own devices. The businesses will live or die by the fairly applied forces of supply and demand. We will also assume that the businesses are not using force or coercion to support their continued existence, such as killing or pillaging the competitors, which often requires the existence of government to counter this by enforcing contracts and protecting private property. The reason for this is that we want to create a scenario in which the survival of the institution depends solely on its ability to be a net producer of resources (to create value) in a freely competitive world of supply and demand. Companies that fail to play this game die quickly, unless they use force or are propped up by a government due to corruption or their "too big to fail" status. With government institutions, on the other hand, they can be propped up and their deaths delayed artificially by a government that compels citizens to provide tax revenue or uses deficit spending, even if the institution becomes a net resource drain on society. For now, then, we will focus our efforts on economic institutions in a notional state of nature.

An important variable that determines whether an economic activity can grow into a large institution is scalability, that is, the ability to accommodate growing demand without losing the profitability of the core business. For example, if a person bakes 10 trays of cookies per day for a local bakery, does this same person have the capacity to bake 100 trays of cookies per day if orders arrive from other stores? The person could buy industrial equipment to make larger batches and then bake them in an industrial oven that holds more trays. However, scalability is not enough. At some point, the business will also have to achieve economies of scale, that is, reducing the unit production cost as sales increase, because these improved margins will be required to hire specialists to run the business behind the scenes (accounting & finance, marketing, human resources, and so on). For example, the person could lower the cost of ingredients by buying bulk quantities or signing exclusive contracts with suppliers. This is not a business book, so I will avoid any more details regarding how to grow a business, but if we think about turning an economic activity into an institution, like turning a garage business into a global corporation like Apple, the company will pass through often predictable phases of organic growth that will involve division of labor and specialization, to the point where many people working for the company will have a limited knowledge of the core business, such as accountants working for a biotechnology company. A business becomes an institution when it becomes a self-sustaining entity that is capable of raising money, creating new products, and in general shifting with the winds and taking steps to ensure its own survival, with the collective whole accomplishing more than the sum of the individuals.

All of this information is available in the local bookstore, so at this point I would like to make the transition from organic growth to what I call the investment bank model of institutions. Let us suppose that we create an invention that blows away everyone's mind, the next super app. We know that everyone in the country will want this product right away. We could start with the family business or the organic growth model, starting with one store or one region, but starting from this position will create inefficiencies along the way that will have to be undone as we take our business to the next level. For example, one particular city might be a wise choice as a distribution hub if we take a regional approach, but the same city might not be a wise choice for a distribution hub if we take a national approach, in which case the growth from regional to national sales will require moving to a new distribution hub, which will take time and money. Therefore, let us assume that we can estimate demand for this product on a national level and go for the gold. In this case, we can develop a national level sales plan, calculate how much money we will need up front, and then create a model that is ready from day one to efficiently cover a national market. Once we go public, every drooling customer will have no problem buying the product quickly because we will have established an efficient production and distribution network that covers the entire country up front, not gradually via organic growth, which can be slow and tedious. If we are successful, the profits will be impressive and no one will be in a position to compete with us. However, if we have miscalculated, even slightly, which tends to happen when growth does not happen organically, or if the national model has to be reduced to a regional model as sales dip, then our business model could quickly collapse and result in bankruptcy. We grew too fast and were probably too leveraged. This model will be more important when we discuss national level public institutions.

The point is that just as politics is often about a balance between left and right, the way we grow an economic institution is often a function of balancing organic growth with the injection of capital or debt that will give us the economies of scale we need to grow more rapidly, to make sure our limited resources are going to the right place. This is called the efficient allocation of resources. In most cases, starting at a point between a family business model and a regional model will work best, taking care to not grow too quickly. If we do not take the leap for some growth, we will remain a family business, which for many people will be a satisfying way to make a living. If we try to bite off more than we can chew, however, we might, to mix metaphors, march beyond our supply lines. If we keep in mind how many businesses fail and how difficult it is to manage the organic growth of a company, we should all have a healthy respect for the economic institutions that have survived the test of time, assuming they did not use illegal means or government favors to achieve success. We should also never forget how fragile many businesses are, as the stock market collapses in 2000 and 2008 showed. (Many people do not calculate how many businesses fail to make one successful business, and therefore are dismissive of businessmen who claim they "deserve" their profits. By not factoring in failed businesses, they overstate the return on capital for businesses as a whole relative to the return on capital for the underlying economy, which in turn creates theories about income disparity that give the false appearance of discrediting capitalism.) If a major economic institution fails overnight, it might take a generation to replace it, taking Detroit as an example. It takes a high level of complexity for a business to establish its own human resources and tax departments, but these jobs could be lost in the blink of an eye if the business is forced to scale back in complexity due to a shock to the business or the economy, in which case these and other functions might have to be outsourced. We would be wise to sustain these institutions, without propping them up artificially, and not take any steps that would threaten *the underlying motivational system that keeps them profitable.* Many people on the left talk about the importance of creating good jobs, but at the same time undermine the incentive system that is required to create those good jobs. The key point to remember is that economic institutions depend on money for their lifeblood, in particular, on their ability to generate positive cash flow by creating value. The corporate culture of the institution will be shaped by this idea, which some people view as a positive or a negative thing, but all people view it as a positive thing when their own retirement pension is on the line. This alone is how we should decide whether or not an economic institution should survive, which, as we will see, is different from how we make life and death decisions regarding public institutions.

Not all economic activities benefit from scalability or economies of scale in the same way. We definitely benefit from the scalability and economies of scale for most technology products, such as cell phones and computers (Would you ever buy a hand-crafted computer?) but nothing beats a serving of homemade lasagna, a bottle of wine from a vineyard in Tuscany, or live music in Memphis or New Orleans. Quality is often more important than quantity, but mass production economic institutions sometimes render craftsmen obsolete or squeeze out the benefits of hand-crafted products with preservatives and machines. If it takes a skilled chef in the Chianti region to make *Pappardelle al Cinghiale* (the best meal I ever had) and an untrained teenager at a fast food restaurant to flip a hamburger, the presence of cheap hamburgers changes the market. On the one hand, more people will be able to buy cheap food, which could be viewed as a good thing, especially for poor people who often cannot afford protein. However, it could also reduce the demand for good food from trained chefs and lower the dietary standards of the population, at least for those who have made the shift from fresh food to fast food. It also does something else. As people move into the lower skilled jobs that are created by highly scalable businesses, such as fast food restaurants, they receive less pay for their work (because it is unskilled work), which in turn limits their ability to buy quality food from a chef. Thus, we start a vicious cycle of lower skilled jobs begetting lower skilled jobs as the process of scalability continues, slowly squeezing the craftsmanship out of many jobs and replacing them with spreadsheets that show a steady return on investment. Granted, one solution to this problem is easy (easy like the design of an iPhone): learn a difficult job skill that is in high demand—one that does not suffer from the forces of scalability, economies of scale, or outsourcing—and spend at least ten years mastering it so you can charge more money for your goods or services, which will allow you to buy quality meals from a chef. In a free market economy where you could barter services with your friends, would you rather be part of a group of friends who are skilled craftsmen or a group of unskilled workers? Another solution involves making unskilled jobs part of a family business model, such as running a family restaurant. If all the family members play their part in the business and all share in the profits of the business (no rational owner is going to share all the profits with strangers), then we can avoid a situation in which people are trying to making a living while working an unskilled job. However, this would require our society to place more value and emphasis on kinship networks and "traditional" families.

The Government Model

Many of the same variables that apply to private institutions also apply to public institutions, such as scalability and economies of scale, but the lifeblood of the institution is usually different. Most public institutions do not generate positive cash flow to sustain their own activities, although some come close. For example, the U.S. Postal Service has a business-like model (it creates value) and could, in theory, run a profit, but some of the decisions that have been made regarding how the business is run, such as defraying costs to remote areas (a first-class stamp will take your letter anywhere), combined with a generous retirement program that a private sector business with actuarial charts would never approve, have made profitability difficult to achieve. Also, many overseas Consulates generate positive cash flow by charging fees for visas, passports, and other services for foreigners and U.S. citizens, which should please taxpayers. These examples, however, are the exception to the rule. Rather than focus on positive cash flow or wealth creation, public institutions tend to focus on the services provided— creating value for the citizens who pay taxes. For example, even though we could probably outsource our judicial system to save money while putting criminals behind bars (if that sounds absurd, keep in mind that many of our prisons are run by private companies that have been known to bribe judges to keep the prisons full), our sense of justice demands that we pursue this activity in ways that a private institution would not. We cannot put a price on justice, although many countries are often forced to. For example, we might spend millions of dollars to put a heinous criminal behind bars, even though the "value" of the trial was not worth millions of dollars in the sense that a successful conviction will not prevent millions of dollars of damages from future crimes yet to be committed. Justice is not easy to calculate, and our contributions to the justice system are not voluntary. We cannot opt out of paying taxes if we are not satisfied with the services being provided, unless by opting out we mean traveling to other states or other countries.

Many government institutions are measured by a standard, such as academic performance in our public schools or crime statistics in our cities. For example, as we manage our public school system, we should focus on what students should be studying at particular ages to create a curriculum that fits their natural organic growth and development (their teleology), teaching subjects at the right time and in the right degree. Not all students learn the same way or at the same pace, which is why we have an honors program track, but there are predictable trends and phases of growth that most students go through. For example, if "normal" students (thinking in terms of a bell curve) need to learn Algebra I in eighth grade, then we should teach them Algebra I in eighth grade, not much sooner and not much later, keeping in mind that there will be exceptions to the rule. The same idea goes for police. If we are going have a law against car theft, we cannot have the police reach a quota for the month and then stop. They must continue to arrest each person who steals a car. That said, we can use financial accounting methods to determine the "price" of these services—how much it costs to teach one student Algebra I, how much it costs to put one car thief behind bars, and so on. If we think of the tax-paying citizens as customers, then we can imagine them paying the police department to do their job, in the same way that they might hire a security guard to protect them (state arbitrage). However, the relationship is not as clear-cut as it is in the case of a private business because the government has the job of preventing the tyranny of the majority and other noble objectives. We would continue to pay the police even if no one committed crimes that needed investigating. In fact, most of us would move to a safe city and gladly pay the police to do nothing if no crimes were being committed. Thus, we could make the argument that some government institutions are driven by or can be measured by the cash flow value creation principles of business, such as the cost to have one child attend fifth grade. This is true, but the primary difference is that paying for the institution is not optional. I can decide which rapid oil change service provider I will use for my car, but I cannot opt out of my local tax bill because I do not like the schools or how the local police take care of business. I can move, but the new place would probably have a similar tax burden. To think about it another way, what would you think if a particular rapid oil change service provider were to get a law passed that compelled you to use his and only his service, with mandatory raises and a generous pension plan? After all, for safety reasons we all have to (or should) change our oil. Many car accidents are due to mechanical malfunction, so perhaps we would all benefit from mandating that everyone use the same rapid oil change service provider.

At the end of the day, government is a service provider, but one that we hold to a higher standard because *we expect it to serve our interests, not its own interests*. In fact, a government should not be thought of as having interests, aside from serving us. We expect Apple to pursue its own profits, not the "greater good," although some people might think of Apple's business activities as contributing to the greater good by creating jobs and new products that make our lives easier or more efficient. National defense, schools, police, and welfare programs—these are all services we pay for. The essential difference between private and public sector institutions is that we are free to choose the former but not the latter, at least not after budget laws have been passed and the tax revenue has been collected. Thus, when making a decision about whether a particular service should be handled by a private or a public institution, we should always keep this in mind. One simple rule of thumb is that public services, at a minimum, should focus on services that people should not be allowed to opt out of, to avoid the free rider problem, or things the private sector could never do in a uniform and consistent manner for all people on an equal basis. In this context, Fukuyama refers to the ideas of public goods, externalities, social regulation, moral hazards, and the importance of controlling elites, which are important ideas to understand but are beyond the scope of this book. For example, everyone for the most part benefits equally from national defense, so it would be odd to allow some people to opt out of taxes to fund national defense, but almost half of all working Americans are not net contributors to federal income taxes, which are used to fund national defense. They might insist that they pay Social Security and other local and state taxes, but the taxes collected for programs do not fund our military. Likewise, we as a society seem to have reached consensus that every child needs a K–12 education with a curriculum that meets certain minimum standards. Thus, it does not seem unreasonable that we should compel all people to pay into the public school system via taxes given that most of us have benefitted from it or expect that our children will benefit from it. We all benefit from having an educated population, at a minimum because democracy depends on the voters understanding the issues, but we also want to avoid a situation where different schools are opening and closing every year due to competition. We are willing to tolerate some inefficiency in our schools to ensure that all students have continuity in schools that are in close proximity to where they live. However, this raises questions about other educational options, such as private schools, charter schools, and home schooling, and at what level these institutions should be managed—federal, state, or local.

To Scale or Not to Scale

Let us assume for the sake of argument that both the left and right sides of the political spectrum agree that the public sector rather than the private sector should manage a particular service—in this case, education—or, at a minimum, that we should have a public school system. The basis for this decision might be that education is (or should be) an investment in our children, which is an empirical question that can be calculated by looking at how much school costs versus the long-term increase in wealth creation by the students and society. Anyone who believes that education for the sake of education is more important than economic results should visit Cuba, where a Ph.D. will barely put food on your table. Given that public schools do not charge direct tuition to the parents of students, we will have to fund the schools with tax revenue. Of interest, even families without children or with children in private schools are forced to pay for the public school system, which shows how much most people value education; think of it as each person paying back what they received as a child or making an investment that will pay long-term dividends for society. The schools do not have a means to sustain themselves directly the same way the U.S. Postal Service can charge for individual transactions, such as stamps, or the DMV can charge a fee for a driver's license. I would not rule this out in the future, though, such as schools asking parents with children attending the public schools to pay additional taxes.

As is the case with any institution, you often get what you pay for. The residents of a school district will have to decide how much of their wealth they are willing to part with to get the desired results in what is often a zero-sum game of opportunity cost because every dollar spent on education is a dollar not spent on something else. If they resort to deficit spending to achieve the desired results, they will have crossed the line and will set the stage for a crisis when the bill comes due. We have to grow organically over time (thinking at least one generation ahead and believing in the power of compounded interest), using debt in a rational way to allow for economic expansion, or we run the risk of collapse. If the schools receive more money and the results are not positive, then the residents should consider cutting back or looking for other ways to improve the results. This raises issues like charter schools, home schooling, unions, and teacher tenure. If we take the perspective that government is a service provider that exists to serve us, then it makes sense to consider other options if the public schools are not performing well, as long as all children continue to have the option to go to schools that meet the basic minimum standards. Why should a given public school have unfettered access to our tax revenue if charter schools or home schooling have better results? Granted, we want to use tried and true educational practices with our children, rather than try something new that we might regret later (you are only a child once), but institutions tend to stagnate if they are shielded from the forces of creative destruction. One reason our military is so successful is that it faces life and death combat, some would say too often. The same goes for teachers and tenure. How is it that the people who receive our wealth to run our schools to educate our children can prevent us from firing them? Why should teachers with radical political beliefs that they voice in school not be fired? What about teachers with poor results? Can you imagine an employee at Apple demanding tenure or Apple compelling people to buy their products so that they do not have to fire anyone? Again, what would you think if the local rapid oil change service provider got a law passed that compelled all citizens to change their oil at his establishment at regular intervals to be decided by him? When it comes down to the left versus right debate in politics, it boils down to what should be the role of government. Should government serve our needs, or should it serve its own needs? Is the government a mere service provider that we toss aside when we are unhappy with the results? Is the government an entity that has a right to exist, with the power to dictate to us how much of our wealth we must give to keep it running? Or is the truth somewhere in between?

With those initial comments out of the way, we can now address the heart of the matter as it relates to institutions and political philosophy. After we reach agreement about what legitimate functions the government should perform—which would be no small achievement, by the way—we then have to ask a more important question that is particularly important in the case of the USA: *at what level?* That is, even if we agree that we should have a public school system, at what level should we manage the program— municipal, county, state, federal? This decision has to be made in the context of the type of government we have. As it turns out, the U.S. public school system has involvement at all levels, but it is mostly run at the local level through school boards and with the states setting academic standards, which is different from most European nations that are structured to run them in a more centralized way. (The way our government is structured by the Constitution prevents us from using the European model.) From the left, we often hear that public schools need more resources to succeed and that many inner city schools are failing because the local tax revenue base is too low, which means that funds should be redistributed to level the playing field. From the right, we often hear that public schools are failing because of tenure and unions, and that the solution lies in making teaching more competitive (eliminating unions and allowing teachers to be fired) or creating other options (charter schools or home schooling) to compete for our tax revenue. At the end of the day, both sides seem to want the same thing—a good education for their children—but the two sides disagree on how to achieve the results and at what cost.

To get to the heart of the matter, I will introduce another controversial issue: healthcare. To get the discussion started, we could ask why people on the left side of the political spectrum, in general, support a decentralized, local or state model for public schools but demand a centralized, national-level program for healthcare. I am not taking sides in the issue as much as I am highlighting a key point: a good rule of thumb for institutions is that *decision-making, to the greatest extent possible, should be decentralized and delegated to the lowest level possible*, especially a country like the USA that has a system of government in which the lowest levels of government are municipal, country, and state, not regional offices of the federal government. The same mechanism that is used to collect taxes to fund our public schools could be used to fund healthcare, assuming a local or state government decided to go in that direction, such as Massachusetts. Institutions have to adjust to local conditions, but a national level model (the investment bank model) will often struggle with managing the multitude of regional issues, many of which fall under the legal purview of municipal, county, or state governments. This does not mean there will be no strategic, national level policies or minimum standards for healthcare that can be enforced, as we have for education; it just means that the municipal, county, and state governments are already in the business of providing social services and that we should leverage them rather than create new bureaucracies, assuming that the people in these states decide to move healthcare in that direction.

If I had to speculate why so many people on the left support the creation of a centralized, national level healthcare system, I would say it relates to the perception of successful programs in other countries, such as Europe. The first problem with this thinking is that it violates a fundamental principle of institutions: *size matters*. Just as Apple would never look to a regional business for advice on how to organize or run itself, large countries like the USA cannot learn much from, say, the Scandinavian model—perhaps local and state governments could, but not the federal government. The best way to structure public institutions for a country with 5 million people in a small territory with a homogeneous population and a limited global leadership role is very different from how you would structure public institutions for a country of over 330 million people in a vast territory with a diverse population and a prominent global leadership role. Even countries like Italy, which has one of the best-rated healthcare systems in the world, manages healthcare at a regional level, not at a national level, and most people buy supplemental private insurance to cover what the public system does not. I would venture to guess that most Europeans would reject the idea of creating a European Union healthcare system. Thus, if the European model appeals to you, you should probably advocate for state level healthcare, not national level healthcare. The second problem with this thinking, as I addressed above, is that the USA has a federal system of government, which includes municipal, county, and state governments that in many ways operate independently of the federal government. The U.S. and Europe have structural differences that do not allow for the copy and paste function.

I believe my home state, Minnesota, which in many ways looks like a Scandinavian country on paper, could establish an effective state level healthcare system, but I am convinced that, beyond a reasonable doubt, any attempt to do so on a national level would fail, for precisely the same reasons that most other states cannot compete with the public schools in Minnesota, where everyone takes pride in being above average. One reason is that institutions, like education and healthcare, are not always scalable in terms of being more effective on a national level. Whereas it makes sense to have a national military because the military does not overlap with municipal, country, or state government functions and has a mission that extends beyond our borders. If we have to build one school building for 500 elementary students, then we have to build another building for the next 500 elementary students, and so on. We do not want an elementary school with 5,000 students and extended bus routes to accommodate large geographic areas. Public schools not do create efficiencies by shifting to a national (or global) level model in the same way that Google or Apple do. The only thing that would grow with a national education or national healthcare system would be the massive bureaucracy to manage it, as opposed to allowing the municipal, country, and state governments manage their regions in accordance with federal oversight.

Again, why does the left generally support a state level education system but not support a state level healthcare system? And why did it take a Republican governor to recognize that such a program could work at the state level (Massachusetts) and was consistent with the Constitution? Likewise, why do so many on the right refuse to listen to an argument for a state level healthcare system but accept a state level educational system? The healthcare industry benefits from creative destruction and from royals from around the world traveling to the USA for complicated surgeries, but the majority of medical treatment involves technology that has not changed in decades, to include basic preventative healthcare. For anyone who thinks people will not become doctors if they cannot make lots of money (many doctors do not make lots of money), they should explain why so many people join the military—to serve. Not all people are motivated primarily by money. The evidence from healthcare in Europe shows that a single-payer system at some level can reduce prices and improve basic services, even if they have to buy supplemental insurance in the private sector to cover more serious medical procedures. At a minimum, we should all want to ensure that all people have enough basic healthcare to avoid long-term health problems that will be a burden on all of us, even if only for selfish reasons. Obviously, there are special interests on both sides of the debate that are feeding us misleading information, and we should do our best to ignore them, but the battle of words must stop and be replaced by the battle of numbers. Both sides need to ground their proposals in mathematics—show me the numbers. Claiming that healthcare is a "right" is no way to start the debate.

In summary, whether we are talking public or private institutions, we should always aim for a model that allows for some flexibility and some delegation to adjust for local conditions, while at the same time using a process of organic growth to take advantage of economies of scale. The result should be a robust web of public institutions that can shift with the wind and sustain small hits (no one should be too big to fail), with the goal of avoiding stagnation. It is not easy to dismantle a massive, national level institution once it is up and running, and it is hard to stop the collapse once it has started, unless we resort to deficit spending or money printing to delay the inevitable. We should also keep in mind that, if we opt to create a public rather than a private institution, we have to take wealth from the private sector to fund it. Printing money or deficit spending will only delay the problem and make it worse. The tax revenue we receive from the salaries of public sector employees is nothing more than a chunk of the tax revenue that was collected in the past to pay their salaries, so the taxes collected from the salaries of public sector employee do not make a net contribution to tax revenue. Thus, we would be wise to keep the number of people on the public payrolls as low as possible while maintaining the services we need. We might all agree that education is important, but if we create a bloated and inefficient school system that results in deficit spending and unsatisfactory results, we should set our emotions aside and fix it, just as we would fix our own finances at home.

Institution Envy

Before moving on to the last section, I will say a few words about the importance of institutions in shaping the rules of the game along the left–right political spectrum. One of the best ways to understand the debate between the left and the right is to listen to what both sides say about different institutions. For example, even though both sides agree that we should have a military, some people on the left have a cynical belief that the "military industrial complex" has nefarious intentions to foment global conflicts as a way to profit from war, whereas the right tends to turn a blind eye to abuses or corruption because they view the military as one of the only essential and legitimate government functions. On the other hand, even though both sides agree that we should have a social safety net for temporary unemployment or other unfortunate situations, many people on the right have a cynical belief that people are inherently lazy and will line up to receive welfare benefits and soak up all the national wealth, whereas the left tends to turn a blind eye to abuses or corruption because they view the welfare system as one of the only essential and legitimate government functions. Each side of the political spectrum seems willing to turn a blind eye to its own pet projects, which is why we have to assess these programs based on mathematics (the prohibition of deficit spending), not emotion.

This kind of finger pointing often involves the genetic fallacy or ad hominem attacks, which amount to assessing someone's arguments based on the origin of the belief or making personal attacks rather than addressing the argument itself. For example, some people on the left argue that people on the right do not want to fund welfare programs because they are racist, even though the argument from the right is focused on how welfare spending is draining the wealth of the country and creating a dependent class of people (empirical observations), which all rational societies should strive to avoid at all cost. Whether or not the people on the right are racist is not relevant to the argument, unless they invoke racial differences as a basis for the argument, which some people have been known to do. Rather than dwell on whether someone might or might not be racist, we should focus on the content of the argument. The mere fact that a person might be racist is not a sufficient basis for dismissing an argument. Likewise, there are people on the right who argue that people on the left want a national healthcare system, not because it will reduce costs or improve basic services, but because they are lazy and want free stuff. Again, we have to assess the content of the argument. If the person can prove the point with numbers, then whether or not the person is lazy or wants free stuff does not matter for the purpose of the argument. However, if we all look at the numbers and they point us in one direction rather than the other, we should have the courage to follow the numbers.

The truth is there probably are many people involved in national defense, such as large defense contractors, who view global warfare as a way to profit—people in the national security business often joke about "job security"—but we could never eliminate our military. Not to mention, we have Congressmen and policymakers who can prevent unnecessary wars by sustaining the national debate and raising ideas in the court of public opinion. And yes, there probably are many people who view the welfare system as a way to avoid work and live off the wealth of others (job applications rise when welfare benefits stop), but we could never eliminate all welfare, and the truth is that much of the assistance is provided to the elderly, so neither party will vote against it, even if it is the rational thing to do. The bottom line is that the existence of large institutions, both private and public, creates the potential for abuse, which is one of the reasons why we should be careful about creating large institutions that have the ability to manipulate the political system and make a power grab for resources to ensure their own survival. But given that we cannot avoid this, because many of our institutions have to be big to work on a state or national level, we have to accept that a certain level of corruption is probably baked into the cake of our democratic system, which allows people with special interests to run for office and run large government institutions. We can do our best to tweak our institutions, with what Popper calls "piecemeal intervention," but we should assume that every government institution will complain about not having enough resources and will make plans to grow larger, even if that means deficit spending. A private business has no claim to anyone's wealth, so the only way it can grow is by generating more business or by using its lobbying power to attain "too big to fail" status, which is a sophisticated form of corruption. A government institution, however, can work the system from within and make promises to voters to gain more resources, or can use fear mongering to demand more money from Congress. The best way to prevent this, of course, is to outlaw deficit spending. This is the judo chop that will break the back of systematic corruption.

Another challenge with large institutions is the problem of political appointees or imposing leadership from the outside. All good institutions take decades to grow and mature organically, to include developing a training program to help people within the institution work their way to the top by merit, but the nature of politics ensures that unqualified people or people with political agendas will often be appointed to run institutions they do not understand or intend to misuse. Granted, presidents often want their own people running the show, to have someone they can trust and control, but the granting of senior level positions to people who have not risen up the ranks the hard way is a form of patronage that often has negative consequences, with the USA handing out more senior level government positions than most other developed countries. For example, the military is designed to fight wars, but some political leaders might decide that nation building or humanitarian relief missions are more important, or that military personnel should be allowed to die in wars without a clear objective. As a result, the institution can lose the edge of its core competency, in this case, fighting wars. Or, large institutions can be used to support political agendas. Clearly, decay has set in when our institutions become tools of policymakers to achieve political ends, rather than performing their primary function of serving the people who provide the tax revenue. Granted, bringing in outsiders can have the positive effect of preventing bureaucratic stagnation or power grabs, but it can also do damage that takes years to recover from. It takes thousands of public service professionals to produce professional quality services, but a few senior leaders from the outside can distort the process to achieve political ends. Given this reality, we should be even more circumspect about giving public institutions too much power.

Two Fundamental Institutions

Regarding the first fundamental institution of resource management and the prohibition of deficit spending, given that a government is a collection of public institutions (society itself is not an institution), the way we should track the growth of institutions is by making sure they never grow to the point where we are using deficit spending to cover their expenses. This must be our line in the sand. The foundation of our budget should be the tax revenue collected during the past year, not a budget proposal based on what the institution would like to do during the next year, the same way that families and businesses are forced to live within their means. Once politicians and large public institutions know that deficit spending is prohibited, they will change their behavior dramatically as the rules of the game change. For example, rather than ask for more money, they might preemptively ask for modest cuts to ensure that they continue to receive money over other institutions that refuse to plan for modest cuts. At the end of the day, this requires governments at all levels to pass balanced budgets.

Shifting gears to the second fundamental institution, procreation, the first social institution, as Aristotle observed, is monogamous procreation:

> He who thus considers things in their first growth and origin, whether a state or anything else, will obtain the clearest view of them. In the first place, there must be a union of those who cannot exist without each other; namely, of male and female, that the race may continue.[1]

Aristotle subsequently talks about the transition from families to villages to city-states, but monogamous procreation (the union of one man and one woman to produce a child, which is the pinnacle of a rational life) is the foundation of civilization and has its origin in ancient Greece. If we read Greek drama, we see that the transition to monogamous procreation was a difficult process, just as it is today, precisely because it is rational. To say that monogamous procreation is not "natural" misses the point. Humans are also prone to violence and greed and hate, but we expect people to rise to a higher level. Thus, monogamous procreation is not natural in the same way that peace and generosity and love are not natural. We have to work hard to achieve them. The family is the first social institution and serves various social functions, such as producing the next generation, giving parents emotional fulfillment, and providing children the altruistic love they need to grow and mature until they are capable of living on their own, at which time the cycle repeats—the circle of life. Parents are the best people to pay it forward because they will do it for free, often at great sacrifice to themselves, and with a level of emotional intensity that no government program can match. This is why we were able to survive for millennium, and why many people continue to survive, without modern states. From time immemorial, men and women have formed unions to produce the next generation, all without handbooks or training classes, and all without government programs.

---

1 Aristotle, *Politics*, 1252a 25.

Chapter Five. Wealth

If we refer back to the first fundamental institution of resource management dealing with the prohibition of deficit spending, there was an important variable underlying the institution that I did not address in detail. If we keep in mind that people must produce and consume resources to survive, such as food, we must also be net producers of resources (wealth creation) to cover other aspects of our lives, such as providing for our family, saving for retirement, and paying taxes during our productive working years. Paying our own bills is not enough. For society to survive, the vast majority of people must be net producers of resources during their productive working years, to offset their years of net resource consumption during youth and retirement, to keep the machine running. These are the laws of mathematics, which are impossible to refute. Therefore, to satisfy our tax obligations (as it relates to the prohibition of deficit spending), we have to use some of our own resources, our wealth, even if that means spending less on ourselves, to contribute to the payment of taxes. Given that the tax bill is paid with money from our wealth, we should address the concept of wealth in more detail. After all, if we do not understand what wealth is (and what it is not), how can we promote a prohibition on deficit spending?

Imagine There's No Money

One of the best ways to understand what money is and the role it plays in society is to imagine a society without it, just as one of the best ways to understand what reason is and the role it plays on our lives is to imagine life without it. If we imagine a band or a tribe living in a village, or a group of strangers living on a remote island as part of a reality television show, how would they survive without money (the paper bills and coins in our pockets)? Clearly, like the people who fled religious persecution in Europe to establish the USA in the New World, they would hunt and farm to get food and develop other skills, such as carpentry to build homes and tailoring to make clothes, all of which they could do without money. They could divide up the work to satisfy their basic needs. It would be a waste of time and energy for each person to try to provide for all of his or her needs if each person could specialize in one or a few jobs, what economists call the division of labor.

The expansion of an economy is linked to the expansion of the division of labor, with primitive societies having a limited division of labor and advanced economies having a division of labor with a complex division of labor, to include people making a living by studying the digestive system of fruit flies. Exactly how the goods and services ultimately get exchanged, such as bartering, is not important, but the members of the village would find a way. For example, how many apples would a farmer need to exchange for a meal with meat and potatoes cooked by a chef (assuming the farmer and the chef are behaving as free rational agents)? It would depend on what the two sides agree is an equitable trade. There is no "correct" exchange rate because it depends on the supply and the demand for the specific goods or services for the specific people involved in the specific trade at a specific time. For example, I might drink water in my house for free but pay $2.00 for a bottle of water during a hot day in an amusement park, or I might pay $2.00 for a gallon of gas today or $5.00 the next year due to limited supplies or excessive demand. This is why price fixing has such limited success and is often counterproductive. Price has no inherent meaning outside of the value of something relative to other products and services (a ratio), just as the square root of two never occurred to anyone until they tried to calculate the diagonal of a square. Again, the specific details do not matter. What does matter is that people would be capable of surviving without money, as billions of people have done throughout history (and now).

Economists refer to this type of economic activity as bartering. A seamstress might demand two pheasants in exchange for a new dress or a blacksmith might demand 20 roof shingles in exchange for two horse shoes, and so on. The key point is that *no one could consume something they did not produce unless they exchanged it for their own goods or services, or unless someone gave it to them.* In the case of a commune, where people freely donate the fruits of their labor to the group for distribution, the same principle applies, to the extent that the people in the commune take steps to ensure that each person contributes his or her fair share and does not become a freeloader. If we were to encounter such a society and try to use our paper money to buy their goods or services, they would probably give us a weird look. In such a society, pieces of paper would be of no value, unless they were to understand that the people in the next village would be willing to accept them in exchange for their goods and services. The limitations of bartering are obvious: bartering is an inefficient way to run an economy because it makes individual exchanges difficult, what economists call high transaction costs. If a person makes dresses, it is difficult to shop at the farmers market to buy fruits and vegetables. A dress might be worth 50 apples, but no one wants 50 apples because they will rot before you can eat them all. This means you will have to waste more time and effort bartering the surplus apples for other goods and services, or collecting five apples per week for 10 weeks. Likewise, a person selling a cow might demand 30 dresses, but have no use for 30 dresses, and will then have to barter the dresses for other goods and services. The transaction costs are high, and therefore inefficient.

Wealth creation and accumulation is possible under a system of bartering. Wealth can be inherited but it can also be created, such as by doubling the number of apples trees you plant. A person over time could create or accumulate enough resources to build a house, which is a form of wealth, to the extent that it maintains value and can be sold later. If a family has a small farm with enough animals and crops to satisfy their dietary requirements, they could use the surplus food to barter with their neighbors for other goods and services, such as silverware, which is also a form of wealth. In fact, if the family gets into a bind or has temporary problems with the farm, they could use some of this stored wealth, such as the silverware, to buy what they need. They could also borrow money from the neighbor (go into debt) and pay it back according to agreed upon terms. This brings us to the concept of real money, such as silver and gold, which is popular with many people on the right and less popular with many people on the left. One of the defining traits of real money is that it cannot be created out of thin air, as is the case with fiat money. In short, real money is anything that can be used to buy goods and services that is itself a form of wealth that people value for its intrinsic properties, such as silver and gold, as opposed to a piece of paper. As noted before, a person could use individual pieces of silverware to buy goods and services from others. The good news is that silver lasts longer than most other objects for bartering, such as apples or cows. This would still be a form of bartering in the sense that the two sides of the exchange would have to agree on the value of a piece of silverware, such as one dress or 50 apples, but the creation of real money opens rational doors that did not exist under a bartering system. To put it another way, the creation of real money involves a level of abstraction that is made possible by the fact that we are rational creatures. All other animals are stuck with satisfying their own needs moment to moment in the perpetual present.

All That Glitters

The introduction of real money, which is a level of abstraction after bartering, resolves some of the inefficiency problems associated with a bartering economy. First, it allows people to acquire wealth over time in a more predictable and measurable manner by acquiring objects that do not decay and can be measured objectively, such as gold. A treasure chest full of apples has value for several days, but a treasure chest of gold lasts forever, literally. Thus, gold is *a store of value* and apples are not, even though both could be used to barter. Houses and horses can also fulfill the role of real money, because they last a long time, but their value changes with time due to age (depreciation), and most barter exchanges could not handle an entire horse or an entire house, which brings us to the second point. Real money allows for *ease of divisibility*, which in turn allows it to become *a medium of exchange* and a *unit of account*. For example, in the case of silverware, if over time we all agree that the silverware is just a fancy form of silver, with silver being the underlying substance of value, we could use silver to promote the exchange of goods and services because it is a homogenous substance and can be melted down or cut into manageable units, such as one ounce coins or pieces of eight, without losing value. This in turn means that society will have to go to great lengths to establish a rational system of weights and measures to confirm the weight and purity of each coin to ensure that the silver content of the coins is not being depleted with base metals (an ancient scam that was a precursor to modern currency devaluation or inflation).

If something is worth one ounce of silver, we can give them one ounce of silver. If something is worth half an ounce of silver, we can give them half an ounce of silver, and so on. The same logic does not apply to a cow or a dress. Cutting a dress in half decreases the value of the dress (the two half dresses together are worth less than the whole dress), but two half-ounce pieces of silver have the same value as a one ounce piece of silver ($\frac{1}{2} + \frac{1}{2} = 1$), in the sense that I could melt the two half-ounce coins at any time to make a one ounce coin, and vice versa. The end result of this is that we can begin to determine the price of all objects in terms of ounces of silver, which provides an objective foundation to how we calculate value and exchange goods and services. We might not use silver in all transactions—bartering is still allowed—but a new level of rational abstraction emerges when people start to think about the value of goods and services in terms of one underlying variable, such as silver, rather than develop complex calculations for the limitless number of possible exchange for all possible goods and services. This is the reason that most currencies are now measured relative to the U.S. dollar, to have a baseline that everyone can understand and to avoid arbitrage. This level of abstraction promoted more efficient thinking and more efficient economic transactions, which reduced the transaction costs. For example, if I am an apple farmer who wants to buy a dress for one ounce of silver and I can sell each of my apples for 1/50th of an ounce of silver, I can sell 50 apples to a variety of customers over time and then use the silver to buy the dress. Not only that, I can plan for the future with more precision by saving money over time.

History has shown that this process of trial and error over time often leads to gold and silver assuming the role of real money, from ancient Greece to Fort Knox. Granted, some societies use cattle or seashells or other objects as real money, but gold and silver from time immemorial have served as a primary way to accumulate wealth. The reasons for this are obvious—gold and silver are a store of value because they never decay; they are a medium of exchange and a unit of account because they are homogenous and can be divided over and over without losing value; their supply is limited, so they cannot be created out of thin air, and so on. However, the introduction of gold and silver introduces new variables to the game. For example, rather than focus on producing normal goods and services that we need to survive, a person might focus on finding new sources of gold. Why grow apples that will rot in a few days after being picked if you can mine gold that will last forever? (Some answers to this question include the fact that gold is hard to find, hard to mine, and hard to convert into coins, whereas apples under the sunlight sprout effortlessly from trees year after year.)

Although these new supplies of silver and gold help facilitate economic transactions, even on a global scale, they also have other effects. As gold or silver flood into or out of a market, the forces of supply and demand change the value of the silver and the gold relative to the products they are used to buy. For example, a dress that used to cost one silver piece now might cost two silver pieces due to inflation if there is too much silver in the system. Just as producing too many apples causes the price of apples to fall, the introduction of too much gold or silver into the economy causes their value to change relative to other goods and services because the price and value have no meaning in a vacuum. We require context and ratios. This is an important point: no matter how we structure our economy, *the value of the money we use will always depend on the supply and the demand of the money relative to the goods and services it is used to buy, whether real money or fiat.* The big difference with gold and silver is that is makes it more difficult for the government to control the money supply, which, as we will see, is not always a good thing.

One of the problems with using gold and silver as money is that people tend to forget that other things can be used as money as well or that we can create value without access to gold or silver. For example, one of the motivations of Spain for conquering the New World was to obtain new supplies of gold to cover its trade deficit with the Orient, which accepted only gold in exchange for its goods. If we think about how much time and money was wasted traveling to the New World to obtain the gold (not to mention how many people were killed or enslaved), the Crown could have found other ways to create wealth, such as improving the production of the agricultural sector or opening a chain of paella & sangria restaurants or Flamenco schools. It is sometimes easier to steal gold or force people to work in gold mines, immorality aside, but we start to see problems when gold becomes an end in itself rather than a means to creating positive cash flow institutions. One of the secrets of accumulating wealth is the insight that *wealth can be created.* Just as we can plant seeds in the soil to make them grow, we can plant investment capital in a project and make it grow. Why divide a pie if you can bake a new one? Why limit yourself to one banana tree if you can plant a second one? Life is not always a zero-sum game, at least not in a free economy that is grounded in liberty.

The second problem with using gold and silver as real money is that the money supply does not necessarily reflect the underlying economic activity, evidenced by the fact that we can have inflation or deflation with gold and silver. Ideally, the amount of money available within an economy should strike a balance between supply and demand and be mathematically linked to the underlying assets of the economy, human motivations, and a system of incentives. If an economy is growing, there should be a rational mechanism to ensure that there is enough money in the system (a mechanism for credit or debt that is linked to the growth of wealth), even if there is no more gold. There should be a way to expand the money supply to facilitate economic growth while at the same time avoiding sky-high interest rates due to a high demand for money, with too few dollars chasing too many goods. Likewise, if an economy is slowing down, there should be a rational mechanism to remove money from the system, or a way to reduce the money supply, to avoid a collapse in interest rates with too many dollars chasing too few goods. This is, admittedly, a difficult feat of abstraction and mathematics for our rational minds, and the propensity for corruption (reckless money printing and deficit spending to achieve political objectives that cannot be achieved in the ballot box) should give us pause when implementing such a system. Thus, whereas gold and silver provide some stability because governments cannot create them out of thin air (this fact alone is a good reason to keep real money an integral part of the financial system), most economies would benefit from a rational fiat currency that structurally closes all doors to corruption and deficit spending.

Returning to gold and silver, we start to see the introduction of modern money and modern banking with the creation of gold or silver certificates, a new level of abstraction after bartering and real money. If a person is worried about someone stealing his gold or silver, he might store it in a safe place in exchange for a fee. As proof of his deposit, he will receive gold or silver certificates, such as one for each ounce, which he can cash in later to retrieve his gold. This creates new opportunities as well. First, it allows the person to protect his gold and use the certificate to make purchases, assuming the person accepting the certificate knows they are backed by gold. If he uses a certificate to buy something, he can sign it over to show the transfer, and then the other person can go to the safe to retrieve his new ounce of gold, which is a safe but inefficient way of doing business—high transaction costs. Or, if someone steals a certificate, the owner can run to the safe owner and tell him what happened (we will assume for now that he is telling the truth). If the thief arrives to retrieve his ounce of gold, they can arrest him. If he does not show up, they could nullify the old certificate and make a new one, like modern traveler's checks. However, even more interesting, it allows the person who is storing the gold to lend some of it out with interest. For example, if the safe has 1,000 ounces of gold and changes in the supply due to withdrawals rarely fluctuates more than 10% during any given month, the owner of the safe could lend 100 ounces of gold to someone for a promising project if the person promises to pay back 105 ounces of gold one year later (a 5% loan). This way, the owner of the safe earns five ounces of gold and the people who store their gold at his vault are none the wiser, unless the deal goes bad, in which case the safe owner will have to find a way to replenish the safe with 100 ounces of gold. Taking it to the next level of abstraction, if the owner of the safe and the clients reach an agreement, they could entrust the owner of the safe to make investment decisions on their behalf, to include printing additional gold certificates such that that the total printed value of certificates in circulation exceeds the total value of the gold in the safe, which opens up the safe to the risk of a run on the bank in a crisis. This is a way of creating what financial experts call leverage, which is the foundation of modern banking. In this case, rather than the depositors paying the safe owner a fee to store their gold, the safe actually owner pays the depositors a percentage of the profits (interest) from the successful investments. If a particular project fails, however, they all take a loss, unless they buy insurance for the investments, which reduces the risk but also reduces the return on the investment because of the cost of the insurance.

With this new level of abstraction, modern banking is born, with the final level of abstraction happening when real money is removed as the foundation of the money supply, which provides more flexibility in terms of expanding and contracting the money supply (which usually results in endless expansion) but opens doors to corruption and a loss of discipline. As we can see, just as the institution of monogamous procreation was a social construct that depended on our rational capacity—animals without reason are incapable of imposing rational order on their lives—the establishment of modern money and modern banking is a social construct that depends on our rational capacity, which in many ways allows us to better manage the natural and unavoidable cycles of nature. Whereas a flood could wipe out a pack of animals, leaving them with no food to eat, a family with a stash of gold (wealth) could travel to a new city and use the gold to start a new life. We certainly benefit from an abstract financial system, but it also imposes new kinds of discipline on us that changes the way we think and behave, assuming we do it correctly and with proper regulations. In other words, the creation of rational money is an important step in helping us achieve our rational potential.

Funny Money

Rather than continue with this analysis, which has involved increasing levels of rational abstraction, I would like to jump from what is generally viewed as the right side of the political spectrum (many on the right like real money) to what is generally viewed as the left side of the political spectrum (many on the left do not like real money, or prefer fiat money). This analysis will set the stage for finding the elusive rational middle ground that culminates in the finding regarding the prohibition of deficit spending. Just as two people who are haggling over the price of something often start on two ends of the price spectrum to find the "fair" price in the "middle," the best way to find the solution to the wealth problem will be to work our way inward from both sides of the political spectrum until we arrive at the rational middle.

At the start of the game *Monopoly*, each person receives $1,500 of funny money to get the game going. It is not clear what each player did to deserve this initial pay out, but there is really no way to avoid it within the context of the game. The process of injecting money into or extracting money out of an economy is a complex and important issue, but in the case of *Monopoly* it involves passing Go. (Of interest, the game *Life* begins with an injection of debt as the players decide whether or not to go to college, which is perhaps a more realistic scenario because it explains the origin of the money.) Most likely, if each player started with only $500, or as much as $5,000 in *Monopoly*, the game would have a different dynamic, just as increasing the distance to first base in baseball by five feet would change the game. We will assume for now that $1,500 is just enough money to get the game going and to keep it on the right trajectory. (If the game gets off to a slow start, each person could probably receive an additional $500 with minimal consequences.) The question we have to ask is whether such a plan would work in a modern state, as opposed to subjecting ourselves to the rigors of organic growth and wealth creation.

Whenever we find ourselves in a recession or a perceived economic crisis, which seems to be more often than not these days, pundits often talk about "stimulating aggregate demand," which is a euphemism for pumping funny money into the system because *supply is demand*. (By "funny money," I mean money that is created out of thin air, such as by the expansion of government debt, or printing money to buy debt from the market.) If an apple farmer in a bartering system cannot buy anything (demand) it is because he is out of apples (supply). Supply is demand and demand is supply. Likewise, in a modern economy, if we cannot buy things, it is because we have no money, which is why it makes no sense to talk about "stimulating aggregate demand." We all certainly "demand" more goods and services—in fact, economics as an academic discipline assumes that demand is virtually unlimited for scarce resources—but we cannot pay for them because we do not have any supply (money). We could use a credit card, but we would need money to pay the balance at the end of the month. If people do not have much money and all we need to do is "stimulate aggregate demand" to get the economy going again, why not take a page from Monopoly and hand out $1,500 for every person? If that does not work, how about handing out another $1,500? At some point, when there is enough new money sloshing around the system, which will allow people to pay off their debts and buy new products, things should get back to normal, right? The reason the answer to this question is a resounding "no" is because funny money is not wealth, which means that the injection of it will not create wealth and will distort the economy. At some point, as in the case of *Monopoly*, the funny money loses value as prices rise to meet the rising supply of money relative to the underlying goods and services in the economy, like boats rising with the tide, except that the people who know how to play the game (the dreaded 1%) will benefit the most as they soak up all the recently printed money with their hedge funds. If we think back to our gold safe with gold certificates, we can print more certificates, without limit, but the value of the contents of the safe (the gold) will not increase unless we increase the amount of gold (wealth) in the safe.

Historically, people on the left have preferred that the system of money and credit should be run by the state (that is, to give the state a monopoly), not by private banks. In fact, this is precisely what Marx demanded in *The Communist Manifesto*. Less than 100 years later, the communists almost got what they wanted with the Federal Reserve, which is a private bank with government oversight that pays a 6% dividend to the private shareholders. (I would recommend reading that sentence again.) The communists rightly observed that the vested interests that control the banking system in the private sector had immense power to decide who succeeds and who fails, as well as the power to manipulate the systems in their favor. As such, the communists aspired to transfer the power of banking to the government (and then foment a revolution to take over the government). If the government wants to build a bridge and only the banking cartel can pool enough money to construct the bridge, then the bankers could choose who gets the loan or offer a loan to the government. Given that the bridge is a government project with a guaranteed profit, the banking cartel has just found a way to gain wealth without fair competition. Or, if two countries are having a war, the bankers could provide loans for both sides to fight, and perhaps event foment the conflict, which would be profitable. In short, given that the system of money and credit plays such an important role in shaping the underlying fairness of a society, the left believes—rightly so—that the government should have some control over currency and banking, especially with a fiat money system.

The government can use its oversight of the central bank and the banking system in a positive and rational way to help break cycles of poverty, but good intentions sometimes backfire. For example, prior to the real estate crisis, the government intervened to make the lending standards more flexible for specific groups, which resulted in many people who were not mathematically creditworthy taking out loans that they could not pay off. The banks were only too happy to do this and collect fees for the loans because they knew they would not be held accountable. (In a rational banking system, in which the banks would be held accountable for bad loans, these loans never would have been approved.) The government can also use its oversight of the central bank and the banking system to directly and indirectly increase or decrease the money supply to smooth over the fluctuations caused by the business cycle, to avoid having too much or too little money in the system at any given time. However, an expansion of the money supply should be in response to an expansion of the economy, *not as the mechanism for expanding the economy*, which is a cart before the horse, pushing a string proposition. This transition from real money, which is wealth or is directly linked to wealth, such as gold, to printed pieces of paper that are enforced as legal tender and are not necessarily directly linked to wealth, brings us to fiat money, which can be a useful, rational tool for any modern state that wants to have the ability to adjust the money supply in response to the forces of supply and demand, often by changing interest rates (the price of money). After all, if faced with an economic depression or widespread starvation, would it not be better to just print the money people need to survive rather than face widespread starvation or violence? This, I think, is the basic idea of how the left side of the political spectrum views the issue.

At first glance, this argument sounds reasonable. However, possible benefits aside, the problems with this model are obvious. First, if we accept that a piece of paper (fiat money) is not real wealth unless it is backed by wealth, which could include gold, a house as collateral on a loan, or some other asset, then although flooding the economy with fiat money might solve some short-term liquidity issues, the injection of fiat money cannot do anything to help the ability of a society to create wealth, which should be the primary goal of any economy. If we could create wealth by printing money, we could print $1 million for each citizen and be done with it. The problem is that most people would spend the money rather than invest it to create wealth, which would result in the money ending up in the hands of the dreaded 1%. At some point, as this money makes its way through the system, prices will adjust (the value of money is based on supply and demand) to nullify the value of the money injection. Taking poker as an example, you could double the number of poker chips on the table without increasing the money in the bank, with the misguided goal of keeping some people in the game, but then the individual chips would lose half their value when it comes time to cash out at the end of the game. Not only that, you would create a scenario in which the people who are currently winning the game and are good at the game could use their skill and existing wealth to win all the new chips added to the table. These misguided intentions to help the poor often give rise to a scenario in which the return on capital exceeds the growth of the underlying economy, as the rich find clever ways to soak up the additional liquidity and grow their wealth exponentially. Even the Federal Reserve has admitted that its loose monetary policies have contributed to creating inequality. If our financial system were based on real money, this never would have happened to the same degree. Thus, although we have achieved the objective of keeping some people in the poker game, we have not created any wealth within the poker game itself, which could upset many people and compel them quit. In fact, some of the players might bail at the original exchange rate for the poker chips as soon as they see the funny chips flooding into the game, possibly leaving the other players with nothing at the end.

It should be clear that willy-nilly money printing (when the money that is printed is not directly linked to real growth in the underlying economy) is not the way to go. Linking the creation of fiat money to tangible assets, however, such as new houses with a 20% down payment, can serve a positive role, assuming the person signs a contract to pay it back with future income (that is, monetizing his future income stream). A modern economy can function and thrive with fiat money, that is, currency that cannot be exchanged for gold, silver, or other tangible assets at a fixed exchange rate. However, the amount of money in the system should be linked to tangible assets, such as homes and paychecks. For example, if a creditworthy person can save up for a 20% down payment on a home, the money supply could in theory be expanded by fiat to cover the other 80% of the loan, even interest-free, with the understanding that this new money would disappear from the system as the debt is paid off. (Please take a moment to consider how money can appear and disappear, and how the entire money supply in such a scenario would disappear if all such debts were paid off.) The money supply must grow and shrink organically with the broader economy, but once deficit spending becomes the norm, the system breaks down as special interest groups take over monetary policy and turn on the printing presses to enrich themselves. History is replete with examples of countries in Latin America, Africa, and other places that have resorted to money printing to artificially stimulate an economy or to achieve political objectives, such as corruption, which often results in hyperinflation. The rule is simple: if people can achieve riches without effort, such as by printing money, they will. If such a path to riches is not possible, they will be forced to achieve riches the old fashioned way: wealth creation via hard work. The specifics of how to implement a rational fiat currency system are beyond the scope of this book, but the basic idea is that the monetary system must have an organic link to the underlying economy—that is, a mechanism for people with wealth to expand their credit or debt limit and a mechanism for people who are losing wealth to reduce their credit or debt limit. We should have a mechanism to increase or decrease the money supply, without raiding gold from the New World, but we should also have a mechanism to prevent abuse.

If we are looking for the rational middle ground between the left and right sides of the political spectrum, we have enough information now to draw a picture. On the one hand, we probably do not want to have a currency that is directly tied to gold or silver on a proportional basis, mostly because we have little to no control over the supply of silver or gold and the value of silver and gold changes over time. That said, we should have a free market for people to buy or sell gold or silver if they are not happy with how the currency is being managed, with no mechanism for the government to interfere. If people believe too much money is being injected into the system relative to economic growth and fear inflation, they should be free to buy gold or silver as a hedge without government intervention, to force discipline on the government. This of course would require transparency by the central bank regarding its activities, which could be achieved with regular audits. (Congress has oversight of many sensitive activities, to include national security, so why not central banking?) Likewise, if the people believe too much money is exiting the system, such as by people saving or paying off debts rather than spending on goods and services, and therefore fear deflation, they should be free to sell gold or silver in exchange for cash without government intervention. *If the government wants monopolistic power over the money supply, it should allow people to behave in a rational manner and provide them information in a transparent way to make rational decisions.* This way, we can use the prices of gold and silver as barometers of the economy.

Without getting into the specifics, if an individual has a good job and has enough income to pay for a car and home loan, we should have a mechanism to ensure that the person gets a loan to make the purchase, but, and here is the key, *the person should value the $20,000 car as much as he values the $20,000 loan he uses to buy it.* That is, we should never get to the point where we treat our money like the funny money of Monopoly. To keep the debt levels stable and avoid bubbles, we could require a 20% down payment on all major purchases, even credit card accounts. If the person defaults on the loan, the bank could sell the asset for up to a 20% loss to close out the loan, with no negative effects on the economy. And people might be more eager to pay off their $10,000 credit card debt if they have to make a $2,000 deposit to qualify. This way, we could reduce the likelihood of asset bubbles and the expansion of the money supply would be grounded on people taking rational risks and setting money aside (savings) to manage those risks in line with real economic growth. Just as deficit spending represents a conceptual leap that is untethered from reality, which is why it should be prohibited, the creation of funny money represents a conceptual leap that is untethered from reality.

Thus, the rational middle of the political spectrum is the point where fiat money is allowed to expand in a rational way that is linked to the underlying economic activity. If we err, it should be on the less easy side (frugality and discipline), with a suboptimal amount of money in the system, because we can always adjust to the middle. However, once the floodgates of funny money open, there is no turning back because people will be less motivated to earn money the old fashioned way.

Engines of Economic Growth

One of the conundrums today is understanding how to stimulate economic growth or create wealth—the wealth of nations. Without any outside assistance or government programs, in many cases with nothing more than a hoe for the soil, the people of the USA established one of the greatest wealth creation machines in the history of humanity, prior to the existence of a modern state or social welfare programs. This should be our baseline for assessing human potential (keeping in mind the role of child and slave labor). On the other hand, many countries today, more than 200 years later, many with ideal climates and abundant natural resources, fail to grow according to expectations, even after receiving hundreds of millions or even billions of dollars in foreign aid (often from the USA) and guidance from people with the modern economy playbook, such as the IMF or the World Bank. However, some have argued that this handholding is precisely what is preventing many of these countries from achieving economic growth because the programs breed dependency or introduce economic models with a level of abstraction that exceeds the complexity of the underlying economy. Some countries, like Switzerland and Japan, established impressive wealth creation machines with limited natural resources. Other countries, like Brazil, have struggled with creating wealth despite having extensive natural resources and an ideal climate. Thus, economic growth cannot be reduced to natural resources or other materialistic considerations alone. As Fukuyama shows, the ability of a nation to succeed is often linked to its ability to establish a capable and autonomous modern state, but the details of this are beyond the scope of this book.

The concept of wealth creation is simple (simple like the design of an iPhone). After you have eaten and paid all your bills, to include taxes, whatever is left over is wealth. For example, if you reach the end of the month, with all your bills paid, and you have $500 in the checking account, you have $500 in wealth to do with as you please. You can spend it, save it, invest it, or give it away to charity if you live in a free country. Likewise, if you are an apple farmer and you pick 1,000 apples during the month and need only 800 to cover all your expenses, your wealth at the end of the month is 200 apples, which you would probably sell to get their full value before they rot. The same principle that applies to individuals on a micro level also applies to society on a macro level. (For reasons that are not clear, some people try to make the argument that a magical transformation takes place from the micro to the macro level, which math demonstrates is not true.) If we as a society produce more than we consume, the remainder is wealth. Simple enough, but why is it so difficult to create wealth?

The reason is that just as good politics is a delicate balance of left and right, the creation of wealth is governed by a delicate balancing act over a treacherous chasm: positive cash flow. As a general rule, the far left tends to downplay how difficult it is to make a positive cash flow business. Some complain that many businesses succeed due to crony capitalism or bemoan the fact that many successful businesses are passed on from one generation to the next, which some consider unfair and prevents the small guy from competing. The far left often takes the businesses that have been fortunate enough to survive as a given (and ignoring the ones that fail) and assume that anyone with a big loan from a bank can make it big. If you want to sell cars, have your rich buddy give you a loan to open a car factory.

Surprisingly, many of the businesses that fail actually have sales but are unable to satisfy their short-term cash requirements—making loan payments, payroll, and so on. For example, if a company has to give good credit terms (cash later) to sell products, this will cause a delay between when the sale is made and when the cash is received, which can cause cash flow problems when it comes time to pay the bills. Or, the company might have to take out big loans up front to buy expensive equipment, which increases the fixed costs associated with paying back the loan, which in turn makes it more difficult to generate enough cash flow on a consistent basis to stay solvent. For this reason, many companies issue equity, which can be paid back at any time but dilutes ownership. Companies that are forced to subject themselves to the cash flow model are forced to impose discipline and rational risk management practices, whereas companies that rise to "too big to fail" status (that is, they know they will get bailed out by the government in the event of failure, and often achieve this status by lobbying) lose discipline and tend to take risks that a normal company would not, which in turn increases the risk of failure.

When an individual or a company assesses an environment for economic activity, there are three important variables to consider: natural resources, the workers, and money (land, labor, capital). For example, if a country has large oil reserves on a per capita basis, like Norway, it is wise to make a strategic decision to focus on fossil fuels to promote economic growth, even if they also want to portray a "green" image. If Norway did not have enough money to get this fossil fuel machine up and running on its own, as is the case with many developing countries with natural resources, it could seek loans or equity from investors who would be more than happy to invest in the Norwegian fossil fuel industry. On top of this, they will have to train a skilled workforce to perform the jobs, but a country can also look at the natural skills of a country to identify business opportunities. For example, many educated people in India speak English, which makes India a good location for businesses that depend on English speakers, such as call centers. Money is also important, but money cannot make oil reserves or specific job skills appear out of thin air. At the end of the day, the business model that is developed will have to produce positive cash flow or the business will go bankrupt, regardless of good intentions. The company can try to pay higher wages than the competition, with the hope of helping the citizens make more money, but such a strategy could backfire if the high salaries cause prices to rise to cover costs, which could price the company out of the market and result in everyone losing their jobs. Just as a person training for a marathon has to follow a rigorous training program to make organic progress over time, all companies must subject themselves to the discipline of the positive cash flow model. Even though the realities of business have proven this over and over, there is a popular idea that often conflicts with it.

Livable Wage

There is a lot of talk today about paying people a livable wage, an idea that has been raised in various forms throughout history. Unfortunately, although the sentiment might feel good, it misses some important points about economic reality. Whether we like it or not, wages are a function of *risk-adjusted value creation*, and the best way to calculate this is to figure out how much money you could make if you did the job on your own as a private business owner. For example, suppose you work at a place that sells hot dogs and are earning minimum wage, say, $7.25. This is clearly not enough money to raise a family if you aspire to middle-class status, but is it a "fair" wage? The answer has everything to do with the value created by the employee within the hot dog business model, which includes the supply and demand for his job skills, and *nothing to do with how much that person needs to survive*.

Suppose the person were to sell hot dogs on his own. He could buy the equipment and supplies he needs to start his own hot dog stand (initial investment). To keep things simple, let us suppose he sells an average of 100 hot dogs per day at $2 each, for average daily sales of $200. If we assume that all the expenses (hot dogs, buns, condiments, equipment depreciation, etc.) run about $120, then he can pocket $80 per day. If he spends eight hours on the street, he will earn $10 per hour. Simple enough. But what if he could not work one day and asked someone to fill in for him. What would be a "fair wage" for that person? Would the hot dog stand owner answer this question by looking at the hot dog business model itself (using break-even analysis) or at the spending habits of the person he hires? Keeping in mind that he would want to make some money each day for himself, because he is the owner, then $7.25 per hour might be a "fair" wage if the owner normally made $10 per hour. We should keep in mind that if it is a slow day or if it rains and there are no customers, the owner might actually take a loss for the day by paying this worker $7.25 per hour. This example serves the purpose of showing that the value of a worker is inextricably linked to the cash flow structure of the business and the risks involved, not to how much money the person needs to survive. Whether a wage is sufficient to raise a family is certainly a legitimate consideration when deciding whether or not to take the job, but the wage itself should ultimately be driven by the risk-adjusted value created for the business and the value of the job skill in the market.

The fundamental problem with the livable wage camp is that they do not appear to consider the cash flow model or business risk, both of which are integral to all business activity. In the case of the hot dog seller, if he has a slow day, he takes home little or no money. He might work all day and have no money in his pocket to cover his expenses. *The entrepreneur cannot pay himself a wage if his business does not make any money.* However, if he hires someone else to work, he has to pay that person a wage, even if the business does not make any money—hence the caveat "risk-adjusted value creation." A guaranteed wage is a low-risk proposition, especially if the job requires limited skills, such as putting a hot dog on a bun. To the extent that a person's daily wages are guaranteed and predictable, he will participate less in the up side (profits) of the business. In the case of the hot dog seller, the worker collects his $7.25 per hour regardless of how many hot dogs he sells, unless he earns a commission, which is one way for him to get some skin in the game. The worker has less of an incentive to sell, whereas how much the owner earns depends on many variables—location, quality of the product, price, etc.—and can results in negative cash flow days and even bankruptcy if things do not work out. If a worker calculates that he generates $200 in profits per day for his company and complains that he takes home only $100 per day, the worker is ignoring two important facts. First, the company has fixed costs that have to be paid, such as the office space where he works and the electricity. Second, the company has to pay him $100 per day even if he has a dry spell. What the company could offer the employee is a commission-based salary, but the employee would have to consider whether the benefit of steady pay ($100 per day) outweighs the risks of a variable income—say, $50 per day plus a commission based on a percentage of the sales. Based on reading case studies in business school, we learned that workers in general do not like basing their wages on the profitability of the company if it means making less money if the profits of the company drop. They like the up side but not the down side.

The critic might agree with my analysis but comment that it misses the point: that many companies are not paying people a fair share of the profits of a company relative to the value they create, even after we factor in the risk-adjusted cash flow business model variables. That is, even if an accountant is creating $200,000 of value within the cash flow model, the company continues to pay him only $75,000 because that is the "market rate" for accountants at his skill level. For example, there is currently a movement to increase the wages of some fast food workers to $15.00 per hour. Let us take a look at the numbers, devoid of emotion, to see whether this idea makes sense. If we make the assumption that each McDonald's franchise has 120 labor hours per day (24 hours per day, averaging 5 people there at any given time, keeping in mind that not all franchises follow this exact model), then we have 43,800 labor hours per year. What this means is that for every raise of $1 per hour, the owner will have to pay out about $50,000 per year in wages plus benefits. Given that many McDonald's owners profit about $100,000–$200,000 per year per franchise, a $4 dollar raise would reduce the owner's profits to about $0, if not a loss, in which case the business closes and no one has a job. If we take the basic rule of thumb that a person will invest in a business if he can recover his money in five years, then if it requires $1 million to start a McDonalds's franchise, the owner will need to make $200,000 per year to make the investment attractive. That is, if the owner cannot make at least $200,000 per year, which would never happen with a $4 raise (let alone a raise to $15 per hour), the restaurant never would have been built in the first place. Thus, the truth of the matter is that any notable raise in the wages would cause the fast food business model to break down. Paying fast food workers $15 per hour violates basic math.

Shutting down the fast food business model might be a good thing (Americans eat too much fast food!) but many people benefit from "access" to the dollar menu, especially poor people, so we should be careful about deciding what people should and should not consume, especially if we are going to allow the sale of alcohol, cigarettes, and soda. But wait, the livable wage person might argue, what about raising prices? If people would be willing pay higher prices (perhaps a tip jar?), we could pass on all the additional profits to the workers and pay them more. This point ignores the fact that prices cannot be raised on a whim—without making other restaurant options more viable—and the store would have to take in an additional $50,000 per year per store to raise wages $1 per hour. This is easier said than done. If the owner can raise prices, why should the employees receive 100% of the benefits? More important, how many customers would stop going to McDonald's if the prices rise?

The point of this analysis is to show that successful business models run a delicate balance to survive (I challenge the reader to investigate the profit margin on one Big Mac). Not to give McDonald's employees a hard time, but the reality is that it is not possible to raise a family to middle-class status with a fast food cashier job and probably never will be. However, if someone is willing to dedicate 10 years to mastering the business, that person will probably make the transition to management. Small tweaks to a business model can have profound implications for the business, just as small changes to a recipe can have profound implications for the taste of the food. One last point to remember is that the forces of supply and demand often determine wages or salaries. An accountant might create $200,000 of value for a company but his $75,000 salary might be justified based on how much it would cost to replace him. Granted, the accountant can negotiate a raise, especially if he establishes himself as an invaluable and trusted asset to the company, but the important question to ask yourself is what you would do if you were forced to use the money in your retirement account, such as Social Security, to start a business. If you were using your own money, would you hire someone at the market rate, or would you pay him a significantly higher salary out of the goodness of your heart? If the person had your trust and was a loyal employee for 10 or 20 years, perhaps, but all things being equal it would not be a rational business decision. If the accountant is really good, he can always leave to start his own business, but then he would face the business risk of losing money, so he will have to weigh that prospect against the benefit of a steady salary.

Two Fundamental Institutions

We have to allow the market to determine the value of someone's work because the market will determine the value of the goods or services he produces, whether we like it or not. Just as profitable companies would be wise to reward good employees with bonuses or other benefits to motivate them, employees would be wise to understand the value of steady pay while profits fluctuate. As most people know, starting a business is risky, but it is always an option for the person who believes he can make more money on his own or is not receiving the salary he thinks he deserves. The alternative to a market-based model for wages is to compel people to pay artificially high wages. We could pass a law making the minimum wage $15 per hour, but many business models would cease to work, such as fast food restaurants, and many jobs would be lost. This might be a good thing—perhaps we do not want business models that depend on people earning $7.25 per hour— because it would force investors to identify business models that include jobs with wages of $15 per hour, but we would have to live with the consequences: many more jobs would move overseas, or many new businesses would not be started as people with investment capital opt for the stock market, bonds, or real estate rather than taking the risk of starting a business. What we should not do is allow profitable business models to emerge under current laws and then change the minimum wage laws dramatically after the fact in an attempt to squeeze more money out of companies. Every action has an equal and opposite reaction. If there are fewer profitable business models, then people will be less inclined to start new businesses. If people are going to expect that good jobs will be waiting for them after they finish their education, they should understand that someone had to take a financial risk to make that job possible.

Shifting gears to monogamous procreation, it is a well-established fact that people who live within the institution of monogamous procreation are more likely to make more money and accumulate more wealth during their lives. In fact, the odds of living in poverty drop precipitously for people who finish high school, get a job, get married, and have children—in that order. The reason for this is that although monogamous procreation is a social construct, it is a construct that is consistent with our rational nature (teleology) and channels our deepest desires and energies in positive ways (it is an institution), for ourselves, for our spouse, and for our children, which in turn makes us more productive members of society and provides our children the altruism they need to grow up to be productive members of society. Many people wait to acquire wealth before getting married, which can be a practical thing to do, but people should also understand that the stability provided by a happy family life will help them acquire wealth by allowing them to focus on work rather than on finding a mate, which can be an expensive proposition in terms of money, time, and energy. Wealth means having stuff left over at the end of the day, after all the bills are paid, and this is difficult to do if we are living beyond our means or running up debts. Wealth is accumulated over years, decades, and generations, not by get-rich-quick scams, so if you were one of the unfortunate many that did not inherit an estate from your family, one of the most satisfying things you can do in this life is try to leave one for your own children.

CHAPTER SIX. JUSTICE

The concept of justice is integral to society. Merriam-Webster defines justice as the maintenance or administration of what is just especially by the impartial adjustment of conflicting claims or the assignment of merited rewards or punishments. At a most basic level, justice means people should get what they deserve, good and bad. To use some obvious examples, on the negative side, if a person commits a crime, he should do the time; or, on the positive side, if a person wins the 100-meter dash in the Olympics without using illegal enhancement drugs, he should receive the gold medal. To use some more controversial examples, if a person is poor and commits a crime to survive, he should get leniency or be found not guilty; or, if a person falls short of qualifying for something for reasons that can be shown to be beyond his control, we should make an exception to the rule.

It would be folly to suggest that I could develop a complete theory of justice in this chapter or explain it with sufficient clarity to cover all the nuances of human life, but we can address some of the basic tenets of justice in the context of political philosophy as well as discredit some beliefs about justice, especially from the "social justice" camp. People often invoke the concept of social justice as a point of departure for political philosophy, with varying degrees of success. However, as I will show in this chapter, the concept of social justice is not a valid point of departure for political philosophy because there are more fundamental issues that have to be addressed first, such as resource management and procreation, which in turn raise doubts about the social justice model. Additionally, some of the most important conclusions of the social justice camp are inconsistent and do not follow from the basic premises, such as the idea that talents are arbitrary from a moral perspective.

As a parent, I have observed in my children that humans from an early age have a deep sense of justice that is innate or natural, not taught, and cannot be ignored. If one child gets one piece of candy and another child gets two pieces of candy, there will be a demand for justice, even if that means the child with one piece of candy throwing one of the other pieces of candy into the garbage to make the score even (each child gets one piece of candy) if obtaining a second piece of candy for himself is not possible. This was never taught to them; they just knew that life should be fair, in a vague and emotional kind of way, which is what allows the concept of justice to flourish and shape our society. A sense of justice is hard-wired into our DNA, similar to kin selection and reciprocal altruism, the natural forms of social cooperation and sociability, which is why people throughout history have often risen up against their oppressors, regardless of the level of brainwashing or suffering. People demand justice. Granted, the concept of justice can be specific to a culture—for example, kinship networks tend to have a different concept of justice than modern states, such as giving the kinship network priority over the individual—and can evolve with time, but all societies have rules for justice, from taking steps to stop a blood feud to suing someone for spilling a glass of Brunello on a polar bear rug.

Most people on the left and right sides of the political spectrum tend to agree on the basic idea of justice—we have police to investigate crimes, lawyers to prosecute them, and judges or juries to give a verdict and impose sentencing. The two sides might have some disagreements on what should be legal or illegal—whether to allow illegal aliens to vote like legal citizens (the obvious contradiction here should render this one easy to rule on), whether to allow the use of deadly force in self-defense, and so on—but we have generally reached a point where most people accept the idea that if you do the crime, you should do the time. Given that people can study the concept of justice on their own or at law school, this chapter will focus on the concept of social justice and why its philosophical foundations are weak.

A Theory of Justice

In 1971, John Rawls published *A Theory of Justice*, revised in 1999, which gave the discipline of political philosophy new life and set its course in a new direction, with the concept of social justice front and center. At over 500 dense pages, it is a difficult read that is rewarded by the effort. I agreed with some of the points passionately and disagreed with some of the points passionately. After reading it, with thousands of passages underlined and hundreds of notes in the margins, I decided to take advantage of someone else's expertise to read *Rawls's A Theory of Justice*, a summary of the book by Frank Lovett, which distilled the argument down to 150 digestible pages, which in turn led me to read the Wikipedia page for an even more concise summary. Either way, whether you are on the left or right side of the political spectrum, it is difficult to have a serious discussion about political philosophy today without a basic understanding of this book. The rest of this chapter will focus on summarizing Rawls's argument and my critique of it, to include a general critique of the idea of social justice.

Rawls's primary motivation for writing this book was to provide an alternative theory of justice to utilitarianism, a school of thought that was the dominant model of the day. According to utilitarianism, which dated back to Bentham and Mill in nineteenth-century England, the primary goal of any society should be to maximize the sum total happiness of a society's members, counting the happiness of each member equally—the greatest good for the greatest number. The specifics of utilitarianism are beyond the scope of this book, but it is important to understand what Rawls was arguing against and the historical context of the debate.

On the flip side, Rawls was inspired by and based his theory on a version of the social contract model of Locke and the deontological ethics of Kant, which are also beyond the scope of this book but certainly merit continued study. It is also important to understand the two foundational ideas that gave rise to Rawls's theory. First, Rawls viewed society as a cooperative venture for mutual advantage. If by this Rawls means that society as a whole is an institution, then I disagree. Society has institutions but is not itself an institution. After all, many people do not cooperate with each other in society and tend to view government as a way to protect them from other people (the opposite of cooperation), but we ultimately do cooperate with other people when we choose to and generally benefit from it, as long as people are playing by the rules.

In fact, Fukuyama defines a state as possessing a monopoly on legitimate coercion, which does not mesh well with Rawls's vision of society. A society is a collection of individuals, not an institution, which tends to include people who are cooperating with each other, but we can certainly accept his point as something to strive for. Second, Rawls focuses on the way in which the major social institutions distribute fundamental rights and duties and determine the division of advantages from social cooperation. The basic idea here is that our success or lack thereof in life within a particular society is only partly due to our individual efforts. As a politician who supports the social justice model once said: "You didn't build that." Some people are born rich with natural talents whereas some people are born poor with limited natural talents, but we all benefit from society, which provides many of the educational opportunities and legal protections that make success possible. According to Rawls, this disparity between people (of family advantages and of talents), especially when it is great, is partly or mostly due to the basic structure of the society we live in. There is some truth to this statement, of course, but Rawls's claim that these differences are *morally arbitrary*, as I will address below, is not sound.

Rawls begins by asking how we can structure the basic rules of society so that the game is fair from the beginning and does not give special benefits to any individuals or groups. To get us moving in the right direction, Rawls proposes a thought experiment whereby we exist behind a veil of ignorance when we make the rules for society. The catch is that we do not have any particular details about the kind of person we will be in this society—gender, height, race, beauty, intelligence, talents, job, etc. For example, if someone is a racist, he might want other races to receive fewer benefits. However, if he does not know which race (or mixture) he will be in this new society, he would be reluctant to give special benefits to one race over the others because he might end up in the race of people without the benefits. To hedge his bets, in the spirit of game theory, he would rule in favor of giving equal rights to all races, and so on. Giving equal rights to all people is the best way to ensure that we live in a fair society.

The tricky part is that the veil of ignorance hides specific facts about society, not general facts. We do not know our gender, race, or socioeconomic position, but we somehow know the basics about society and human nature. It is not clear how the people behind the veil could sustain such a balance of knowledge and ignorance but we can try to follow the argument to see where it goes. The other tricky part is that Rawls has to give the people behind the veil of ignorance a certain level of intellectual sophistication, which he does by saying that everyone behind the veil of ignorance is "rational," which should please the readers of this book. Otherwise, if we include irrational or uneducated people, they would vote for the rules they already understand, rules that educated people would not want to live by. (The problem, of course, is that apparently rational people often reach diametrically opposed conclusions.) The basic idea makes sense—no individuals or groups should receive special benefits or privileges, and we should not allow our current knowledge of ourselves to bias our opinions—but there is a sense in which Rawls is stacking the deck with people who would agree him. After all, what if it turns out that we are not so rational after all or that truly rational people do not agree with his argument? Perhaps there are higher principles we are not yet aware of and that will require many more years of social progress to grasp? The rational person argument is precisely what Hegel argued against, noting that rational people are the end result of a social process, not the beginning. Rational people can certainly tweak society after they reach the level of rational thought, but many people and institutions will resist the change. Another problem behind the veil is that we do not know what kind of society we will belong to or in what stage of development. This is extremely odd because the rules that govern a particular society are inextricably linked to the cultural and socioeconomic development of the society. (This is why imposing "Western" values on developing countries often does not work as intended.) I am skeptical that we could use the socioeconomic model of suburban Minnesota with a village in Afghanistan.

With the veil of ignorance in place, Rawls proceeds to develop two principles he believes everyone would support. (The best way to do this, of course, would be to poll rational people about what rules they would want to live by.) The first principle states that all people would favor the equal assignment of basic rights and duties, to include basic liberties and freedoms, equal access to offices and positions, income and wealth, and self-respect, to name a few. From the start, we already have major problems. Rawls seems to be mixing terms, in particular, the concepts of rights and entitlements. Most would agree that we have a right to life, liberty, and the pursuit of happiness, as outlined by the Founding Fathers, but the key to rights is that *they must be thought of in the negative*; that is, no one should have the right to take away our life, our liberty, or our pursuit of happiness. A right does not grant us something tangible, such as money or other resources. This is by definition an entitlement. Rawls is correct that normal people would always prefer more of his basic rights, not less, but how does he account for income? No one has a right to an income. An income is earned by our labor, whether a product or a service. No one should be able to prevent you from earning an income (in this sense, we have a right to an income), but that is not the same thing as saying you have a right to an income. Depending on how we establish our society, we might have some entitlements, such as unemployment or retirement benefits, which we receive after paying into the system, but entitlements are not the same as rights. Entitlements can be taken away and depend on the current budget and laws, but rights by definition do not depend of the whim of government and cannot be voted out of existence. What if Rawls simply had said no one would be allowed to violate the rights of anyone else? Unfortunately, Rawls does not distinguish between rights and entitlement, so it is difficult to understand exactly what he means by the first principle. Oddly enough, Rawls states, correctly, that society should never be allowed to ask people to have their rights violated for the greater good, but he then proceeds to talk about how things, like income, which he claims is a right, might have to be taken away from us for the greater good. After reflecting on this first principle, as a self-proclaimed rational person, I am convinced I would never select this principle behind veil of ignorance.

The second principle states that social and economic inequalities are just only if they result in compensating benefits for everyone, in particular, the least advantaged members of society. Rawls was widely considered an egalitarian, but he was clear that inequality would exist in a just society. I agree. Thus, we could say he believed in equality of opportunity, not in equality of results, which is a key distinction. The reason for this is that Rawls was focused on making the game of life fair from the beginning, that is, reducing or eliminating those artificial rules or structures that make the game unfair from the beginning. He does not set out to make people equal at the end of the process, even though he might prefer that things turn out that way. As long as the rules are fair for all from the beginning, with no privileges or fast-track options, Rawls was prepared to accept some level of inequality as the people play by the fair rules of society. Again, most people get the basic idea, but I doubt anyone would select this rule after a process of rational deliberation. The biggest problem is how do we make such a calculation? If I wanted to use some money from the family fortune to start a business (which Rawls would consider arbitrary luck), how would I calculate whether or not the least advantaged members of society received compensating benefits? To state it simply, the principle is too abstract and too difficult to confirm, like basing a legal system on the premise that people should be "good." Just as utilitarian philosophers were unable to define happiness or how to measure it, at least to my satisfaction, this principle does not provide a clear way to confirm whether we are in compliance. The basic idea makes sense—if we are going to allow people to play by the rules of the game to make money and move up or down the social ladder, we should structure the game in such a way that the least advantaged members of society do not systematically take it on the chin—but it is not clear how we should do this when devising the rules. Would each person with a business plan have to explain to the bank how he or she would achieve this prior to receiving a loan? Would we have to shut the business down if we discovered later that the least advantaged members of society were not receiving compensating benefits? If so, who would make the decision? Who would compensate the people who got fired? How would they make the calculation? Would this apply to all economic projects or only those initiated by rich people? Who would define what rich means? And so on.

Admittedly, I am glossing over some of the finer points of the argument, but I am inclined to say that many rational people behind a veil of ignorance would not select Rawls's two principles. Here are some principles that come to mind:

1. All rights shall apply to all people equally.

2. All people shall be equal under the law.

3. No one may violate the rights of another person.

4. People may not obstruct other people from participating in the free exchange of goods and services.

5. People may not use their majority status to oppress or seize assets from the minority.

6. Deficit spending shall be prohibited.

7. Monogamous procreation shall be the sanctified law of the land.

This list is not complete—it might be a fun game to play with others during dinner parties to develop such a list—but they are relatively simple and clear points that most people can understand and might even support. In the end, I question the premise that there are any fixed rules that all rational people would agree to behind a veil of ignorance precisely because the two sides of the political spectrum disagree on what it means to be rational and what it means to be fair. As a result, we often have to focus on rules that prevent people from abusing the system rather than providing people opportunities.

The Genetic Lottery

Rawls goes to great lengths to argue that the circumstances of our birth, both the wealth of our family and our natural talents, are arbitrary from a moral perspective. Rawls is arguing that people born into wealthy families or with great talents have no moral claim that their situation at birth entitles them to a successful life, any more than we can say that someone who is born into a poor family with limited talents deserves a life of poverty, an idea that Rawls calls moral deserts. According to Rawls, the basic structure of society played a role in arbitrarily loading the game one way or another, and that one of the primary functions of social justice was to ensure that these arbitrary differences between people play a minimal role in shaping the basic rules of the game at the beginning, and to take steps to ensure the starting positions are as fair as possible. For example, if a particular group of children is born into poverty (regardless of race, gender, etc., I would assume), which is not their fault, we as a society have a moral obligation to shift resources to them—for education or nutritional assistance, for example—to mitigate the weakness of their starting point, even if the goal is merely to avoid dealing with statistically predictable social problems later in life. Most people would agree that this claim has merit—children should not be totally dependent on their parents, especially if their parents neglect them—but is this the same thing as saying that birth and natural talents are arbitrary from a moral perspective? If we accept that people will be born into different social strata with different natural talents, is blind luck not the best way? I wonder what Rawls would think if these things were not arbitrary, that is, if there was a systematic way to manipulate the procreation game to make our talents the result of rational planning? Most people have a basic belief that two people who are smart, beautiful, or athletic will tend to have children who are smart, beautiful, or athletic, but this is not always the case. As I noted earlier, the ancient Greeks struggled with the fact that many (self-proclaimed) virtuous men had children who lacked virtue, despite a formal education. My guess is that if the technology is ever invented, rich people will find a way to ensure that their children are born with even more natural talents and advantages as possible.

The odd part of Rawls's argument is that he seems to suggest that we could have been born into other circumstances. The only way for an injustice to occur is if things could have been otherwise. Thus, if we can show that a person's birth could not have been otherwise, it would strike a blow at the foundation of the social justice argument. I am reminded of Plato's *Phaedrus*, in which pre-existing souls circle the heaven prior to entering a body:

> All soul looks after all that lacks a soul, and patrols all of heaven, taking different shapes at different times. So long as its wings are in perfect condition it flies high, and the entire universe is its dominion; but a soul that sheds its wings wanders until it lights on something solid, where it settles and takes on an earthly body, which then, owing to the power of this soul, seems to move itself.[1]

If we set aside the beautiful and esoteric poetry of Plato, I will make the bold assertion that Rawls would probably recognize that each person is a combination of one unique egg and one unique sperm cell provided by a unique mother and a unique father, respectively. A particular person could not have been born otherwise. It does not make much sense to talk about a particular person as having been born into different circumstances, other than as an abstract argument. (It does, however, make sense to say that a person's parents could have been living in difficult circumstances due to unjust oppression.) Granted, a person might be born into poverty, but he probably would not have been born otherwise: consider the fact that small changes in society probably would have resulted in his two biological parents never meeting, in which case he never would have been born. If his parents had not been poor or middle-class or rich, there is a good chance they probably never would have met, in which case the person never would have been born, unless you believe, like Plato, that souls exist prior to birth and select a body to inhabit, which is something I suspect most people do not believe.

---

1 Plato, *Phaedrus*, 246c.

Thus, *from a first person perspective*, we should be thankful just to be alive. How many people would trade poverty for non-existence? From the *third person perspective* of society, however, we can take steps to encourage people to delay procreation until they are ready to raise a child—as far as we are concerned, one sperm cell and egg combination is as good as the next—but we only have to reflect on our own lives to turn this argument inside-out. To the extent that we steer away from the sanctity of life, we chip away at our own claim to a right to life, if our focus is fairness. This of course does not mean we should demand that people born into poverty be happy with their lot and suck it up or that rich people should be given special privileges regardless of effort, which is an argument made by caste societies that believe in reincarnation, but it does mean that those people would not have been born otherwise. The truth is that *each of us won the genetic lottery just by being born.* If you consider the odds of not being born, it is really quite staggering, unless you believe, like Plato, that your soul existed prior to your birth and that you selected a body to inhabit, in which case you are responsible for selecting your parents. Getting back to a more scientific approach, in order for you to have been born, one unique sperm cell and one unique egg in the whole history of the universe had to unite for the brief window of time that gives life. Again, not to downplay the lot of many people, but beginning with the miracle of life seems like a more tenable position when thinking about life and the world we live in. For the people who support the so-called "right to choose," especially after the fetus is viable, how many of them would be willing to roll the dice to give their mother a second chance to go back and choose differently? Millions of us are probably alive today because abortion was illegal when we were born. This is not to suggest that we should prohibit abortion as much as it is a thought experiment to provide more context to our beliefs.

Returning to the topic of the wealth or poverty you are born into, Rawls seems to have forgotten an important point: one of the fundamental rights (his first principle guarantees basic rights to all) we have is the right to earn an income *and to dispose of our income as we see fit*, which includes transferring it to our children. As Robert Nozick observed in *Anarchy, State, and Utopia*:

> Since in a capitalist society people often transfer holdings to others in accordance with how much they perceive these others benefitting them, the fabric constituted by the individual transactions and transfers is largely reasonable and intelligible.[1]

As Nozick points out, this basic freedom to dispose of our income as we see fit conflicts with a fundamental tenet of social justice, which focuses on distributing resources to where they "should" go, not where individual

---

1 Nozick, Robert, *Anarchy, State, and Utopia*, pg. 159.

people (the owners of the resources) want them to go. We can equalize incomes but we cannot dictate how those incomes will be spent. Suppose a man works hard, has financial success, marries a beautiful woman, and gives her proper nutrients during pregnancy, which results in a healthy baby who receives breast milk and love every day before sending him down the path of a good education. Is this not what we hope for all of our children? To say this child's situation is "arbitrary from a moral perspective" conflicts with the rights of parents to provide for their children and denigrates their efforts to play a positive role in shaping the life of the children they bring into the world. From this perspective, the social justice position looks downright offensive.

Taking it to the next level, what if the child is born into a strong kinship network that provides for his education and helps him make the transition to a successful career and provides for him in his old age? Is this child fortunate? Yes. Does this child deserve this? Yes, with an important caveat, which brings us back to kinship networks and the second fundamental institution regarding the sanctity of monogamous procreation. If a child is born into favored status with all the blessings of wealth and education, we can talk about the child deserving this leg up on the competition as long as, and this is the key, *he pays his debt forward to his own children or to his own kinship network.* In the case of government, we pay our debt to society by paying taxes in accordance with the law. Nothing more is required, which is not to say that our (charitable) giving should stop there. If we are born with a heavy debt to our parents or kinship network, we can pay off that debt by paying it forward to our own children or to the kinship network that made our success possible. (I believe the efficacy of monogamous procreation and kinship networks for accumulating wealth and providing advantages to its members over multiple generations is precisely why the far left has a history of trying to tear down these social arrangements.) Again, this does not mean that such a person should receive any special benefits or privileges from society, such as stipends from the government or honorary titles—we should all be treated equally under the law—but neither should the person be made to feel that his life situation is "morally arbitrary."

In the real world, it is difficult for children born into poverty and broken families to compete with children born into wealth and strong families, no doubt about it, and Rawls does have a good point about how we should treat them. These children are not to blame for their situation and we should take reasonable measures to help them. It makes sense to talk about investing in social programs to help these children break the cycle of poverty, especially if the programs pay dividends, but it should be with the understanding that we promote the social values that will make them successful in life, such as monogamous procreation and avoiding deficit spending. We should not promote the social values that tend to result in poverty. For example, simple things like having a good lunch at school can help kids stay healthy and alert and avoid long-term health problems, which would have to be managed by the government later. Education is another example. If we want poor child ren to get on the right track so that they can work, become net producers of resources, pay taxes, and produce the next generation, as opposed to ending up on welfare or in jail, we as a society would be wise to invest money in educating them. However, we have to be realistic. First, we will never be able to provide all poor children the same level of education the wealthy receive (precisely because we cannot stop wealthy people from spending money on their own children, to include private schools and tutors), with the understanding that many poor children will have better SAT scores than many wealthy children. Second, we can calculate the return on investment to see what we are getting for our money, so our spending should be driven by facts, not by an abstract sense of social justice. There is no doubt that wealthy people, all things being equal, begin the game of life from a position of advantage, but given that the top 10% of households pay about 70% of all federal income taxes, the wealthy are already paying their "fair share" to fund government programs, some of which provide assistance for the poor. Not to mention, society benefits from many of these rich children who attend the finest schools because they often create new companies and technological innovations.

Before moving on to the next topic, I wanted to say a few words about how Rawls views what he calls natural talents and our place in society. As was the case with wealth, Rawls goes to great lengths to argue that our natural talents are arbitrary from a moral perspective. If the Muses were responsible for determining salaries, an artsy novelist would probably make more money than the typical romance novelist, but the fact that some people are born with limited natural talents does not mean that we should allow society to subject them to abject poverty. Beyond the fact that it is not really clear what Rawls means, I think he exaggerates the idea of "natural talents." In the case of professional athletes, novelists, or singers, it is true that natural gifts, such as physical strength, a gift for language, or pristine vocal chords play a major role in determining who rises to the top, and that there is limited room at the top in this winner-take-all economy, but the truth is that most jobs do not depend on a metaphysical concept of "natural talent." Some people are good with people and other people are good with numbers, but as long as the career we choose is a good fit for our character, we should have no problem achieving a level of mastery in our work—some studies suggest at least 10,000 hours or ten years of dedication to the craft—which in turn should equate with earning a good income. The problem is that many people are not willing to take the painful steps to achieve mastery in a particular skill, which should be one of the goals of our educational system and any person with a career. If people master the skill of plumbing, they will make good money. If people master the skill of accounting, they will make good money. At some point, they might have to take some risks to go it alone, as opposed to hoping for someone else to offer them an even job, but most people should have no problem carving their own niche and achieving enough mastery in their chosen profession to make a comfortable living.

Regarding our place in society, Rawls speaks about not knowing what our place, class position, or social status will be while contemplating our hypothetical society behind the veil of ignorance. For example, he might argue that we should respect all jobs because we might end up as a street sweeper after the veil of ignorance is lifted, even though Rawls probably would not allow a street sweeper to design the rules for his ideal society behind the veil of ignorance.

It is not clear what Rawls means by this because our place, class position, and social status in society are determined by what we do in life over many years, and we can always make changes. Our roles are not assigned, at least not in a free society. Granted, we can be born into wealth or poverty, and that status can stay with us through life for reasons sometimes beyond our control, for better or worse, but this premise seems to ignore the possibility of social mobility. There are many poor people who move up the social ladder, from street sweeper to CEO, and many rich people who fall down the social ladder in two to three generations. Few families on the Forbes 400 list from the 1950s are still on the list today, which should be viewed as a positive thing. This "role" thinking seems to apply to a stratified, zero-growth society, characterized by a person's social role being determined by birth—such as the son of a blacksmith becoming a blacksmith—and a zero-sum, fixed-pie economy in which one person's gain is another person's loss. Granted, we do not have complete social mobility, because the room at the top is limited and the people at the top go to great lengths to ensure their children replace them, but the truth is that it does not make sense to talk about what our place, class position, or social status will be after the veil of ignorance is lifted because we can always change it after the fact. This might sound optimistic, but it is not clear what the alternative is.

Distribution and Access

Rawls addresses two important concepts in the social justice lexicon that also raise concerns. More often than not, when someone talks about "distribution," usually in the context of income, they are in the social justice camp. In this context, the word distribution has two meanings, both of which cause more confusion than clarity. The first meaning of the term is to divide and dispense in portions. For example, if a parent has a bag of 21 candies and three children, the parent might distribute seven candies to each child. Clear enough, but the problem is that this definition does not apply to society in most circumstances, especially to people living in a modern state. If we lived in a world where all of our basic needs could be satisfied by nature without effort, such as fruit growing on trees, we could distribute these goods to each member of society and live in peace. (In fact, people are free to form a fruit tree commune.) This model breaks down, however, as soon as we introduce goods and services that are the product of rational human labor. In this case, assuming people do not live in a commune and do not agree to share their goods, goods and services are no longer available for "distribution." Who would be chosen to distribute? Based on what principle? With what justification?

> There is no central distribution, no person or group entitled to control all the resources, jointly deciding how they are to be doled out. What each person gets, he gets from the others who give to him in exchange for something, or as a gift...There is no more a distributing or distribution of shares than there is a distributing of mates in a society in which persons choose whom they shall marry.[1]

In short, even at an early stage in our social development we progress from a distribution model to an exchange model, which is evidence that the desire of some people toward collectivism or communism represents intellectual regression, not progress. In this case, people will be free to exchange their goods and services with other people in society. We will collect some resources (taxes) to fund social programs, such as roads or schools, but a central authority will not collect the fruits of our labor to distribute as they see fit. Thus, the idea of society distributing the fruits of individual labor is a contradiction in terms and a violation of our basic rights as defined by Rawls. To repeat, this does not mean that we will not collect taxes or that the wealthy will not pay a greater percentage of their wealth in taxes, which they do, but it does mean that people are free to do with whatever money is not collected in taxes. The basic premise behind the social justice camp of wealth distribution is that the goods and services that constitute GDP should be spread out more evenly, ignoring the fact that the most productive people would stop being as productive if they had to bear an even greater burden of distributing their wealth to other people. (There are good examples of this phenomenon when students in a class are forced to "distribute" their test scores, which usually results in a collective failing

---

1 Nozick, Robert, *Anarchy, State, and Utopia*, pgs. 149-150.

grade for the class because the good students refuse the carry the bad or lazy students.) In the case of natural resources, like water and oil, which are waiting to be exploited and are often on federal lands, I agree that we should treat these resources differently than the fruits of individual labor and that a society would be wise to ensure that no one is allowed to claim all the profits. For example, we would be unwise to allow private companies to take control of our water supply and then use a business model to maximize profits while selling the water back to us at a massive profit. There is no need to subject water to the forces of private sector supply and demand (at least in most states in the USA, for now) because there is nothing to gain from competition—no innovation. Water is water and always will be, despite what the marketing companies tell us. Not to mention, there are health and sanitary issues to consider that might not mesh well with a traditional business model.

The second idea of "distribution" relates to how wealth is spread out at a given point in time. For example, if the top 1% own 40% of the wealth and the bottom 50% own 2% of the wealth, we could represent this data visually to see how it is distributed. Many people would argue that such a wealth distribution would be unjust, but we have to consider one important point: how was the wealth obtained? In Nozick's chapter on Distributive Justice, he says the following:

> The subject of justice in holding consists of three major topics. The first is the original acquisition of holdings, the appropriation of unheld things...The second topic concerns the transfer of holdings from one person to another...The complete principle of distributive justice would say simply that a distribution is just if everyone is entitled to the holdings they possess under the distribution...The existence of past injustices...raises the third major topic under justice in holdings: the rectification of injustice of holdings.[1]

Nozick acknowledges that the existence of a past injustice could result in an unfair distribution of goods, and highlights that such injustices should be rectified, which is fertile common ground for the left and the right, *but this is not the same thing as saying that the mere existence of a wide disparity of wealth between rich and poor is proof of injustice.* If a wealthy person violated no rules to acquire his wealth, then the acquisition of the wealth was just, regardless of how many people acquire little to no wealth or how the wealth of a society is distributed. The social justice advocate might grant this argument but point out that the rules of the game should never be structured in such a way as to make such a disparity of wealth possible. That is, wealth disparity is *ipso facto* proof that the rules of society are not fair. That might be so, but I would

---

1 Nozick, Robert, *Anarchy, State, and Utopia*, pgs. 150-152.

ask that person to devise a set of fair rules that would ensure a more equal distribution of wealth, one that is achieved by the rules themselves, not by the seizure of wealth after the fact and not in a way that would destroy the system of incentives. If one side believes the rules are not fair, they can vote to change the rules, as long as they do not violate the rights of others. What is not just is establishing social rules and laws and then seizing the wealth after the fact of those who succeed by playing by the rules. In fact, even Rawls did not support such a plan: he believed we should focus on making the game as fair as possible from the beginning, rather than focus on undoing injustices after the fact, especially if people are playing by the fair rules. The social justice camp seems to have an *a priori* belief that the wealth disparity between rich and poor is due primarily to the injustice of the system itself, not to the inherent differences between people.

Shifting gears to "access," another favorite term of the social justice camp, this term is also misused to achieve political objectives. When rational people use the word access, they mean an ability or permission to enter or pass, such as having access to a road or access to the back stage of a concert. For most of us, when someone asks us whether we have access to a school or a hospital, we assume the person wants to know whether the doors are unlocked. In the case of the social justice camp, however, the word access refers to a moral right to something. For example, they might say they should have "access" to good education or affordable healthcare. This statement is literally silly because anyone has access to anything as long as they have money to pay for it. Supply is demand. Would it make sense to say that I do not have access to a Ferrari if I could not afford one? The social justice camp would have us believe that a good education and affordable healthcare are out there for all to enjoy, but that unfair barriers are keeping them out of reach, like bouncers outside a club blocking access with a velvet rope. They point out that they would improve their chances for success if they could have access to a good college education. I suppose, but that applies to all people. We would all benefit from a perfect diet and a perfect exercise program with a personal trainer, but not all of us can have those things. We would all benefit from an Ivy League education and a home in the suburbs, but not all of us can have those things. Because the social justice camp's use of the word "access" does not make sense (they use "access" to suggest "right"), it is clear that it is being used to manipulate the narrative—Who would deny this person access to education?—but this simple and short analysis shows that it has no place in serious debate.

Self-Respect and Equal Opportunity

According to Wikipedia, social justice is the ability people have to realize their potential in the society where they live, where the set of institutions will enable people to lead a fulfilling life and be active contributors to their community. At first glance, it is difficult to argue with this view of life, which in many ways encapsulates the American dream. However, as is common with many arguments that are politically motivated, there is a lot of rhetoric about how people should be given opportunities to succeed without a lot of details about how these opportunities will be paid for or what would be expected from the people in exchange for these opportunities. Likewise, there is a lot of talk about promoting equal opportunity as a way of giving special treatment to select groups of people. Thus, we should now get beyond the rhetoric and to the heart of the matter.

Rawls goes to great lengths to argue that self-respect is one of the most important basic rights of his first principle, perhaps even the most important. He insists that each person should have the opportunity to seek a fulfilling career and map out his own life journey. Again, who could disagree with that? Well, the problem is that Rawls insists that tax dollars (the wealth of society) should be used to structure society with institutions and social programs in such a way as to help people with their life journey. If a person needs a college education, he should have "access" to a college education. If the person needs a fulfilling career to achieve happiness, he should have "access" to a good job, even if it is not clear who will take the financial risk to create such a job. And to top it off, society should allow each person to pursue his or her own life journey, without judgment and without expectations. Obviously, Rawls would not endorse a life of crime, but he suggests that we should not use any moralistic standards of perfection to judge people, which would not please Aristotle or other adherents of perfectionist teleology.

What is oddly missing from Rawls' analysis of self-respect is any reference to what we in society can expect from these people while they are on their life journey or who will provide all the "access" they need to stay on their life journey. Rawls says they will perform their chosen profession, which might or might not be of benefit to society, but who is to say whether this profession will generate enough wealth to cover all of their obligations—to include consumption for self and family, savings for retirement, and taxes? To be specific, what tax policies will we implement to fund all of this access, and what impact will it have on the economy? Why does society owe each individual a fulfilling life journey? Perhaps they would benefit from a healthy diet as well, or from driving a nice car. On the other hand, perhaps we should hold them accountable for building this infrastructure? Also oddly missing from this discussion, but not surprising, is *any reference to procreation* (a fundamental social institution, no less) or sacrificing one's own life journey for the sake of family, which is precisely why most of us here today are in a position to talk about a life journey. At birth, our debt is paid, but we are obligated to pay it forward to our own children, rather than self-absorbedly view ourselves as the end product of a long evolutionary process, as if history has been waiting for us to go on our life journey. In fact, Rawls only reluctantly acknowledges the need for the monogamous family, and even suggests that society might benefit from another model, which harkens back to Plato and the contradictory views of the radical left regarding family. This suggests that there is a conflict between his theory and the institution of monogamous procreation, as Nozick noted.

> We should note in passing the ambivalent position of radicals toward the family. Its loving relationships are seen as a model to be emulated and extended across the whole society, at the same time that it is denounced as a suffocating institution to be broken and condemned as a focus of parochial concerns that interfere with achieving radical goals.[1]

Rawls makes no reference to expecting that these individuals use their own wealth to create jobs for others or to limit their life journey to raise children for the next generation. If they have the right to demand that a good job is waiting for them after college, do we have a right to demand that they create good jobs for others at some point? The creation of good jobs is one of the greatest contributions someone can make to a society, so we should strive to motivate more people to create jobs, and even reward them and celebrate their achievements.

Does everyone have a right to self-respect? Assuming that a person is living in accordance with the laws and paying taxes, of course, but does that mean we cannot hold people to certain standards of behavior? There is a difference between criminalizing behavior, condemning behavior, tolerating behavior, accepting behavior, respecting behavior, and celebrating behavior. Most things are not black or white or binary. For example, if a talented person—say, someone who got accepted to medical school but decided not to go—dedicates his life to drinking and gambling, we can judge this person in moralistic terms even if he insists he is on his life journey. We probably will not criminalize his behavior but we might tolerate or accept his behavior, because it is his life to live. However, we certainly will not respect or celebrate his behavior. This person has no right to demand anything from society, aside from equal treatment under the law. And if we reserve the right to judge people, we must have a standard for judging them, which was addressed in the chapter on human nature. We all have a general

---

1 Nozick, Robert, *Anarchy, State, and Utopia*, pg. 167.

idea of acceptable behavior. If a family or kinship network invests a lot of time and resources in a child, perhaps at the expense of other children, the family or kinship network has a right to have some reasonable expectations about what the child does. We cannot force a child to become a doctor or inherit the family business (even though rational people would leap at such opportunities, if they were capable), but the person should think carefully before wasting all the sacrifices his family or kinship network made for him while growing up. Of course, if the person wishes to abandon the family or kinship network, he should also be prepared to abandon the benefits so that the precious resources can be used on family members who are more eager to enjoy the benefits of membership. Perhaps the other, less talented brother should get the money for college if he is willing to take over the family business.

Shifting gears to equal opportunity, Rawls also speaks about the importance of ensuring that every person who is willing, eager, and capable of working be given the opportunity to do so. The odd part about this is that he seems to suggest that this is not the case. Is there anything preventing people from working? Would a company or government agency not hire someone who was willing, eager, and capable of working? Once again, when we peel the onion, we see that something more fundamental is at work here, something political. What Rawls is really talking about, I think, is breaking down barriers ("access") and taking proactive measures to identify diamonds in the rough of the lower strata to break the cycle of poverty, which is a noble objective. Clearly, any company or government agency that uses race or gender as a way of choosing who gets a job is in violation of civil rights (discrimination), unless that job is so clearly designed for one race or gender so as to be obvious. My guess is that no one would balk at the NAACP hiring an African-American president or at the LPGA hiring a female president. For most other positions, we seem to have reached consensus that people offering jobs should look at qualifications when choosing candidates, with the understanding that people should be allowed to associate with people of their choice. For example, a man can hire his own children, wisely or unwisely, to take over the family business, even if there are more qualified candidates, because that is his right. However, most people would balk at a government agency giving preferential treatment to a person because his father or mother had a prominent position in the government. This is called nepotism.

Getting back to Rawls' point, there is a certain logic to offering good jobs to diamonds in the rough who did not benefit from wealth and a private school education, as a way to break the cycle of poverty and attract the best talent. However, this also raises some problems, all good intentions aside.

First, can we really expect a business owner to make such a selfless decision? The candidate might be good, but there might be other candidates who grew up in wealth and who attended private schools who are much better candidates. Rawls argues that meeting the basic qualifications should be the threshold, but he seems to ignore the fact that many candidates far exceed the basic qualifications. Is it really reasonable to ask a business owner to select a less qualified candidate in the name of social progress? If so, why? Based on what principle? Is it fair to punish wealthy kids who attend private schools and have better qualifications? Would Rawls ever support picking a rich white man who "meets standards" if a poor black woman was the most qualified candidate? The answer is probably no, which brings us to government jobs, which is one place where these diamonds in the rough can be given opportunities to excel. All things being equal, the best and the brightest from the wealthiest families do not apply for government jobs, so this seems to be a reasonable place to help people move up the social ladder, to break the cycle of poverty, and to provide their children a leg up in the next generation. (Ironically, many government officials who complain about the privileges of rich people take measures to help their own children get jobs with the government.) By seeking new talent, we avoid nepotism and stagnancy. My sense is, however, that Rawls and others in the social justice camp would like to see even more drastic measures. We should do our best to level the playing field (by raising up the poor, not by dragging down the rich) and give people opportunities, but not if it interferes with the rights of others to seek the same opportunities. Granted, no one has a right to a particular job or to attend a particular university, but if we are going to base selection for jobs or school on things other than merit, such as the idea of diversity, then we have to explain why this basis of selection is morally just.

The basic idea of social justice provides a good framework for helping a society transition from being ruled by oligarchs and kinship networks (tribalism) to the creation of a modern state that protects individual rights and promotes fairness, which is a common theme in this book. Individuals and society as a whole benefit from kinship networks, as should be clear, but there are also benefits to be had from reducing the power of kinship networks and creating a modern state. Children should not be forced to submit themselves to any customs or traditions of a kinship network that by rational standards violate their basic human rights, such as child labor or the right to choose to not marry someone. People should also be allowed to participate in the benefits of a kinship network, and the state should not attempt to dissolve kinship networks that are not attempting to manipulate the political system. Obviously, for those areas where the kinship networks no longer have sovereign authority, the state must fill the vacuum, which requires that taxes must be collected to establish a network of public institutions—that is, a modern state—but we must never forget that real wealth has to be collected from real people to run the government, whereas kinship networks will perform many of the same functions for free. For every dollar we demand in benefits to fund our life journey, society has a right to demand a dollar plus interest from us down the road to keep the programs funded. And society should also reserve the right to expect that each person do his or her part to produce and raise the next generation.

Two Fundamental Institutions

Looking back to the two fundamental institutions in Part I, the prohibition of deficit spending is relevant because it sets a rational limit on how much a government may spend to promote the social justice model. If the math is done for any particular society, without deficit spending, I believe it will be difficult or impossible to achieve the level of social spending and government intervention needed to achieve the results the social justice camp wants, not without doing damage to the underlying economy—eating the seed corn, so to speak. The reason this is difficult or impossible to achieve is that each individual will struggle to produce the wealth he needs to keep making progress—consumption for himself and his family, retirement planning, and paying taxes. Given that society is nothing more than a collection of individuals, the sum total of national wealth is the sum total of individual wealth. That is, *there is no magic in the wealth creation process when transitioning from the micro to the macro*, unless we resort to deficit spending. If our society has one million households and each household has one dollar available to pay in taxes, the government budget should be one million dollars. No other money will magically appear during the process of collecting taxes. Thus, we can grant the social justice camp that they have a basically good idea for helping people achieve their potential, especially those who are living in difficult circumstances, and helping us make a lot of the social progress we have seen during the past 100 years, but with the caveat that we will prohibit deficit spending as a way to prevent abuse and the disruption of organic economic growth. Society cannot transcend itself, any more than an individual can transcend himself—we can only fulfill our rational potential, our teleology—so we cannot use deficit spending as a way to "prime the pump" to artificially grow the economy to the point where the deficit spending goes away after tax revenue magically rises in response to the magical economic growth. Once the deficit spending starts, it will take us down the one-way road of growing interest payments and ballooning debt, if history is any indicator.

The same idea applies for monogamous procreation. Every person should be free to pursue his or her dream, assuming that no laws are broken and that all the taxes are paid, but each person needs to understand that no one is the end product of history. Each of us was the product of one man and one woman, ideally within the institution of monogamous procreation, which is the best way to strike a sustainable balance between satisfying our own desires with the need for social stability. Just as every person benefitted from some degree of altruistic love to make them the people they are today, we all owe it to society to perpetuate society by producing the next generation and giving our children all the altruistic love they need to promote the virtuous cycle of wealth creation, even if that means sacrificing our own dreams and making compromises. If not, we face social disintegration. Again, after we look at reality and do the math, for most people this will mean giving up on some aspects of our life journey, but only to find new doors. Working as a starving artist—without paying customers—in an industrial warehouse might seem cool, but at some point we all have to grow up. Although this might sound depressing or frustrating to some people, I should highlight that getting married and having children will, for most rational people, be the most fulfilling part of the life journey. In fact, you will probably find that the blind drive that compels most people to succeed in their life journey was nothing more than this lingering primal desire to produce the next generation, at which time a calm satisfaction will fill your days.

Part III. Parerga and Paralipomena

Within the continuum of reality that constitutes political philosophy, I have attempted to construct an abstract model, which inevitably requires carving out and highlighting certain aspects of reality at the expense of others. Concepts by definition highlight what is essential to something and set it apart from all other things, often leaving the particular details to the imagination. For example, I took some political science classes in college but did not really understand the core concepts until I had lived for many years in foreign countries, especially developing countries, where I saw firsthand the tragic flow of human activity that provides the seeds for the concepts of political science. As Schopenhauer observed (I owe the odd title of this chapter to him), one of the fundamental problems of the educational system is that we often begin with concepts and conceptual models and only later learn what they really mean, often learning after the fact that the concepts do not mesh well with reality (black magic concepts), and that these false concepts and false conceptual models often distort how we learn, like using a broken telescope to observe the universe. A real education, Schopenhauer says, involves immersing ourselves in the world of particulars, the primordial soup of life, with the concepts we form being the end product of our education, not the starting point, all the while using the concepts of our wise elders to keep us on the right track but always aware of the need to modify them as needed.

Like relics, some concepts age and decay, or can be refined or polished, so we must not take them as irreducible molecules of reality, which was the insight Aristotle used to attack Plato's theory of Forms. Words like "alienation" and "praxis" are not necessarily meaningful just because we continue using them in sentences, and children do not desire to have sex with the opposite sex parent just because it happens in one Greek myth. (For what it is worth, as Rene Girard observed, the children are probably imitating the behavior of the same-sex parent, not actually desiring the opposite sex parent, which should be a relief for many parents.) For example, when I was in college I thought I understood what it meant to say institutions are the key to good governance because I read a book that said something along those lines. Looking back, I did not understand it, but I do now. During college, I understood it on an abstract level, like admiring a trophy in a glass case, but I could not feel it within me or use the concept as a tool for shaping my thoughts in new ways, like the members of the team who won the trophy in the fire of competition. Unfortunately, most people on the left and the right inherit flawed concepts and flawed conceptual models that keep them trapped in flawed thinking and prevent them from seeing reality for what it really is. This is especially true in disciplines like economics, where social theories posing as science can lead to tyranny, economic collapse, or even death camps. The economist John Maynard Keynes made one of the most prescient quotes regarding this phenomenon, despite being seen by many as one of the people he criticized.

> The ideas of economists and political philosophers, both when they are right and when they are wrong, are more powerful than is commonly understood. Indeed, the world is ruled by little else. Practical men, who believe themselves to be quite exempt from any intellectual influences, are usually slaves of some defunct economist.

The fact that we inherit a conceptual model with a long history (over hundreds or thousands of years) often means is has worked; it is not 100% correct forever just because it once worked, and it is not false just because it is old. And we most certainly should never throw out the baby with the bathwater in the name of revolution unless we have a better solution to offer in its place, a problem we are still living with as a result of the flower children of the 1960s. As I addressed in the chapter on human nature, it is precisely these flawed concepts and conceptual models that lock us into left and right ideologies. Therefore, to avoid leaving the reader with a tidy six chapters broken down into two parts, with two fundamental institutions and four pillars, I will take this opportunity to address a variety of other topics (Parerga and Paralipomena) in a less formal way to put some additional meat on the bones of my theory.

In the spirit of honesty, I will begin with a critique of the historical so-called conservative or so-called Republican position. As a former College Republican, I accepted without question most of the so-called conservative core beliefs that were promoted (as do many people regarding their own political beliefs), but I have since had time to take a more systematic approach. What I have found over the years is that some of the core beliefs have a weak foundation and some of the core beliefs have a stronger foundation than I originally had imagined. For example, I now see that monogamous procreation is one of the keys to social stability and personal fulfillment, whereas I once thought people were crazy to get married and raise children. After I cleaned up the hard drive and let the dust settle, to mix metaphors, what I was left with was what most people would consider a moderate right political philosophy, with the understanding that *a political philosophy is as much about having correct beliefs as it is about establishing a system of social values that has the best chance of keeping individuals and society on the right path of organic growth and maturity*, which will allow us to flourish with a life of virtue.

Mea Culpa

Conservatives often accuse liberals of being naïve about human nature (too much hope and change), which is sometimes an accurate criticism; the same goes for many conservatives, however, but in a different way. If we look at the history of so-called conservative ideas related to liberty and free markets, there should be no doubt that most of the regular people who espoused these ideas really believed them and wanted to live by them, such as liberty and free markets, but there should also be no doubt that some people used these ideas to justify their corrupt or criminal activities or to perpetuate their favored positions or privileges within society.

Hold your breath, but many of Marx's observations were accurate and insightful. Rather than being free societies based on liberty and true capitalism, many societies during the middle of the nineteenth century when Marx wrote were driven by patrimony, clientelism, cronyism, exploitation, and corruption, which made positive social change difficult to achieve, and for which we owe a debt of gratitude to the Marxists. The rich people who controlled the banking system and bribed government officials while Marx was writing often did invoke concepts like "free trade" and "free markets" to justify their grip on the economy. In theory, every person was free to do as he or she pleased, but when a few families at the top (oligarchy) controlled the universities, government institutions, and major corporations, there was no doubt that their own children would succeed in the game of life, often with special favors and at the expense of others, even if they would not win in a game with fair competition. That is, rather than merely shower their children with economic benefits to give them a leg up on the competition, which will happen in any free society, they possessed unchallenged *political power* that allowed them to control the outcome of the game. The system was set up to prevent new families from rising up in the power game, often in the name of "conservative" values.

Having lived, worked, and traveled in different countries throughout Latin America, Europe, and Asia, I saw the same story over and over. A small group of families had a lock on power and invoked so-called conservative principles to justify their positions and privileges, such as "free markets," "free trade," or even religious beliefs that emphasized obedience to authority, all the while using the military to prevent uprisings by the poor masses. These poor masses, because they were born with an innate sense (teleology) of justice and equal rights, eventually reacted by turning to communist ideology to fight back. With time, reactionary leftist movements formed around the world (reactionary to the people who were oppressing them), which usually triggered a violent backlash from the powers that be. The narrative is similar in each country, with a series of military dictatorships—in many cases supported by the USA, as painful as it might be for us to admit—delaying the inevitable, until free and fair elections are held that eventually result in victory for the masses, which more often than not results in the new government turning to corruption, theft, and constitutional changes to ensure its own grip power—wash, rinse, repeat.

The reason for this is that these (mostly leftist) movements were focused on defeating the existing system in a dialectical way, not on reforming the system to help us find our social teleology. Many of their leaders wanted their time at the trough to line their pockets before retirement, at least the ones who rose up within the party power structure. I have lost track of the number of rich conservatives in Latin America who told me about how hard they have worked or how economic success depends on free markets. The truth is that many of them did not work all that hard to get where they are and many of them equate free markets with the survival of their own companies, which often have a monopolistic grip on the local economy. I have also grown tired of revolutionary leftists who talk about how they want to help the poor but often behave in ways that are worse than the oligarchs they defeated to assume political power. Then as now, both sides invoke noble philosophical principles to justify their quest for power, but the ideas have no substance—all propaganda. The goal of political philosophy should be to escape this dialectical narrative of rationalizations (thesis, antithesis, synthesis) and start living by abstract principles that keep the game as fair for everyone as possible, without violating the rights of individuals and with the understanding that we should have no preconceptions that equality of opportunity will result in equality of outcomes. The children of rich parents will continue to have advantages over the children of poor parents because parents have the right to pass their legally acquired wealth to their children, and society will reserve the right to help poor children.

Many conservatives in the USA probably are not familiar with how the conservative platform around the world and throughout history has been used to justify what is often immoral or criminal behavior, but many people on the left are aware of it and often unfairly invoke the "exploitation" or "colonialism" models to justify their activities. There is no doubt that some conservatives use buzzwords like "free markets" and "liberty" to justify their activities, such as Wall Street banks getting bailed out or energy companies receiving subsidies, or because they are unaware of their own privileged status, but nothing like what we still see today in Latin America or other regions. For example, anyone who believes big banks on Wall Street are not abusing the system in the name of "free markets," such as getting bailed out by the Federal Reserve and Congress or using 0% interest rates to make risk-free gains in the stock market, is missing the big picture and places far too much trust in people who do not deserve it.

The problem with many on the far left is that they are still trapped in this revolutionary narrative of the common man fighting the oligarchy, whereas most conservatives are not even aware of this narrative or have tossed it aside as a sad relic of the past. Many on the far left do not seem to recognize that their ideology is reactionary, and that their obsession with tearing down the powers that be is preventing them from seeing the big picture, or from helping society grow and develop by refining the idea of promoting the free exchange of goods and services. That is, we can recognize that some people are invoking conservative principles for nefarious reasons, *but this does not mean the principles are false.* Does anyone seriously believe we should not have liberty or that one central government can micromanage a $17 trillion economy with over 330 million people living in over 50 different states and territories, especially when we live in a federal system that grants most powers to the states? Ironically, there is now a movement in California, that bastion of liberal thought, to break California down into smaller states because—get this—California is too big to manage! Liberty means that each individual shall have the right to decide how to live his or her life, even if that means giving up the revolution to focus on more mundane things like working, paying the bills, and making sure the kids finish their homework before going to bed. If so, then we have to abandon all hopes of creating a Utopia or a state that interferes in our daily lives to the point where it sucks away our ability to produce wealth. Likewise, does anyone seriously believe that we should not try to keep government as small as possible while at the same time providing the basic services we all need? Does Apple hire as many accountants as possible or as many as it needs to handle the accounting? We should never forget that government is a service provider, in much the same way that we pay someone to change the oil in our car. We grant certain powers and authorities to the government that we would not grant to the person who changes our oil, for sure, but we have to drop the belief that there is an enlightened group of people out there capable of leading us to the Promised Land. We are "they."

I could address other points, such as how conservative ideas were used to justify racist policies or how conservatives opposed universal suffrage, universal education, eliminating child labor, or the 40-hour work week, but we should not forget that the people who invoked these ideas were stealing conservative ideas for their own selfish purposes, to "vote their interest"; they were not using them as a philosopher would. The true conservative philosophy really is compassionate and really does believe that conservative ideas can be used to create prosperity for as many people as possible. Thus, with this mea culpa for the history of some false conservative prophets, we can wipe the slate clean and develop our genuine conservative ideas in a way that are designed for everyone, not to protect our own interests. Any political philosophy that begins with the adage "vote your interest" has no place in rational discussion.

Taxes

In many ways, the battle between left and right boils down to the collection of taxes. We all agree that we need government and a modern state that is capable and autonomous, but how big should it be, what should it do, and how should we pay for it? These are the questions that matter. If we are to believe the left, government spending is too low, relative to other countries, and the rich are not paying their "fair share" of the taxes, but the facts say otherwise. If we begin with the fact that U.S. GDP for 2012 was about $16.2 trillion, we see that tax revenue and government spending were as follows:

2012 Tax Revenue		2012 Government Spending	
Local:	$1.1 trillion	Local	$1.6 trillion
State	$1.4 trillion	State	$1.5 trillion
Federal	$2.5 trillion	Federal	$3.5 trillion
Total	$5.0 trillion	Total	$6.1 trillion*
	30.9% of GDP		37.7% of GDP

* Less intergovernmental spending.[1]

---

1 www.usgovernmentrevenue.com and www.usgovernmentspending.com.

To put this in perspective, according to the Social Security Administration, in the USA in 2012 there were 153,632,290 workers who earned $6.53 trillion, with an arithmetic mean of $42,498 and a median of $27,519. The most noticeable gap in the above chart is the $1 trillion deficit between revenue and spending at the local and federal level and the near lack of net deficit spending at the state level. It is worth noting again that a prohibition on deficit spending is a rational policy based on the first fundamental institution of political philosophy (resource management) and would strike a decisive blow to the corrupt elements on the left and rights sides of the political spectrum at the local, state, and federal level. It would also prevent the interest payments of our ballooning debts from eating away at our ability to grow the economy. You can ignore the apocalyptic fear mongering from people who decry austerity, balanced budgets, and living within our means. Deficit spending is the reason we are in this position in the first place. We will eventually have to pay the piper, even if that means years of pain and suffering now to avoid collapse later. Not only that, it would require us to regain the discipline necessary to promote economic growth. It does not mean government spending cannot increase or that the government cannot issue debt, but it does mean that an increase in government spending should be the result of economic growth and additional tax revenue, not of deficit spending. And we should not believe that we can stimulate the economy by spending more tax dollars because we collect tax dollars by removing them from the economy—like siphoning your own gas to fill your own gas tank—which by definition limits growth. (Of course, some government spending, such as building infrastructure, can stimulate economic grow, as long as we use wealth, not deficit spending, to pay for it.) With these numbers in mind, we should look at how the USA compares to other G-20 countries for total government expenditures as a percentage of GDP.[1]

Country	Tax Burden	Government Expenditures
Argentina	34.6%	40.9%
Australia	25.6%	35.3%
Brazil	34.8%	39.1%
Canada	31.0%	41.9%
China	19.0%	23.9%
France	44.2%	56.1%
Germany	37.1%	45.4%
India	7.0%	27.2%

1 2014 Index of Economic Freedom, www.heritage.org.

Indonesia	11.8%	18.5%
Italy	2.9%	49.8%
Japan	27.6%	42.0%
Mexico	10.6%	26.6%
Russia	29.5%	35.8%
Saudi Arabia	3.7%	35.1%
South Africa	27.3%	32.1%
South Korea	25.9%	30.2%
Turkey	25.0%	34.9%
United Kingdom	35.5%	48.5%
USA	25.1%	41.6%

I selected the G-20 countries for government expenditures as a percentage of GDP from the report because these are the 20 largest economies in the world, which includes both relatively wealthy and relatively poor countries. As I addressed in the chapter on institutions, it does not make sense to compare large countries to small countries when talking about the size of the government (as a percentage of GDP) any more than it makes sense to compare large companies to small companies. At some point, we reach the point of diminishing returns and the various institutions can handle more people with minimal additional expenses. For example, as the economy grows and military spending stays stable, military spending as a percentage of GDP will decrease even if the actual spending increases. No doubt, many people will demand that we compare ourselves to small countries in northern Europe, but we will not allow their apples and oranges comparison in this context to cloud our analysis (although I will compare us to them in a different context). As should be clear from the data, the USA is definitely on the high end of the spectrum for total government expenditures as a percentage of GDP. Therefore, the argument that our government desperately needs to spend an even larger percentage of GDP does not hold water. Anyone who makes this claim has not looked at the numbers or does not care about math. My guess is that many people would be surprised to know how large our government expenditures are relative to other countries, probably because many sources do not include local or state taxes when making the calculation. Rather than focus on how to spend even more tax dollars, which will eventually damage the economy, if it has not done so already, we should focus on cutting out waste and spending our money more wisely, which would probably reduce government spending, especially if we were to prohibit deficit spending.

Shifting to the tax burden and the claimed need of the wealthy to pay their "fair share," this might be a good sound bite for crowds that do not understand math, but the facts clearly show otherwise. Beginning with Social Security and Medicare, which are called "taxes," we should remember that the money collected for these programs is earmarked for the people paying into them—not directly, of course, like a 401(k) investment account—but they will know the benefits in advance. (I refer the reader to the discussion of defined benefit versus defined contribution retirement programs in the chapter on the prohibition on deficit spending.) This money is not used to fund federal programs, such as defense spending or education. Some people highlight that the poor and middle-class pay their "fair share" of federal taxes because they contribute to these two programs. What they fail to acknowledge is that many or most of the poor and middle-class people who pay into these two programs will receive more in benefits than they pay in during their lives, which makes the program a net drain on the federal budget, not a net contribution to the federal budget. That is, the argument could be made that these programs are entitlements and wealth redistribution, not a tax burden.

I would never begrudge anyone's participating in these programs, but we should all be clear that we are not contributing to anyone other than ourselves (in the future) by paying into them now. We are not contributing to national defense, the federal courts, or other federal programs by paying into Social Security or Medicare. They are paternalistic, mandatory retirement programs, so there is nothing hypocritical about Republicans demanding their social security checks, although there is something inconsistent about demanding more money than was paid into the system. Given that roughly 50% of the federal budget is for Social Security and Medicare, this means that roughly 50% of the federal budget consists of mandatory retirement programs, not spending on institutions or social programs. The biggest problem with these two programs, as I discussed before, is that the decisions being made to regulate them are often driven by politics, and only secondarily by math or actuarial charts, evidenced by the growing insolvency of the programs. Finally, I should note that many taxes also get paid at the local and state level. To the extent that poor, middle-class, and others pay these taxes they are most certainly contributing to government programs, and their contribution to these programs should be duly recognized.

Shifting to federal income taxes, many on the left have finally, albeit quietly, acknowledged that the wealthy in the USA pay the vast majority of federal income taxes. According to the National Taxpayers Union, in 2009 the top 1% paid 36.73% of federal income tax revenue, with the top 5% paying 58.66%, the top 10% paying 70.47%, the top 25% paying 87.30%, and the top 50% paying 97.75%, which means the bottom 50% contributes (net) only 2.25% of the federal income tax bill. To repeat, this does not include Social Security and Medicare. These numbers are irrefutable and available to everyone, yet the rhetoric from the left still suggests that the wealthy still are not paying their "fair share." According to an Organization for Economic Cooperation and Development (OECD) study, the United States "has the most progressive tax system and collects the largest share of taxes from the richest 10% of the population," and that the U.S. stands out as "achieving greater redistribution through the tax system than through cash transfers."[1] So much for the claim that the top 10% are not paying their "fair share." The numbers for the tax burden of the top 10% in each c ountry, from the same report, are telling:

	Share of Taxes	Share of Income	Ratio
USA	45.1%	33.5%	1.35
Ireland	39.1%	30.9%	1.26
Italy	42.2%	35.8%	1.18
Australia	36.8%	28.6%	1.29
United Kingdom	38.6%	32.3%	1.20
New Zealand	35.9%	30.3%	1.19
Canada	35.8%	29.3%	1.22
Netherlands	35.2%	27.5%	1.28
Czech Republic	34.3%	29.4%	1.17
Germany	31.2%	29.2%	1.07
OECD-24	31.6%	28.4%	1.11
Finland	32.3%	26.9%	1.20
Slovak Republic	32.0%	28.0%	1.14
Luxembourg	30.3%	26.4%	1.15
Belgium	25.4%	27.1%	0.94
Austria	28.5%	26.1%	1.10
South Korea	27.4%	23.4%	1.17
Poland	28.3%	33.9%	0.84
Japan	28.5%	28.1%	1.01
Norway	27.4%	28.9%	0.95
France	28.0%	25.5%	1.10
Denmark	26.2%	25.7%	1.02
Sweden	26.7%	26.6%	1.00
Iceland	21.6%	24.0%	0.90
Switzerland	20.9%	23.5%	0.89

---

1 "Growing Unequal? Income Distribution and Poverty in OECD Countries," 2008.

As should be clear from the chart, the top 10% in the Unites States earns a large percentage of the national income (33.5%, which is second only to Italy at 35.8%) but pays a disproportionately larger tax burden, both in absolute terms (45.1%) and as a ratio of their share of their income (1.35). What this means, however painful it might be for many people to swallow, is that *the top 10% of income earners in the USA are the most heavily taxed group in the entire OECD.* I attribute this as much to the actual tax burden of the top 10% as to the limited tax burden on the bottom 50%. I should highlight that all of the admired Scandinavian countries are below the OECD average, with the top 10% in Norway, a darling of the left, earning 28.9% of the national income but paying only 27.4% of the taxes (compared to 45.1% for the United States), for a ratio of less than 1.00, less than their "fair share." How could the top 10% in the USA carry the heaviest tax burden in the OECD but the left continues to spout a false narrative about the rich not paying their "fair share" of taxes? The answer is that clever people on the left know full well that the top 10% pay far more than their fair share but also know full well that this false message resonates with their voter base to win elections. However, nothing speaks louder than facts, so I encourage everyone on the left and the right to look at the numbers before making conclusions.

Given that this book is not an apologetics for the rich—quite the contrary—we should take a closer look at some legitimate tax issues that should be raised. There probably is some truth to the claim that rich people designed the tax system for the benefit of rich people, so you would be wise to learn the rules of the game and play by them. In fact, many of the good books on the topic highlight that the tax system is designed to benefit people who accumulate and transfer wealth from one generation to the next via the institution of monogamous procreation, which is telling. If this is what the elite teach themselves, why is it not taught in our public schools? For example, as any book on investing will tell you, the single worst way to make money is earned income (due to the requirement to pay Social Security and Medicare taxes), which is how most working class people make money. Why is this not taught in our public schools? Far better ways to earn money include long-term capital gains, dividends, passive income from real estate, and royalties, which is how rich people make most of their money. Why is this not taught in our public schools? The left would be wise to promote financial education for all children. Bickering about the marginal income tax rate for the rich will not address any fundamental issues, even though the rich pay the majority of federal income taxes.

One solution to achieve fairness would be to treat all income the same, regardless of the type. Thus, people in the top tax bracket would pay the top tax rate for all income, not only earned income. Why should someone in the

39% tax bracket pay only 20% on long-term capital gains? Not to mention, the tax laws provide incentives to the rich to avoid earned income, so they will focus their efforts in other areas that have a lower tax burden, which we should expect from any rational person who seeks to minimize his tax burden in accordance with the law. Many rich people will argue that we need low taxes on capital gains to encourage investment, but low-income people would pay lower taxes because they are in a lower tax bracket. Not to mention, when someone buys a share of stock, the money goes to the person who sold the stock, not to the company, so the buying and selling of stocks on an exchange does not directly affect the cash flow of the companies and is therefore not an "investment" in the company in the sense that it does not provide them a new source of cash to invest in new projects. Companies receive new injections of cash (investment capital) only during an Initial Public Offering (IPO), subsequent equity offerings, or bond issuances. Why is this not taught in our public schools? Thus, my advice to the left is that you are barking up the wrong tree with marginal income tax rates. If we were to treat all income the same, there would be a dramatic shift in the way rich people work and invest their money, which would probably have a mixture of positive or negative consequences for the economy.

Diversity

One of the signature ideas on the left these days is diversity. It certainly sounds good and feels good, right? Who could be opposed to diversity? We live in a diverse world and are a nation of immigrants. Besides, the opposite of diversity is university (a deliberate play on words). The concept of diversity is one of those ideas that probably had good intentions from the beginning but has since transmogrified into what it is today: a mechanism to receive unfair benefits, which is precisely what the left should fight against. In other words, just as some conservatives have wrongly invoked conservative ideas like free markets to justify questionable activity on the right side of the political spectrum, there are people on the left side of the political spectrum who have invoked good ideas for questionable purposes as well. And just as the mere fact that people are misusing concepts on the left does not mean the concept is false or should be eliminated, we should use a scalpel to excise the misused part of the concept so that all that remains is the original concept in its purest form.

To dive right in, if we keep in mind that every person on the planet except a white male generally counts as "diversity," in the current parlance, then it should be clear what the left hopes to achieve with diversity: tearing down the so-called institution of "white male privilege." There is some merit to this goal if you believe that white men have abused the system or have received unfair benefits, but like many concepts along a spectrum, we can sometimes overshoot or ignore the fact that many of these white males received their money or benefits from their parents, not from the government, which is a legitimate way to transfer wealth. The primary concern should be taking steps to ensure that no one receives unfair political power, that is, the authority to coerce people to act—the separation of politics and economics.

Even if we grant to the left that old white men have traditionally wielded power, both economic and political, at least in Western Civilization, it should be clear that the goal of diversity (for the most radical elements, at least) is not to level the playing field or to make the game fair for all, but to give special treatment or privileges to everyone except white males, to create their own special club with benefits and privileges. For example, from 1950 to the present, the labor force participation rate for white men over 20 has dropped from 90% to 70%, but we do not hear anyone talking about the crisis of white males losing jobs or how to fix it. If we keep in mind that even conservative thinkers like Nozick recognized the importance of rectifying injustices of the past, there is nothing wrong with leveling the playing field, if by that we mean making sure the game if fair and that no one receives special treatment from the government. (Many people will receive special treatment from their own families or kinship networks because it is their right to spend their money as they wish, so we will not address that again here.) For example, if a university or government agency were to give special preferences to white males, as a matter of policy, this would not be fair. I as a white male would be opposed to any such policy and would refuse to study or work there. However, if you remove "white male" from the previous sentence and replace it with "minority," it somehow sounds reasonable and noble to some people. The hypocrisy is staring us in the face.

One of the biggest problems with the word "diversity" is that it is misleading. A good concept was stolen and distorted to achieve political objectives (black magic concept), just as some people have stolen good conservative concepts to justify their actions. If we think about diversity in the abstract, we should think of things like diversity of personality, beliefs, talents, or academic background. For example, we know that many groups benefit from having a diversity of personality types, such introverts and extroverts, or thinkers or feelers, and so on. We do not want a room full of type-A personalities making all the decisions that will affect an entire institution, especially if the type-A personalities are a small segment of the institution. Or, if we want to discuss a particular project, such as a school or a water treatment facility, the discussion would probably benefit from having a diversity of people on the left and the right side of the political spectrum to ensure the project is looked at from a variety of perspectives. One side or the other might win in the end, but at least all ideas were heard. Or, if a company wants to develop a new product, such as a smart phone, the team would probably benefit from having a diversity of academic backgrounds, such as people from engineering and the liberal arts, to ensure the technical and aesthetic ideas work together. All of these scenarios make sense and give the word diversity the respect it deserves. There are also many scenarios in which having diversity is not a good thing, such as creating a government. Do we really want a mixture of radical left and radical right ideas to define how we write our constitution, or would we not benefit more from a university of ideas in the middle of the political spectrum?

If we dig a little deeper, we see that social change is slow and that we might have to take some proactive measures to get us moving in the right direction, to rectify injustices of the past, which even conservatives like Nozick acknowledge is important. For example, if a particular group of people, such as the bottom of the socio-economic pyramid (regardless of race, gender, etc.), traditionally never applies for certain universities or jobs because they do not view themselves as competitive, perhaps because they lack role models or perhaps because their diet or education prevent them from being competitive, we could take some reasonable steps to improve their education and encourage the most qualified people in these groups to apply to break the cycle. For example, if a poor person sees his neighbor get accepted to Harvard or the Air Force Academy, this might create positive momentum as young people in the community gain inspiration and try to follow in the person's footsteps—positive role models.

We could take this to the next level by understanding that marginalized groups might have lower academics standards for systematic reasons and that the bar might have to be lowered just a bit (without announcing it) as a way to gain momentum. People who achieve top 10% status in a poor neighborhood cannot always be compared to people who have similar test scores in a wealthy neighborhood but who might test at the 30% level. This all makes sense and I defer to all the voters around the country to make rational decisions along these lines, keeping in mind that there are many poor white males who need help and many middle-class minorities who do not. But we must also never forget that any wider perception that a particular group is being selected with lower standards, specifically because they are a minority group, not due to their socioeconomic status, would cause more harm than good because this would remove the incentive to work harder and because this would create resentment from other groups who are not being given special treatment. Also, there is a legal issue that prevents discrimination or preferable treatment due to race, gender, or other protected categories, so many of these programs violate the principle of fairness they seek to promote.

In theory, we could promote diversity as a social value (after all, no one has a right to a particular job or to attend a particular university), but then we have to explain why it is morally right or just. Why should skin color, as opposed to personality type, be a legitimate basis for selection? Two wrongs do not make a right, so if you are opposed to white men receiving special treatment, you should be opposed to minorities receiving special treatment. As always, good intentions do not suffice.

When we start introducing words like gender and race to the discussion, it is not clear how these variables, on their own, contribute to diversity. Gender can contribute, I suppose, such as a discussion about procreation and family, but never race because the mere fact that someone belongs to a particular race contributes nothing to diversity in and of itself, unless the argument is made that different races have innate differences that are not linked to culture and affect how they think and behave, which would require some empirical evidence. Some people talk about the importance of our institutions reflecting the diversity of our population, such as not having an all-white police force in a city that is predominantly African-American, which is fine, but it should be with the understanding that qualified African-Americans are applying to be police officers. We can encourage qualified people to apply for jobs but we cannot and should not force people to apply for jobs. Given the dearth of conservative college professors, I would be interested to hear what the left would think about making a concerted effort to make universities more diverse by hiring more conservative professors at the expense of liberal professors, to better reflect the diversity of our country. I attended a fairly liberal college that had a relatively diverse student body, by Minnesota standards, but what was lacking most was a diversity of ideas. I knew many groups of students that included different races and genders, but most of them thought exactly the same way—the emotional, left-wing idealism that is typical of so many college students and often fades with age as reality set in. Regardless of the issue, I could predict with precision exactly how they would respond to any issue, and when they met as a group they immediately reached consensus because they all thought the same way. Talk about a lack of diversity. On the other hand, when I joined the Air Force, what many people probably consider a bastion of conformity, I can truly say it was one of the most interesting and diverse groups I have ever had the pleasure of working with. With uniform standards for dress, we judged each person by the content of his or her character because that was the only way to distinguish ourselves, regardless of race, gender, beliefs, educational background, or profession.

Human nature being what it is, what probably started out as a good idea has taken a wrong turn. There is no doubt that the word diversity is being used to justify the same types of decisions that were decried regarding white males. The same people who fought against white male privilege are now celebrating minority privilege. Minorities—some, not all—are being selected for positions because of their race or gender, which in many ways defeats the entire principle of what the left has been fighting for—fairness. The rational thing would have been to prevent white males from being selected because they were white males (that is, fix the problem) and then open up everything to free and fair competition, but we have unfortunately crossed a line where people will continue to invoke "diversity" to shame and silence people, with no concern for any of the poor white males who might be left behind.

For many years people bemoaned the fact that most college students were men, which was no doubt due to social and systematic factors that they were right to challenge. However, now that women make up the majority of college students, in some cases by as much as a 10% margin over males, no one is talking about this particular gender gap. Why are women celebrating this inequality? Why are they not promoting a "fair distribution" of slots in colleges for men? The answer is obvious. The intention was never to attain equality. It was to create a power structure similar to the ones used in the past by white males to justify selecting their own. It is no surprise that feminist philosophy focuses on power. Just as many politicians in Latin America are using the leftist banner to win elections and enrich themselves, while the masses continue to live in poverty and misery, many people realize that they can further their career, contrary to fairness, by invoking diversity. We hear a lot about the benefits of diversity and the need for diversity committees run by diverse people to ensure that we have enough diversity, but I am still waiting for the evidence to show the tangible benefits of diversity for society as a whole. As the education bubble bursts and college education experiences a major transformation, some of these artificial social rewards will go away, but we would all benefit from rethinking the idea of diversity now.

Radical Feminism

We all owe a debt of gratitude to the left for its efforts over the decades to ensure equal rights for women. I have to admit, if the far right (the false conservatives, that is) had had its way, women still might not have the right to vote, but that is speculation because social forces other than left-wing activism were already moving society in that direction. Before the left cheers too much, we should remember that social institutions develop slowly over time, and that change is often difficult—institutions are "sticky"—even if the need for change is obvious to all. This is why it took so long to eliminate slavery. If we embrace the basic concept of rights for all, rather than rights specific for women or other groups, which can never move us in a positive direction, then it makes sense to say that women should not be forced to marry someone they do not want to marry, that they should not be forced to have babies when they do not want to have them, that they should not be prevented from voting or going to school, that they should not be prevented from working, and so on, while at the same time holding them to a reasonable standard regarding monogamous procreation (just as we should hold men to a reasonable standard), but as is often the case, the radical feminists resort to irrational arguments anytime someone challenges their ideas.

The fundamental error of radical feminism is the conclusion that because the men who suppressed them for so long had a flawed view of women, then *everything* about that flawed view, from soup to nuts, must also be wrong, reversed in the opposite direction, and pushed to the opposite extreme. For example, because men expected women to have many babies and to raise them, usually at the expense of an education or a career, the radical feminist concludes, incorrectly, that having babies was therefore not in any way essential to her nature, an unfortunate part of life that men obsessed about and can therefore be ignored without any consequences. Because the view was part of the flawed view of men, it can be dismissed completely. This logic is obviously flawed.

Even if men intentionally created an unfair system with bad intentions, as judged from our eyes today, we should never forget that the unfair system might have been a matter of survival at one point in our history. For example, given that the number of children who died before reaching adulthood hundreds or thousands of years ago, it should not surprise us that the societies that survived were the ones that took steps to ensure that women had enough babies to ensure the survival of society, which most likely involved, let's be honest, some coercion. After all, childbirth is a painful process, so it is unlikely that most women would eagerly agree to have 12 or more babies. The societies that did not do this probably died out. The societies that had many babies probably continued doing it because that was how thing were always done. Given that few men were educated in these times, it should not surprise anyone that educating women was not a priority. People do what they have to do to survive. Given that it takes 2.11 babies per woman to sustain a population in a modern state, women in tribal or less developed societies would need to have many more babies, if we assume many might die before reaching adulthood. With a life expectancy of about 35 years for most of human history, this means that most women would have to start having babies in their teens and not stop until almost death just for their society to avoid extinction. This was a matter of survival, not a matter of oppression, even if oppression was used. I doubt the social rules were driven by malice or spite, but they might have transformed into a way to control women. Many people today, living in the luxury of a modern state, seem to not realize just how brutal life was for most people throughout history or the sacrifices that were made. We ought not to forget the hundreds of millions of women who dedicated their lives to procreation so that we might live today, just as we ought not to forget the hundreds of millions of men who fought wars so that we might live in peace today.

Granted, now that we have progressed to a modern state with a life expectancy that has more than doubled and an infant mortality rate that has plummeted, we have the luxury of placing fewer demands on women, but we should never forget that the historical pressures on women made the modern state possible, just as the historical pressures on men, such as facing an early grave by working in coal mines, made the modern state possible. The path to civilization is best forgotten or transformed into mythology. The $64,000 question is what minimal steps we should take today to prevent from slipping back into a situation where the old model returns and women have to start having many more babies again to avoid extinction. As we see in many modern states today, the fertility rate is dropping to dangerously low levels, as low as 1.3 children per woman for some European countries. (Those who believe the world population is too large might consider this a good thing, as long as you accept that the pension funds for the elderly will implode at some point.) As noted before, a modern state needs a fertility rate of 2.11 to sustain the population, so assuming that we want to at least sustain our population, it is not unreasonable to structure our society in such a way as to promote these results, such as providing incentives for monogamous procreation. If we can educate children to get jobs and pay taxes, why can we not also steer them in the right direction for monogamous procreation to avoid predictable social problems, such as the correlation between broken families and poverty? We obviously do not want to compel people to have babies, even though we have no problem compelling them to go to school or to pay taxes, but I think an educational program that addresses the importance of having children, for the benefit of society and for personal fulfillment, not to tickle our fancy, would help, especially a curriculum that encourages— nay, demands—that men and women be held responsible for all of the babies they bring into the world, even at the expense of their own happiness. The obvious way to do this is to sanctify monogamous procreation.

If I could identify one area where the radical feminists have caused damage to society, it is in making women believe that the monogamous procreation model is tantamount to failure.

> Being a housewife is an illegitimate profession...The choice to serve
> and be protected and plan towards being a family-maker is a choice
> that shouldn't be. The heart of radical feminism is to change that.
>
> —Vivian Gornick

> The nuclear family must be destroyed...Whatever its ultimate
> meaning, the break-up of families now is an objectively revolutionary
> process.
>
> —Linda Gordon

The list of similar quotes from radical feminists is endless, and they all have one thing in common: tearing down the sanctity of monogamous procreation between men and women and the rational gender roles that tend to follow from such a social institution. That is, radical feminists clearly do not like the second fundamental institution of political philosophy regarding the sanctity of monogamous procreation. In fact, I would argue that attacking monogamous procreation is the primary objective of radical feminism because this is one of the most fundamental issues of the political debate. Whoever wins this issue wins the debate and determines what path we will take as a society. Sadly, many women buy the radical feminist agenda (or refuse to fight against it) and feel ashamed about embracing their maternal side or wanting to start a family. Over the years, women have told me privately that other women have verbally harassed them about their plans to stop working after the baby is born, as if taking care of a baby is not legitimate work. My own wife has received many cold shoulders when it was learned that she was "just" a stay-at-home mother, even though she was running home-based businesses that involved more talent and creativity than many of the office jobs many of these women had. In fact, the early radical feminists knew full well that most women, left to their own devices—that is, if they were to base their choice on genuine and honest reflection—would choose monogamous procreation, just as most normal men would, which is why the radical feminists opted for a shock-and-awe platform to shame women into compliance. Oddly enough, the things that most women have complained about men since the beginning of time—war, power, profits—are the same things radical feminists now celebrate, such as women in combat, anything to show that male and female gender roles are the result of socialization, not of innate differences. We are seeing the negative consequences of these ideas in our schools, which reward children for compliantly sitting in their seats, which comes more natural to girls, and punish other forms of behavior that are more natural for boys, which explains the surge of academic success girls are having and the number of boys who are prescribed ADHD drugs. Rather than accept the raw material of boys and take the disciplined approach of shaping their character (teleology) over several years, the current system judges the behavior of boys as abnormal and as something to be suppressed or medicated. If we consider that helping boys make the transition to adulthood is one of the most important and difficult challenges of any society, then it should be clear that this will not end well. Underlying all of this, unfortunately, is the fact that we as a society have not valued motherhood the way we should. As a result, it should not be a surprise when many women are less than eager to be a traditional mother and instead look for social recognition in other ways.

At the end of the day, each woman will have to decide what her priorities will be, with whom she will procreate, how they will divide the work of raising their children, and so on, but we should not be so foolish as to think that men and women are equally suited to raising children. (Ask a room full of women whether men are equally suited and you will hear uproarious laughter.) Just as we should tap into the natural altruism that exists between parents and children, we should also tap into the natural bond that exists between mother and child when making a rational plan for how to produce the next generation. We can argue until we are blue in the face about whether life is fair, but anyone who believes a father can replicate the love of a mother is living in denial, just as anyone who believes a single mother can make up for the role of a father is living in denial. As all fathers know, mothers have an internal strength and a bond with children that no man can ever hope to match, something that should give women a deep sense of joy and pride, as it does for most mothers I know. Does this mean women should be barefoot and pregnant in the kitchen? Of course not, but why go to extremes? Does it mean mothers will play a role in the life of the children that fathers never will? Yes. What a mother and a father decide to do about this is up to them.

The odd part is that many people do not embrace this simple fact of life, as we would embrace any natural talent or ability. We are reluctant to have a public discussion about which genders are better at different roles, although we laugh about it all the time in the steady stream of romantic comedies. I would think that being better at raising children would be something to celebrate and define who we are, especially given that raising children is one of the most satisfying and important things that most of us will do during our short lives. On a practical level, the families that tap into these natural forces, on average, will do better than the families that do not, which will give their own children advantages over other children that they will deserve, as long as they pay the debt forward. This is why I propose that we sanctify monogamous procreation within society. If we do not, not only will we continue to see high divorce rates and broken families, with many of them living on welfare, which creates a vicious cycle of poverty, we will create a divide between those who raise traditional families and those who do not. The people who use a kinship network model and have the discipline that goes with it will create a virtuous cycle of wealth creation, which will give their children a better education, which will lead to better jobs and better income, and so on. At some point, the radical feminists will have to look in the mirror, recognize that they are not motivated by love or compassion, and recognize that the union of one man and one woman for the purpose of procreation is the pinnacle of the rational human life.

Education

As I already addressed, both the left and the right sides of the political spectrum value education, especially for their own children, but the two sides often do not see the issue the same way. The right side of the political spectrum tends to view education as a process of honing our relatively fixed nature over a process of many years, which takes us back to the perfectionist teleology of Aristotle. It is no surprise that aristocrats throughout the ages have aspired to the classical virtues and a life of rational reflection—they studied Aristotle's *Nicomachean Ethics*—which they believed separated them from the masses, whom they assessed were ruled by their passions. Naturally, the wealthiest people have used the educational system to their advantage by sending their own children to elite schools and by offering them jobs at their own elite businesses (jobs they probably would receive even if they did not attend elite schools), but this is a fact of life that we will have to accept in a free society, as long as they do not use the government to support their agenda. As long as wealthy families have the right to spend their money as they wish, which should never change while acquiring wealth legally, they will find a way to give their kids a leg up on the competition in terms of education. But we should not forget that the wealthy spend so much money on education precisely because they understand the value of a good education for shaping character. They are less worried about giving their kids opportunities, because they know their children will inherit their wealth and businesses, and are more worried about intellectual and moral development.

Shifting to the left side of the political spectrum, they have a different approach to education that focuses on ideology and opportunity. I defer to the social scientists for the specifics, but anyone who has met teachers knows that the majority of them vote Democrat. Why? I will not speculate too much aside from saying that teaching apparently resonates with people on the left side of the political spectrum, and, dare I say, they view it as a way to shape the minds of the next generation. It is true that the educational system needed some reforms during the past 200 years, and certainly we owe many of those reforms to the good people on the left, but reforming and pushing an ideology are two different things. I have lost count of the numbers of news stories I have read about teachers pushing a left-wing agenda and attacking anyone on the right who has the courage to speak up. I have no doubt that their hearts are in the right place and that many mean no harm, but they should keep in mind that the good taxpayers do not care what they believe and do not want those beliefs imposed on their children, especially if they are going to hide behind unions and tenure to prevent an honest dialog.

The first flaw of the left regarding education is their belief in the extreme plasticity of human nature (their rejection of teleology), which they believe education plays a key role in shaping. Rather than seeing humans as having a relatively fixed nature that is fulfilled by developing the classical virtues (teleology), the left tends to view humans as a work in progress that can transcend their nature. In fact, some even go as far as saying humans do not have a specific nature and that it is for us to decide what our nature is (for those of you who enjoy existentialist literature). Extreme and irresponsible cases from this camp are parents who raise girls as boys, or vice versa, or any other claims that gender differences are merely social constructs. As any parent knows, boys and girls are truly from two different planets, different by nature, down to the bone marrow, not because we teach them to be that way.

Getting down to brass tacks, many on the far left are not satisfied with human nature, which can be a good thing to the extent that it energizes us to do better, but the premise is flawed. The far left is correct that we have seen progress during history, but this has been the manifestation of a potential that was there from the beginning (teleology), not a change in our nature or the imposition of structure on a blank slate. We are animals of a specific nature (rational) but we have to work hard to manifest that potential. To use an analogy, if we compare education to exercise, the job of a teacher or a personal trainer is to help us train the brain or the body in accordance with its nature. Just as there is a proper way to train a bicep and a properly trained bicep will take a predictable shape, there is a proper way to train the brain and a properly trained brain will take a predictable shape. That is, teachers are not putting information into the minds of children as much as they are training the brain to think and process information. The brain is a muscle. Where the left and the right differ is on how they view the proper end of human nature—teleology. For example, even though people on the left will recognize that people, all things being equal, even the most rational and enlightened people, will naturally provide altruistic love to their own children at the expense of strangers, they seem to view this as unfair and demand that people should transcend their limitations and see the benefits of providing altruistic love to all. People on the right recognize such a belief as not only unrealistic but misguided. Altruistic love is a finite good that must be distributed carefully. Therefore, we look for ways to structure society in a way that resonates with our true nature. In this case, given that we naturally have altruistic love for our own children, we should harness that force by building our institutions around it rather than bemoaning it and trying to change it.

The second flaw the left has regarding education is what I call the cart before the horse problem. We hear it all the time—people who go to college will earn $1 million more dollars during their career, or that people who go to elite schools make more money. Therefore, if you want to be successful, you should go to college. The flaws in this view are obvious, but we should take a closer look nonetheless. The first problem is that it ignores the supply and demand nature of a college degree, with the number of people going to college skyrocketing during the past 50 years. As we push more and more people to go to college, we have more college graduates competing for jobs and the inevitable lowering of standards. Thus, we become a victim of our own success, with the unemployment rate for recent college graduates hovering around 50%, a stunning number that should make us all pause, but instead we continue to hear about the value of a college education. The reason a college degree used to be so valuable was that *few people attended college*. I am not saying that college is not valuable, because I attended college and valued it, but the truth is that the people who succeed in life in terms of income probably would have succeeded anyway, either because of skill or family ties.

The problem is that by making a college degree an all-encompassing prerequisite, people will do it to punch the ticket, without necessarily having any high-demand job skills on graduation day. Many of the people who are successful today would have skipped college 40 years ago and probably would have risen up the ranks due to hard work and dedication. And many of the wealthy people who go to elite schools and get elite jobs do so within a wealthy family network. These jobs are not open to outsiders, so we should not dwell on the incomes of graduates from Ivy League schools. Membership is exclusive. It is true that most of the best paying jobs require a college degree, such as being a doctor, but we unfortunately have shifted the emphasis from learning a craft (medicine is a craft) or a job skill to just checking a box, even if that means majoring in gender studies. Rather than look at college as a way to slide into a middle-class life, where good jobs will magically be waiting for us, we should instead focus on learning critical skills that will allow us to create the value that is required for achieving a middle-class life, combined, we hope, with a general love of learning, such as art, literature, and philosophy, which help us grow and mature as humans. Instead, the left in its quest to help everyone succeed with a college degree has created the bloated debt problem of student loans (now in excess of $1 trillion), apparently oblivious to the fact that easy loans caused tuition to skyrocket and that the lingering debt at the end of the college experience would saddle many of these students for decades. Again, good intentions do not suffice. This, in turn, will make it difficult for them to accumulate wealth and climb the social ladder.

The third flaw relates to the second flaw in that the left is trying to use education as a way to transform society. This is evident with the cries about the so-called wage gap between men and women. Without beating a dead horse, there is simply no truth to this claim once you factor in the relevant variables that determine salary, such as the type of degree, the type of job, the level of stress, the number of hours worked, the level of responsibility, and so on. In fact, in many cases women are making more money than men and there are more women going to college than men. It all boils down to the coveted college degree. If the far left had its way, our income would be a function of the degree we have (to be granted by them), not the value we create for other people in society, as determined by the free market forces of supply and demand. For example, people on the left will often bemoan the fact that a social worker or a teacher with a master's degree makes less money than a plumber with a high school diploma, or that a woman with a master's degree in political science does not make as much money as a man with a bachelor's degree in engineering. This should surprise no one. The incomes are not the same for the same reason that people on the left demand to pay the market rate for the things they buy in stores. The money we earn is a function of the value we create as decided by consumers who buy and sell goods and services, not the degree we have. The value of a master's degree depends on the context in which it is used. The money we make is a function of the value we produce, as calculated by the free market. The relevant question is why do people pursue college degrees they know prepare them for low-paying jobs (if any) and then demand to get paid more? Why not pursue the difficult degrees that lead to high paying jobs, if income is the priority? Granted, to the extent that the left is focused on breaking the back of the old system that gave unfair privileges, I understand and sympathize with their motivation, but the far left clearly wants to create their own privileged network. Thus, they can make a gender studies department and give high-paying, tenured university positions to like-minded people who in the end produce nothing of value. Rather than fix the problem and promote the fairness they claim to champion, they resort to the same tactics they fought against. The tragic but good news is that this broken system is coming to an end. There are simply too many unemployed people paying too much tuition to keep the train rolling. As this model breaks down and we go back to making success a function of creating value and not of having a piece of paper, we will see this model lose sway.

There are other practical considerations as well, such as spending per child in our public school system. We currently spend about $7,700 per year per school-aged child. To put that in context, Japan and South Korea spend about $3,700 per child, less than half of what we spend. However, students in Japan and South Korea score much higher on math and science tests. Once again, we are facing a situation where more money is being spent and more money is being asked for, with results that are not improving and at a price that is too high. Any attempt at logic on this topic is met with resistance and demands for more spending. Without discussing unions, bloated administrations, or tenure, there should be a better way to produce better results for less money. Granted, it would be difficult to run K–12 schools on the business model of profit maximization, but we can calculate the cost of an education and identify ways to make the system more streamlined. As is often the case, the left begins with what appears to be good intentions—transform society by educating all children—and then turns it into a power play along the same lines that they had fought against at the beginning. I have seen this repeatedly in Latin American and other places where the left campaigns on a platform of "helping the people" only to become corrupt like the people they just replaced. This is not a matter of a left-wing autocrat unfortunately not getting it right; it is a case of the inevitable consequence of power. This is, in many ways, the prescient insight of the conservatives: *that there is no class of leaders who can be entrusted with absolute power at a national level, especially when voters are encouraged to "vote their interest."* We should always be skeptical of anyone who promises us things we know we cannot afford. This is why government has to be understood in the context of setting limits on its power rather than granting it powers, especially in our system that is based on federalism.

Dependency

One of the common complaints today by the right against the left is that the left has created a dependent class of people to win votes in exchange for tangible benefits, what Fukuyama would call clientelism. To analyze this issue, we will consider the two fundamental institutions of political philosophy: resource management, the prohibition of deficit spending; and procreation, the sanctity of monogamous procreation. According to the CNN exit polls for the 2012 presidential election, people who make less than $50,000 voted 60%-38% in favor of Obama, but those who make between $50,000-$100,000 voted 52%-46% in favor of Romney and those who make more than $100,000 voted 54%-44% in favor of Romney. As should surprise no one, as people have financial success in life, and thus learn how to earn more money in our economy by creating value, they are more likely to vote Republican. In theory, the argument could be made that people who are successful become greedy and therefore vote Republican, or that their high incomes are a function of inherited wealth, but someone will have to show me the evidence. If we look at marriage, we see that married people voted 56%-42% for Romney and unmarried people voted 35%-62% for Obama, whereas married people with children voted 54%-45% for Romney and all other categories voted 45%-53% for Obama, a notable difference. As should surprise no one, as people step up and settle into the challenging but rational institution of monogamous procreation, they are more likely to vote Republican. Granted, the argument could be made that Republicans are more predisposed to monogamous procreation and Democrats are more predisposed to other family models, but this ignores the fact that monogamous procreation is a rational institution. That is, monogamous procreation differs qualitatively from other family models. Shifting to age, which usually correlates with maturity and wisdom, we should also see how people vote as a function of age. To wit, the 18–24 age group voted 60%-36% for Obama, the 25–29 age group voted 60%-38% for Obama, the 30–39 age group voted 55%–42% for Obama, the 40–49 age group voted 50%–48% for Romney, the 50-64 age group voted 52%–47% for Romney, and the 65 and older age group voted 56%–44% for Romney. The trend is clear: as people age, they become more conservative (even the flower children of the 1960s are more conservative). As they say, if you are not liberal in college, you do not have a heart; if you are not conservative as an adult, you do not have a head.

The bottom line is that as people make the difficult climb up the social ladder, as measured by age, financial success, and family status—that is, as they live increasingly in accordance with their teleology and the two fundamental institutions of resource management and procreation—there is a steady trend to vote Republican over Democrat. I have no doubt that this will not resonate well with many Democrats, who often view themselves are more educated or enlightened (for reasons that are not clear), but they are a minority (45%–55%) of the people on the top of the income ladder. Just as we can ask what motivates people to vote Republican as a response to their success, we can ask what motivates people to vote Democrat as a response to their lack of success, keeping in mind that many successful people vote Democrat and many unsuccessful people vote Republican. (We are talking big numbers and bell curves for over 330 million people.)

With the facts established, we can move on to the important question: do Democrats target people who are young, poor, and single or from broken homes? Are the Democrats deliberately creating a dependent class of people supported with generous social programs (clientelism) to maintain political power? Clearly, if there are Democrats who are doing this, it is a small minority at the most senior levels of the party leadership, because most good-hearted Democrats I know would abandon the party if this were true. Rather than speculate on the existence of a shadow organization within the Democrats that is focused on sustaining a dependent class of voters, we should look at the facts.

First, regarding income, the left seems to focus most of their efforts on steering people toward college, despite the fact that people are going into debt and unemployment rates are close to 50% to recent college graduates. We hear almost nothing from the left about going to trade schools and learning valuable job skills that can be used to create value in a free market. There are literally millions of skilled jobs that are not filled today because people lack the skills to do them, yet we continue to send millions of students to earn relatively low quality degrees from relatively low quality universities. Thus, it appears that either the left is giving bad advice to people or they do not want people to get good paying jobs. Part of this, I think, stems from the fact that people on the left, bless their hearts, want each person to shoot for the stars to fulfill his or her potential, with less consideration for the reality of the job market or the competition. They perhaps fear that any plan to move poor or low income people into trade schools would stratify a social divide of haves and have-nots, with blacksmiths begetting blacksmiths, even though some trade school jobs result in millionaire status.

Second, regarding marriage, the left is not promoting monogamous procreation by any stretch of the imagination. If fact, the far left media often celebrate everything except monogamous procreation, and actively highlight the collapse of the "traditional family" as proof that it should not be celebrated. If they do make reference to monogamous procreation, it will always be with the caveat that "other family models" are important as well. In my assessment, this stems partly from the fact that they see the institution of monogamous procreation as a threat to their political agenda.

Third, shifting to the delicate topic of race, with whites voting 59%–39% for Romney in 2012, a clear majority, it should be clear that Democrats depend on the overwhelming majority of the non-white vote, with African Americans voting 93%–7%, Latinos voting 71% to 27%, and Asians voting 73% to 26% for Obama. I assesses that there would have been cries of outrage if whites had voted 93%–7% for Romney, both because Romney would have won by a landslide and because it would have been viewed as racism. Clearly, if these skewed numbers were to shift, the Democrats would have a difficult time ever winning another presidential election.

Based on this, can we conclude whether Democrats are purposefully trying to create a dependent class of voters to stay in power via clientelism? I think the answer is yes and no. For the no side of the answer, I think Democrats are so focused on implementing their social justice agenda that everything depends on that, for better or worse, just as the USA did some misguided things to hasten the decline of the Soviet Union. For the yes side, I believe Democrats view many things as a means to an end, just as many Republicans do. If they have to appeal to a minority vote with questionable tactics to combat a surge in conservative support, such as playing the race card or offering welfare benefits to people who are in the country illegally, they will. If they have to pander to poor voters by attacking businesses that provide jobs, they will. Granted, the fringe members of the Democrats are leading this charge, but they are loud and influential, just as the fringe members of the Republicans are loud and influential. The Democrats believe their model for society will produce wealth and prosperity, to include equality and social justice, so I believe they will tolerate a certain level of poverty and broken homes for now, if that means people will not vote Republican. On the other hand, Republicans would love for everyone to make more than $50,000 per year and have a "traditional" family because these people are more likely to vote Republican.

Laboratories of Democracy

I would be remiss if I did not offer some tangible solutions to the issues raised in this book. Given that the far left and far right positions are grounded in broken conceptual models, the first thing we have to realize and accept is that *there is no solution to the current political divide.* As long as the extreme wings of both parties are allowed to shape the narrative, it will be difficult to break the two party system and reach consensus in the rational middle, unless enough Americans agree to abandon their parties to join a third party in the middle, which history has shown is difficult. Another approach is to simply accept that, for reasons that are not clear—the way our brains develop, and so on—people are just different. Some people drift toward left-wing ideology and some people drift toward right-wing ideology, with a large group of people in the middle. If so, then we have to accept that no rational middle ground will be found between the two extremes, which means that we will have to find a way for these different people to live together without allowing either side to gain too much power or to violate the rights of others. Again, life is short, so rather than obsess about finding the perfect middle ground for everyone to live in harmony, perhaps we should instead take steps to see which ideas work as a matter of fact. The Republicans should accept that not all people will embrace their model and the Democrats should accept that not all people will embrace their model, and that any more attempts to try to convince people will not be successful.

The USA has a federal system of government with 50 states that in many ways regulate how most people live day to day, from schools, to zoning laws, to police departments, to criminal law. This fact makes the left-wing quest for a centralized, modern state based on the European model doomed to failure. Rather than bicker and fuss about who is right, why do we not see who is right? Like a reality TV show, we can point the cameras at different groups of people to see which model actually works in practice. Therefore, I propose we try an experiment. Rather than allow the federal government to impose nation-wide compromise solutions on big problems like abortion, taxes, marriage, and guns, why not allow the states to decide and then allow people to go where they believe they would want to live? (Many of our individual states are larger than many countries, so the proposal is not as crazy as it sounds. In fact, California would be a member of the G8. Minnesota is similar to Norway, and so on.) Why should people be forced to live in a place if they despise the laws? If the people of California or Texas want to push their own agenda, why allow the federal courts to stop them? I can only assume that most liberals in California would love to establish a Utopia of liberal values, just as most conservatives in Texas would love to establish their version of small government, without the federal courts interfering. These states, in turn, could have the centralized power (like Europe) to enforce a liberal or conservative agenda. As states change their laws and people move to states that fit their political beliefs, we will eventually have an answer to the question of which party is right. If California thrives and Texas crumbles, the liberals will be right, and vice versa.

The liberals might complain that a state-based model is precisely what conservatives want and would therefore give conservatives an unfair advantage, but my counter to that is, so what? Perhaps the conservatives are right on this point. If the liberals are so confident their model is correct, they should jump at the opportunity to prove their point in the crucible of battle because they will never achieve 100% of their political objectives on a national level, but they could achieve them at the state level. Most conservatives I know are confident of their model and would jump at the opportunity to prove it in the crucible of battle. Part of the liberal concern with such a plan, no doubt, is the recognition that their model depends on the redistribution of wealth, and if most of the wealth producers were to move to the conservative states, the liberals would have less wealth to tax for their social programs, which would force them to take steps to make their states more attractive for businesses. The liberal states would certainly enjoy many perceived benefits, such as "(fill in the blank) rights," diversity, and a minimum wage that few companies could afford to pay, but reality would soon catch up. Eventually, the people who were expecting generous benefits in California would move to Texas to get a job after California failed to deliver on its promises. Likewise, if Texas did not offer sufficient social programs, such as education, people would move to other states. Of course, there would be many states in the political middle that would blend the two models, so the beauty is that people have many options to choose from and the flexibility to move if things do not work out. The liberals might also object that a state-based model, with limited federal oversight, would allow states to violate the rights of its residents. This point is obviated by the fact that people are free to move and that any such laws would reflect the will of the people. The federal government would still exist and would still play a crucial role in keeping our country safe and keeping us on the right track in the areas where federal oversight is required by the Constitution, but the fact remains that we live in a federal system and this will not change, absent a violent revolution or a rewriting of the Constitution, so the dream of establishing a centralized modern state based on the European model is off the table.

To the extent that we allow people to live by the principle of liberty, the left has to give up its quest for a centralized state and Utopia, keeping in mind that many people, myself included, would not want to live in their hypothetical Utopia, even if it was possible. From an organizational perspective, given the size of our population and the diversity (the proper use of the word) of our states and regional economies, we really have no option but to decentralize and allow the states to serve as laboratories of democracy. If one state makes a mistake, at least the whole country does not make a mistake and the damage is minimal. If we are honest and rational enough to admit that abstract models do not work forever and that success is often a function of trial and error, we should employ the empirical method to see which ideas work as a matter of fact and then tweak them as necessary. If the people of California see the errors of their ways and shift to the right, so be it. If the people of Texas see the errors of their ways and shift to the left, so be it.

The important thing is that people will be free to choose and to live and learn. I cannot predict the future, but the states that prohibit deficit spending and sanctify monogamous procreation probably will have the most prosperity over the long run. If I had to use my pruning shears to clip the bonsai tree of our society, I would start with those two clips first.

Selected Bibliography

Compiling this selected bibliography turned out to be a surprisingly rewarding part of the writing process. By making a list of the best or most influential books I read during the last twenty years, which does not include the books I read as part of my undergraduate and graduate studies, it helped me recall my own intellectual journey that led me to develop the ideas in this book. Some of the books are long forgotten or were not consulted for this book directly, but I recall that they were influential or important to me at one point and kept me moving along a pleasant yet sometimes circuitous journey that eventually led, like all roads, to Rome. As the list of books makes clear, it is important to study subjects other than political philosophy to gain insights on the subject because political philosophy in many ways embodies the collective wisdom of the ages.

Abbott, H. Porter, *The Cambridge Introduction to Narrative* (Cambridge: Cambridge University Press, 2002).

Aeschylus, *The Complete Greek Tragedies*, Vol. I, edit. David Grene and Richmond Lattimore (Chicago: Chicago University Press, 1991).

Aristophanes, *Four Plays by Aristophanes*, trans. by William Arrowsmith, Richmond Lattimore, and Douglass Parker (New York: Meridian, 1994).

Aristotle, *The Basic Works of Aristotle*, edit. Richard McKeon (New York: Random House, 1941).

_____. *The Complete Works of Aristotle*, Vol. 1, edit. Jonathan Barnes (Princeton, Princeton University Press, 1995).

_____. *The Complete Works of Aristotle*, Vol. 2, edit. Jonathan Barnes (Princeton, Princeton University Press, 1995).

Baghavad-Gita: The Song of God (New York: Signet Classic, 2002).

Bal, Mieke, *Narratology: Introduction to the Theory of Narrative* (Toronto: University of Toronto Press, 1999).

Barzini, Luigi, *The Italians: A Full-Length Portrait Featuring Their Manners and Morals* (New York: Touchstone, 1996).

Baumohl, Bernard, *The Secrets of Economic Indicators: Hidden Clues to Future Economic Trends and Investment Opportunities* (Upper Saddle Valley, NJ: Prentice River, 2008).

Becker, Ernest, *The Denial of Death* (New York: Free Press, 1973).

Bernstein, Peter L., *Against the Gods: The Remarkable Story of Risk* (New York: John Wiley & Sons, 1998).

_____. *Capital Ideas: The Improbable Origins of Modern Wall Street* (New York: Free Press, 1993).

Booth, Mark, *The Secret History of the World: As Laid Down by the Secret Societies* (New York: Overlook Press, 2008).

Calasso, Roberto, *Literature and the Gods*, trans. Tim Parks (New York: Knopf, 2001).

_____. *The Marriage of Cadmus and Harmony*, trans. Tim Parks (New York: Vintage, 1994).

_____. *The Ruin of Kasch*, trans. William Weaver and Stephen Sartarelli (New York: Belknap Press, 1994).

Campbell, Joseph, *The Hero with a Thousand Faces* (Princeton: Princeton University Press, 1973).

Casebeer, William D., *Natural Ethical Facts: Evolution, Connectionism, and Moral Cognition* (Cambridge, MA: The MIT Press, 2003).

Cassirer, Ernst, *The Philosophy of Symbolic Forms: Language*, Vol. 1, trans. Ralph Manheim (New Haven: Yale University Press, 1955).

_____. *The Philosophy of Symbolic Forms: Mythical Thought*, Vol. 2., trans. Ralph Manheim (New Haven, Yale University Press, 1955).

Castiglione, Baldesar, *The Book of the Courtier*, trans. George Bull (New York: Penguin Books, 1976).

Childers, J. J., *Asset Protection 101: Tax and Legal Strategies of the Rich* (Hoboken, NJ: John Wiley & Sons, 2008).

Coll, Steve, *Ghost Wars: The Secret History of the CIA, Afghanistan, and Bin Laden, from the Soviet Invasion to September 10, 2001* (New York: Penguin Books, 2004).

Collingwood, R. G. *The Principles of Art* (Oxford: Oxford University Press, 1958).

Copleston, Frederick. *A History of Philosophy, Vol 1: Greece and Rome From the Pre-Socratics to Plotinus* (New York: Image, 1993).

_____. *A History of Philosophy, Vol. 2: Medieval Philosophy: From Augustine to Duns Scotus* (New York: Image, 1993).

_____. *A History of Philosophy, Vol. 3: Late Medieval and Renaissance Philosophy: Ockham, Francis Bacon, and the Beginning of the Modern World* (New York: Image, 1993).

_____. *A History of Philosophy, Vol. 4: Modern Philosophy: From Descartes to Leibnitz* (New York: Image, 1993).

_____. *A History of Philosophy, Vol. 5: Modern Philosophy: The British Philosopher from Hobbes to Hume* (New York: Image, 1993).

_____. *A History of Philosophy, Vol. 6: Modern Philosophy: From the French Enlightenment to Kant* (New York: Image, 1993).

_____. *A History of Philosophy, Vol. 7: Modern Philosophy: From the Post-Kantian Idealists to Marx, Kierkegaard, to Nietzsche* (New York: Image, 1994).

_____. *A History of Philosophy, Vol. 8: Modern Philosophy: Empiricism, Idealism, and Pragmatism in Britain and America* (New York: Image, 1994).

_____. *A History of Philosophy, Vol. 9: Modern Philosophy: From the French Revolution to Sartre, Camus, and Levi-Strauss* (New York: Image, 1994).

Cornford, F. M., *From Religion to Philosophy: A Study in the Origins of Western Speculation* (Mineola, NY: Dover Publications, 2004).

Covel, Michael W., *Trend Following: Learn to Make Millions in Up or Down Markets* (Upper Saddle River, NJ: FT Press, 2009).

Damasio, Antonio, *The Feeling of What Happens: Body and Emotion in the Making of Consciousness* (New York: Mariner Books, 2000).

Dawkins, Richard, *The Blind Watchmaker: Why the Evidence of Evolution Reveals a Universe Without Design* (New York: W. W. Norton & Company, 1996).

_____. *The Selfish Gene* (Oxford, Oxford University Press, 1990).

Defoe, Daniel, *Robinson Crusoe* (New York: Bantam Books, 1982).

Dodds, E. R., *The Greeks and the Irrational* (Los Angeles, University of California Press, 1997).

_____. *Pagan and Christian in an Age of Anxiety* (Cambridge: Cambridge University Press, 2001).

Dulles, Allen W., *The Craft of Intelligence* (Guilford, CT: The Lyon's Press, 2006).

Durant, Will, *The Story of Philosophy* (New York: Pocket Books, 1991).

Elder, Dr. Alexander, *Trading for a Living: Psychology, Trading Tactics, Money Management* (New York: John Wiley & Sons, 1993).

Elderman, Gerald M., *Wider than the Sky: The Phenomenal Gift of Consciousness* (New Haven, CT: Yale University Press, 2005).

Elderman, Gerald; Tononi, Giulio, *A Universe of Consciousness: How Matter Becomes Imagination* (New York: Basic Books, 2001).

Euripides, *The Complete Greek Tragedies*, Vol. III, edit. David Grene and Richmond Lattimore (Chicago: Chicago University Press, 1992).

_____. *The Complete Greek Tragedies*, Vol. IV, edit. David Grene and Richmond Lattimore (Chicago: Chicago University Press, 1992).

Fauconnier, Giles; Turner, Mark, *The Way We Think: Conceptual Blending and the Mind's Hidden Complexities* (New York: Basic Books, 2003).

Ferguson, Niall, *The Ascent of Money: A Financial History of the World* (New York: Penguin Books, 2009).

_____. *Civilization: The West and the Rest* (New York: Penguin Books, 2011).

Fox, Robin Lane, *Alexander the Great* (New York: Penguin Books, 1986.)

Fromkin, David, *A Peace to End All Peace: The Fall of the Ottoman Empire and the Creation of the Modern Middle East* (New York: Holt Paperback, 2001).

Flew, Anthony; with Varghese, Roy Abraham, *There is a God: How the World's Most Notorious Atheist Changed His Mind* (New York: Harper One, 2008).

Fukuyama, Francis, *The End of History and the Last Man* (New York: Free Press, 1992).

_____. *The Great Disruption: Human Nature and the Reconstitution of Social Order* (New York: Free Press, 1999).

_____. *The Origins of Political Order: From Prehuman Times to the French Revolution* (New York: Farrar, Straus and Giroux, 2010).

_____. *Political Order and Political Decay: From the Industrial Revolution to the Globalization of Democracy* (New York: Farrar, Straus and Giroux, 2014).

_____. *State-Building: Governance and World Order in the 21st Century* (Ithaca, NY: Cornell University Press, 2004).

_____. *Trust: The Social Virtues and the Creation of Prosperity* (New York: Free Press, 1996).

Gardner, John, *On Becoming a Novelist* (New York: W. W. Norton & Company, 1999).

Gilpin, Robert, *The Political Economy of International Relations* (Princeton, Princeton University Press, 1987).

Girard, Rene, *Deceit, Desire, and the Novel: Self and Other in Literary Structure* (Baltimore: John Hopkins Press, 1976).

_____. *Things Hidden Since the Foundation of the World* (Stanford: Stanford University Press, 1987).

_____. *I See Satan Fall Like Lighting* (Maryknoll, NY: Orbis Books, 2001).

_____. *The Scapegoat* (Baltimore: John Hopkins University Press, 1989).

_____. *Violence and the Sacred* (Baltimore: John Hopkins University Press, 1979).

Gladwell, Malcolm, *Blink: The Power of Thinking Without Thinking* (New York: Back Bay Books, 2007).

_____. *Outliers: The Story of Success* (New York: Back Bay Books, 2011).

_____. *Tipping Point: How Little Thinks Can Make a Big Difference* (New York: Back Bay Books, 2002).

Gracian, Baltazar, *The Art of Worldly Wisdom*, trans. Joseph Jacobs (Boston, Shambhala, 2000).

Greene, Brian, *The Elegant Universe: Superstrings, Hidden Dimensions, and the Quest for the Ultimate Theory* (New York: W. W. Norton & Company, 2003).

Greene, Robert, *The 48 Laws of Power* (New York: Penguin Books, 1998).

_____. *Mastery* (New York: Viking, 2012).

Griffin, G. Edward, *The Creature from Jekyll Island: A Second Look as the Federal Reserve* (Westlake Village, CA: American Media, 2002).

Hamilton, Edith, *The Greek Way* (New York: W. W. Norton & Company, 1993).

Hanson, Victor David; Heath, John, *Who Killed Homer?: The Demise of Classical Education and the Recovery of Greek Wisdom* (New York: Free Press, 1998).

Haqqani, Husain, *Pakistan: Between Mosque and Military* (Washington, DC: Carnegie Endowment for International Peace, 2005).

Hawking, Stephen, *A Brief History of Time* (New York: Bantam Books, 1998).

Hearder, Harry, *Italy: A Short History* (Cambridge: Cambridge University Press, 2007).

Heilbroner, Robert L., *The Worldly Philosophers: The Lives, Times, and Ideas of the Great Economic Thinkers* (New York: Touchstone, 1999).

Hesiod, *Theogony and Works and Days* (Oxford, Oxford University Press, 1988).

Hesse, Hermann, *Siddhartha* (New York: Bantam Classic, 1981).

Hofstadter, Douglas R., *Gödel, Escher, Bach: An Eternal Golden Braid* (New York: Basic Books, 1999).

Homer, *Iliad*, trans. Richmond Lattimore (Chicago: Chicago University Press, 1961).

_____. *Odyssey*, trans. Richmond Lattimore (New York: Perennial Classics, 1999).

Hughes, James E., Jr., *Family: The Compact Among Generations* (New York: Bloomberg Press, 2007).

Hunt, Morton, *The Story of Psychology* (New York: Anchor Books, 2007).

Huxley, Aldous, *Brave New World & Brave New World Revisited* (New York: Harper Perennial, 1965).

_____. *The Perennial Philosophy*, (New York: Harper Perennial, 2009).

Innis, Robert E., *Susanne Langer in Focus: The Symbolic Mind* (Bloomington, IN: Indiana University Press, 2009).

Jaynes, Julian, *The Origin of Consciousness in the Breakdown of the Bicameral Mind* (Boston: Houghton Mifflin, 1990).

Johnson, Paul, *Modern Times: The World from the Twenties to the Eighties* (New York: Harper and Row, 1985).

Joyce, James, *A Portrait of the Artist as a Young Man* (New York: Penguin Books, 1993).

Kenny, Anthony, *A New History of Western Philosophy*, (Oxford: Oxford University Press, 2010).

Kiyosaki, Robert T., *Rich Dad's Increase Your Financial IQ: Get Smarter with Your Money* (New York: Business Plus, 2008).

Kindlon, Dan; Thompson, Michael: *Raising Cain: Protecting the Emotional Life of Boys* (New York: Ballantine Books, 2000).

Kinzer, Stephen, *All the Shah's Men: An American Coup and the Roots of Middle Eastern Terror* (Hoboken, NJ: John Wiley & Sons, 2003).

Lakoff, George; Johnson, Mark, *Metaphors We Live By* (Chicago: University of Chicago Press, 2003).

_____. *Philosophy in the Flesh: the Embodied Mind and its Challenge to Western Thought* (New York: Basic Books, 1999).

Langer, Susanne K., *Philosophy in a New Key: A Study in the Symbolism of Reason, Rite, and Art* (Cambridge, MA: Harvard University Press, 1979).

_____. *Feeling and Form* (New York: Charles Scribner's Sons, 1953).

Le Bon, Gustave, *The Crowd: A Study of the Popular Mind* (Atlanta, Cherokee Publishing Company, 1994).

Lieven, Anatol, *Pakistan: A Hard Country* (New York: PublicAffairs, 2012).

Lovett, Frank. *Rawls's 'A Theory of Justice': A Reader's Guide* (New York: Bloomsbury Academic, 2011).

Machiavelli, Niccolo, *The Prince*, trans. George Bull (London: Penguin Books, 2003).

Magee, Bryan. *Confessions of a Philosopher: A Personal Journey Through Western Philosophy from Plato to Popper* (New York: Modern Library, 1999).

_____. *The Philosophy of Schopenhauer* (Oxford: Oxford University Press, 1998).

Marx, Karl; Engels, Friedrich, *The Communist Manifesto* (New York: Penguin Books, 2002).

McCullough, David, *The Path Between the Seas: The Creation of the Panama Canal, 1874-1914* (New York: Simon & Schuster, 1978).

Menand, Louis, *The Metaphysical Club: A Story of Ideas in America* (New York: Farrar, Straus and Giroux, 2002).

Merzbach, Uta C.; Boyer, Carl B., *A History of Mathematics*, Third Edition (Hoboken, NJ: John Wiley & Sons, 2011).

Meyer, Stephen C., *Darwin's Doubt: The Explosive Origin of Animal Life and the Case for Intelligent Design* (New York: HarperOne, 2013).

_____. *Signature in the Cell: DNA and the Evidence for Intelligent Design* (New York: HarperOne, 2009).

Modell, Arnold H., *Imagination and the Meaningful Brain* (Cambridge, MA: The MIT Press, 2006).

Murray, Gilbert, *Five Stages of Greek Religion* (Mineola, NY: Dover Publications, 2002).

Nabokov, Vladimir. *Lolita* (New York: Vintage International, 1997).

Nozick, Robert. *Anarchy, State, and Utopia* (New York: Basic Books, 2013).

Paglia, Camille, *Sexual Personae: Art and Decadence from Nefertiti to Emily Dickenson* (New York: Vintage Books, 1991).

Pears, David. *The False Prison: A Study of the Development of Wittgenstein's Philosophy*, Vol. 1 (Oxford: Oxford University Press, 1987).

_____. *The False Prison: A Study of the Development of Wittgenstein's Philosophy*, Vol. 2. (Oxford: Oxford University Press, 1988).

Piaget, Jean; Inhelder, Barbel, *The Psychology of the Child* (New York: Basic Books, 1969).

Pinker, Steven, *Words and Rules: The Ingredients of Language* (New York: Perennial, 2000).

Plato. *Complete Works*, edit. John M. Cooper (Hackett, 1997).

Pons, Frank Moya, *The Dominican Republic: A National History* (Princeton: Markus Wiener Publishers, 1998).

Popper, Karl. *The Open Society & Its Enemies* (Princeton: Princeton University Press, 2013).

Prigogine, Ilya, *The End of Certainty: Time, Chaos, and the New Laws of Nature* (New York: Free Press, 1997).

Rand, Ayn, *Capitalism: The Unknown Ideal* (New York: Signet, 1986).

_____. *Introduction to Objectivist Epistemology* (New York: Meridian, 1990).

_____. *The Romantic Manifesto* (New York: Signet, 1975).

_____. *The Virtue of Selfishness* (New York: Signet, 1964).

_____. *The Voice of Reason: Essays in Objectivist Thought* (New York: Meridian, 1990).

_____. *Philosophy: Who Needs It* (New York: Signet, 1984).

Rawls, John. *A Theory of Justice*, Revised Edition (Cambridge, MA: Harvard University Press, 1999).

Reid, Michael, *Forgotten Continent: The Battle for Latin America's Soul* (New Haven, CT: Yale University Press, 2007).

Ridley, Matt, *Genome: The Autobiography of a Species in 23 Chapters* (New York: Harper Perennial, 2006)

Roberts, J. M., *A Short History of the World* (Oxford: Oxford University Press, 1997).

Ross, Sir David. *Aristotle* (New York: Routledge, 2004).

Rothbard, Murray N., *A History of Money and Banking in the United States: The Colonial Era to World War II* (Auburn, AL: Ludwig Von Mises Institute, 2002).

Ryan, Alan. *On Politics: A History of Political Thought: From Herodotus to the Present* (2 Vol. Set) (New York: Liveright, 2012).

Schopenhauer, Arthur. *On the Fourfold Root of the Principle of Sufficient Reason*, trans. E. F. J. Payne (La Salle, IL: Open Court Classic, 1999).

_____. *Prize Essay on the Freedom of the Will*, trans. E. F. J. Payne (Cambridge: Cambridge University Press, 1999).

_____. *The World as Will and Representation*, Vol. 1, trans. E. F. J. Payne (Mineola, NY: Dover Publications, 1969).

_____. *The World as Will and Representation*, Vol. 2, trans. E. F. J. Payne (Dover Publications, 1969).

Scruton, Roger. *Beauty: A Very Short Introduction* (Oxford: Oxford University Press, 2011).

_____. *Kant: A Very Short Introduction* (Oxford: Oxford University Press, 2001).

_____. *Modern Philosophy: An Introduction and Survey* (New York: Penguin Books, 1996).

_____. *A Short History of Modern Philosophy: From Descartes to Wittgenstein* (New York, Routledge, 2002).

Skinner, Stephen, *Sacred Geometry: Deciphering the Code* (New York: Sterling Publishing, 2009).

Sophocles, *The Complete Greek Tragedies*, Vol. II, edit. David Grene and Richmond Lattimore (Chicago: Chicago University Press, 1991).

Talbot, Michael, *The Holographic Universe* (New York: Harper Perennial, 1992).

Taleb, Nassim Nicholas, *Antifragile: Things that Gain from Disorder* (New York: Random House, 2012).

_____. *The Black Swan: The Impact of the Highly Improbable* (New York: Random House, 2007).

_____. *Fooled by Randomness: The Hidden Role of Chance in Life and in the Markets* (New York: Random House, 2004).

Tarnas, Richard, *The Passion of the Western Mind: Understanding the Ideas that have Shaped Our World View* (New York: Ballantine Books, 1993).

Thomas, Even, *The Very Best Men: The Daring Early Years of the CIA* (New York: Simon and Schuster, 2006).

Turner, Mark, *The Literary Mind: The Origins of Thought and Language* (Oxford: Oxford University Press, 1998).

Weatherford, Jack, *Genghis Khan and the Making of the Modern World* (New York: Broadway Books, 2005).

Weiner, Tim, *Legacy of Ashes: The History of the CIA* (New York: Anchor Books, 2008).

Wright, Lawrence, *The Looming Tower: Al-Qaeda and the Road to 9/11* (New York: Vintage, 2007).

Wright, Robert, *The Moral Animal: Why We Are, the Way We Are: The New Science of Evolutionary Psychology* (New York: Vintage, 1995).

_____. *Nonzero: The Logic of Human Destiny* (New York: Pantheon Books, 2000).

Printed in the United States
By Bookmasters